BEST DOG STORIES

BEST DOG STORIES

Introduction by
GERALD DURRELL

Edited by
Lesley O'Mara

Brockhampton Press
London

First published in Great Britain by
Michael O'Mara Books Limited
9 Lion Yard
11-13 Tremadoc Road
London SW4 7NQ

Best Dog Stories copyright © 1990 by Michael O'Mara Books Limited

A CIP catalogue record for this book is available
from the British Library.

This edition published 1995 by Brockhampton Press,
a member of Hodder Headline PLC Group

ISBN 1 86019 107 X

Design: Richard Souper

Printed and bound in Great Britain by
Mackays of Chatham PLC, Chatham, Kent

Contents

CONTENTS

Acknowledgements

The Publisher has made every effort to contact the copyright holders of material reproduced in this book, and wishes to apologise to those he has been unable to trace.

Grateful acknowledgement is made for permission to reprint the following:

'Can I Be Your Dog?' from *Best of Dogs* by Eric Parker (Century Hutchinson Limited); 'Tricki Woo' from *James Herriot's Dog Stories* by James Herriot (Michael Joseph); 'Having No Hearts' by Sir Hugh Walpole, reprinted by permission of Sir Rupert Hart-Davis; extract from *Jimmy, the Dog in My Life* by Sir Arthur Bryant (Lutterworth Press); 'Gone Wrong' by P. G. Wodehouse (Random Century Limited); 'The Great Lad' © 1990 by Joyce Stranger, by permission of the author; 'Some Sunnybank Dogs' by Albert Payson Terhune, reprinted by permission of Albert Payson Terhune, Inc; extract from *Intelligent and Loyal* by Jilly Cooper (Methuen London); 'The End' from *Flush* by Virginia Woolf (The Hogarth Press), reprinted by permission of the Executors of the Estate of Virginia Woolf.

The illustrators are:

Cecil Aldin: 120, 122/3, 138, 140, 197, 200, 202, 204, 207
C. G. Ambler: 167
Honor C. Appleton: 127
K. F. Barker: 27, 34, 42, 76, 79, 89, 98, 189, 211
Mil Brown: 16, 24, 31, 87, 238, 242
G. L. Stampa: 108
Dilys Watkin: 60, 72, 245, 252

Introduction

GERALD DURRELL

THE dog is, I think, one of the more successful animals that man has domesticated. We have, in fact, outdone nature itself, for we have produced by our manipulation more different types of dog than are found in nature. They come in a most bewildering number of colours, shapes and sizes, from Irish wolfhounds and mastiffs to Pekinese and Chihuahuas. They have jowls and wrinkles, ears that droop or stand up, blunt docked tails or ones that sway from side to side like plumes. We have them brown, black, golden or speckled all over like a quail's egg, as in the Dalmatian. The one thing they all have in common, however, in spite of their differing appearances, is their highly developed personality, and yet no two dogs' personalities are the same, as this wonderful collection of stories will demonstrate.

Dogs have, since they entered 'domestic service' as they say, cared for us in a hundred different ways. They give us solace and companionship when we need it; they help us in hunting our food or in rounding up and guarding our flocks. They help us in ice and snow by pulling sledges or, if we are stupid enough to get ourselves lost in a snowdrift, they rescue us with the (possibly apocryphal) keg of brandy round their necks. They act as police in sniffing out crime and they become the eyes of those who can't see. They guard our possessions from barges to country houses, from cottages to castles. In them we have indeed created the multipurpose friend.

Dogs are strange and wonderful creatures to share your life with and no life is complete without a dog, providing, as Chesterton wisely observed, you do not spell it backwards. They have a wit and wisdom of their own. I have seen three of my own dogs snarling and barking and backing away from a

11

corner of a huge, ancient kitchen we had on the island of Corfu. There was nothing that either I or my family could see in the corner, just medieval brickwork. I have been followed twenty-five miles on horseback over the Argentine pampa by three arthritic and very elderly dachshunds who refused to go home when I told them to and who, when the grass became too high, had to leap up like grasshoppers to see which way we were going. I have seen my dog rescue a puppy that had fallen into the sea and could not swim, plucking it out of the water by the scruff of its neck. I have met good dogs and bad dogs, stupid ones and intelligent ones, but I would not be without one. As the Greeks say, a house is not a home unless it has a swallow nesting under the eaves, so I think a house is not a home until it has a dog.

My most recent dog was a boxer, a breed for which I have a great love. He came to me fully grown and his name was Keeper—Keeper of the Keys—which was singularly appropriate since he was coming to live in my zoo on the island of Jersey. He was a very large dog with his ears fortunately uncropped and a massive blunt tail which he never ceased wagging. His prominent brown eyes were capable of more different expressions than any other dog's I had owned. I viewed with a certain trepidation the introduction into a zoo of a two-year-old dog who had—according to his owners—never seen another animal apart from a dog—not even a cow. However, Keeper, oozing goodwill, shambled his way into everyone's hearts and was an immediate success. His day would start with him visiting all his friends, exchanging kisses through the wire with the tapirs, saying good day to the peccaries and being greeted by a clatter of tusks, for these pigs were not fond of him. He would go and say hello to the spectacled bears and the gorillas and orangs, have a limbering-up race with the cheetah, say good morning and give a quick lick to the zoo cat, Mimi, and to Trumpy, our trumpeter bird, who stalked the zoo like the squire of the manor. Having done all this exuding of goodwill, it was time to go and meet his friend, Dick, the big Labrador from next door, and after much kissing they would set off shoulder to shoulder, a formidable but harmless pair, to see how the world wagged. Keeper lived with me for eight years and not once in that time did he show anything but extreme benevolence to any of the vast array of strange animals he was to come in contact with. I think this was pretty extraordinary for a dog who, until he was two, had never even seen a cow.

I think this book will demonstrate what elaborately complex and fascinating animals dogs are. Read on and enjoy some of the best stories of dogs ever written.

23rd February 1990

Can I Be Your Dog?

ERIC PARKER

IT was in the years when wars had been forgotten, that I was taken by a friend who knows more about dogs than I shall ever know, to see a famous kennel. It was a kennel of which I had heard much, and about which I had often wondered, guessing how the owner could plan to house, feed, and exercise its occupants, which were Great Danes; I forget how many, but they were more in number than I had supposed any single owner of dogs would ever be likely to have under his own single control.

Even so, guessing as I might, when I found myself actually on the spot, faced with the long lines of enclosures I realized that I had under-estimated everything—the numbers of the dogs themselves, the prodigious quantities of their daily diet, the size of the runs allotted to each separate inhabitant. It was all a marvel of organization, of efficiency, of cleanliness, even— comparatively—of quiet, for I had anticipated echoes re-echoed, dog-shows outdone in the din, and here most of the dogs moved about their runs in silence.

But more than that! Silence was not the first, the dominating impression, almost the pervading spell of the place. It was solitariness, loneliness. I walked from enclosure to enclosure— no, I walked from dog to dog. Each dog as I came to his allotted parallelogram of wire-walled soil, came to the side and walked along it, and I looked at each in turn, at each massive frame, each noble head, but at more than that. For I have looked at many dogs in turn at many dog shows, passing down the long lines of benches in order, and I have seen many things in their eyes, but I never before that day saw what I saw then. For here, I realized, it was not I who was looking at the dogs, but the dogs who looked at me, and each dog with the same look in the

15

eyes that belongs to no other creature, and in those eyes the same hope, the same hopelessness. 'Can I come with you? Can I be your dog? Can't I be your dog? No?'

And I had to say, or rather to be, No, cage after cage. Each dog, as soon as it looked at me, knew my answer. Each dog, when any person came to visit those cages, in the casual, curious, sight-seeing way in which I went to visit them, knew what the visitor's answer would be. I think that my friend who took me to see that kennel, had guessed no more than I what would be the effect of the mere numbers of dogs we saw. There, in the autumn sunshine, through the years that have passed since, the memory, the vision remains; every care, every provision, for health, every physical comfort . . . and in the eyes of those dogs, each in turn, the same question and the same answer.

I have memories of another kennel. To visit it I had driven by roads and through woodlands of the South Country as I love best to see them on an April day, to come near the end of our journey to the light on a Dorsetshire salmon river and flood-water falling to fishing level; and after that through Dorsetshire roads again to find ourselves on a sudden within sound of what we had come to see—I remember the unexpected greeting of the sound. We were to choose, out of a kennel bearing a name honoured in the annals of shows and field trials, a single young creature, trained we hoped in the rudiments of spaniel lore and performance; a spaniel who was to be given into the charge of a trusted friend, a gardener who in his youth had learned from a gamekeeper what good gun dogs should know and be and do. With the gardener the chosen spaniel was to be housed, fed, and generally looked after, for the benefit of its owner, one of the family whose daily business took him to London, and who hoped thus when September came round to be able to go out into field and covert with a spaniel-retriever—whether him or her we had not made up our minds—so to speak ready-made.

So much for the plans of mice and men. As things turned out, the spaniel never came into the care of the gardener, who—we did not know it—at the moment when our choice from the kennel was made, lay on a bed from which to our sorrow he never rose; so the spaniel came not into a gardener's cottage, but into a home in which she lived and was loved all her life. But here the tale may be taken up by the would-be spaniel-owner's sister, to whose lot it fell to introduce the inmate of a kennel of some thirty or forty of its kind into a new and surprising world.

Lytchett (I transcribe) was a mistake. That is to say, she was never intended to be our dog. The garden was overrun with rabbits, and we thought it might help to have a spaniel to find them. So my father decided to buy a spaniel for my brother, and give it to the gardener to train and look after. The gardener had had a spaniel before (in fact he had had two, called Shot and Missed, but they were both gone) and we wanted another. As it turned out, however, the spaniel came to live with us instead of him.

We went to choose our puppy from a large kennel of springers. We saw a great many spaniels there, but only two of them were for sale. One was a quite young puppy which had not had much training, and the other was nine months old. We saw the younger one first, but it was so timid that it would not show us what it could do; it merely looked miserable, poor little thing, so we tried the other one.

As soon as it was let out, it rushed up to us and said How do you do?—after which it showed us how to retrieve a stuffed rabbit. It was not perfect, but it was very pretty, and we decided to buy it.

I had brought the foot-bath in which I had fetched Patsy (a black Labrador)—but it was useless as far as this new puppy was concerned. Patsy had only been seven weeks old when she came, and this creature was nine months. So she sat on the floor of the car.

At least, that is what we had intended that she should do. But it was clear from the first that her great idea was to be a lap-dog. She had lived for five months in a kennel where she shared a master with fifty or so other dogs, and now she had someone all to herself and she was going to make the most of it. First one paw came up on our laps (my younger brother's and mine), only to be pushed down again. This was quickly followed by the other paw, which was as quickly repulsed. But Lytchett was not to be repulsed. Eventually we allowed one foot to remain, after which the other took courage and came up also, and I regret to say that when we drove up to the front door, the dog was lying at full length across our knees.

We could not take her over to the gardener's cottage at once, as he was ill, so we took her indoors and introduced her to Tess and Patsy. But the gardener, instead of getting better as we hoped, grew suddenly worse, and we realized that Lytchett was ours for keeps.

She spent the first two or three days investigating everything. She had apparently never been in a house before, and everything was new and exciting. When anything was too high for her to see, she jumped up, or stood on her hind legs. I was sitting alone at lunch the day after she came, with Lytchett lying by my side, and I went out of the room to answer the telephone, leaving my lunch half finished. When I came back my plate was empty and shining, and Lytchett was again lying on the floor.

Although not exactly a puppy, she is the most childish creature. She has invented a game, in which she seizes hold of a piece of stick or just as you are about to pounce on her she springs up and rushes round in circles, dodging anyone who attempts to catch her, in a way that any Rugger player would envy. Then she suddenly flops down again, and waits till you are once more ready to pounce before she darts away. Sometimes, instead of merely running round in circles, she goes down to a big oak tree at the bottom of the lawn, jumps up on the bank where it is growing, and then races back again, or else she runs right round the tree and back again.

That is the tale, ordinary enough in its details, of how a puppy belonging to a kennel, but to no individual in particular, became herself an individual. And in process of becoming an individual, she became known by an individual name; she was renamed Lytchett, after Lytchett Matravers where she came from, who before had been Norah, a name difficult to call a dog by. As Lytchett she was a dog definitely belonging to someone; a dog with a home of her own, living in buildings of which she knew every wall and floor, with a garden and among woods and fields and roads made familiar day by day, above all surrounded by scents and smells that belonged to her own people and places and to nobody and nowhere else. And as Lytchett she herself in turn became known to quite a large number of persons, to neighbours with dogs of their own, to farmers, gardeners, chauffeurs, schoolchildren. Lytchett was a Somebody, a personage. Norah had been a nobody, nothing to anybody, a Waif.

That was the change, and it is a change that does not come to every dog. It is a change that comes to different dogs in different ways. It may never come at all. But it must happen, in any case, that most dogs start their lives as waifs. Only a few are somebody, or somebody's dogs, before they are born. Most of them have to wait—some indeed are given no time to wait, either to be chosen or given or sold as tiny pups, or as growing dogs like Norah who became Lytchett.

Here, in these following pages, are stories of Lytchetts and Norahs under other names: of dogs who belonged through purpose or by accident to many masters and mistresses. Sometimes the owner tells the story, sometimes the story builds itself.

Memoirs of a Yellow Dog

O. HENRY

I DON'T suppose it will knock any of you people off your perch to read a contribution from an animal. Mr Kipling and a good many others have demonstrated the fact that animals can express themselves in remunerative English, and no magazine goes to press nowadays without an animal story in it, except the old-style monthlies that are still running pictures of Bryan and the Mont Melée horror.

But you needn't look for any stuck-up literature in my piece, such as Bearoo, the bear, and Snakoo, the snake, and Tammanoo, the tiger, talk in the jungle books. A yellow dog that's spent most of his life in a cheap New York flat, sleeping in a corner on an old sateen underskirt (the one she spilled port wine on at the Lady 'Longshoremen's banquet), mustn't be expected to perform any tricks with the art of speech.

I was born a yellow pup; date, locality, pedigree, and weight unknown. The first thing I can recollect, an old woman had me in a basket at Broadway and Twenty-third trying to sell me to a fat lady. Old Mother Hubbard was boosting me to beat the band as a genuine Pomeranian-Hambletonian-Red-Irish-Cochin-China-Stoke-Pogis fox terrier. The fat lady chased a note round among the samples of gros grain flannelette in her shopping bag till she cornered it, and gave up. From that moment I was a pet—a mamma's own wootsey squidlums. Say, gentle reader, did you ever have a 200-pound woman breathing a flavour of Camembert cheese and Peau d'Espagne pick you up and wallop her nose all over you, remarking all the time in an Emma Eames tone of voice: 'Oh, oo's um oodlum, doodlum, woodlum, toodlum, bitsy-witsy skoodlums?'

From a pedigreed yellow pup I grew up to be an anonymous yellow cur looking like a cross between an Angora cat and a box of lemons. But my mistress never tumbled. She thought that the two primeval pups that Noah chased into the ark were but a collateral branch of my ancestors. It took two policemen to keep her from entering me at the Madison Square Garden for the Siberian bloodhound prize.

I'll tell you about that flat. The house was the ordinary thing in New York, paved with Parian marble in the entrance hall and cobblestones above the first floor. Our flat was three fl—well, not flights—climbs up. My mistress rented it unfurnished, and put in the regular things—1903 antique upholstered parlour set, oil chromo of geishas in a Harlem tea house, rubber plant and husband.

By Sirius! there was a biped I felt sorry for. He was a little man with sandy hair and whiskers a good deal like mine. Henpecked?—well, toucans and flamingoes and pelicans all had their bills in him. He wiped the dishes and listened to my mistress tell about the cheap, ragged things the lady with the squirrel-skin coat on the second floor hung out on her line to dry. And every evening while she was getting supper she made him take me out on the end of a string for a walk.

If men knew how women pass the time when they are alone they'd never marry. Laura Jean Libbey, peanut brittle, a little almond cream on the neck muscles, dishes unwashed, half an hour's talk with the iceman, reading a package of old letters, a couple of pickles and two bottles of malt extract, one hour peeping through a hole in the window blind into the flat across the air-shaft—that's about all there is to it. Twenty minutes before time for him to come home from work she straightens up the house, fixes her rat so it won't show, and gets out a lot of sewing for a ten-minute bluff.

I led a dog's life in that flat. 'Most all day I lay there in my corner watching that fat woman kill time. I slept sometimes and had pipe dreams about being out chasing cats into basements and growling at old ladies with black mittens, as a dog was intended to do. Then she would pounce upon me with a lot of that drivelling poodle palaver and kiss me on the nose—but what could I do? A dog can't chew cloves.

I began to feel sorry for Hubby, dog my cats if I didn't. We looked so much alike that people noticed it when we went out; so we shook the streets that Morgan's cab drives down, and took to climbing the piles of last December's snow on the streets where cheap people live.

One evening when we were thus promenading, and I was trying to look like a prize St Bernard, and the old man was trying to look like he wouldn't have murdered the first organ-grinder he heard play Mendelssohn's wedding-march, I looked up at him and said, in my way:

'What are you looking so sour about, you oakum-trimmed lobster? She don't kiss you. You don't have to sit on her lap and listen to talk that would make the book of a musical comedy sound like the maxims of Epictetus. You ought to be thankful you're not a dog. Brace up, Benedick, and bid the blues begone.'

The matrimonial mishap looked down at me with almost canine intelligence in his face.

'Why, doggie,' says he, 'good doggie. You almost look like you could speak. What is it, doggie—Cats?'

Cats! Could speak!

But, of course, he couldn't understand. Humans were denied the speech of animals. The only common ground of communication upon which dogs and men can get together is in fiction.

In the flat across the hall from us lived a lady with a black-and-tan terrier. Her husband strung it and took it out every evening, but he always came home cheerful and whistling. One day I touched noses with the black-and-tan in the hall, and I struck him for an elucidation.

'See here, Wiggle-and-Skip,' I says, 'you know that it ain't the nature of a real man to play dry nurse to a dog in public. I never saw one leashed to a bow-wow yet that didn't look like he'd like to lick every other man that looked at him. But your boss comes in every day as perky and set up as an amateur prestidigitator doing the egg trick. How does he do it? Don't tell me he likes it.'

'Him?' says the black-and-tan. 'Why, he uses Nature's Own Remedy. He gets spifflicated. At first when we go out he's as shy as the man on the steamer who would rather play pedro when they make 'em all jackpots. By the time we've been in eight saloons he don't care whether the thing on the end of his line is a dog or a catfish. I've lost two inches of my tail trying to sidestep those swinging doors.'

The pointer I got from that terrier—vaudeville please copy—set me to thinking.

One evening about 6 o'clock my mistress ordered him to get busy and do the ozone act for Lovey. I have concealed it until now, but that is what she called me. The black-and-tan was called 'Tweetness'. I consider that I have the bulge on him as far as you could chase a rabbit. Still 'Lovey' is something of a nomenclatural tin-can on the tail of one's self-respect.

At a quiet place on a safe street I tightened the line of my custodian in front of an attractive, refined saloon. I made a dead-ahead scramble for the doors, whining like a dog in the press dispatches that lets the family know that little Alice is bogged while gathering lilies in the brook.

'Why, darn my eyes,' says the old man, with a grin: 'darn my eyes if the saffron-coloured son of a seltzer lemonade ain't asking me in to take a drink. Lemme see—how long's it been since I saved shoe leather by keeping one foot on the foot-rest? I believe I'll—'

I knew I had him. Hot Scotches he took, sitting at a table. For an hour he kept the Campbells coming. I sat by his side rapping for the waiter with my tail, and eating free lunch such as mamma in her flat never equalled with her home-made truck bought at a delicatessen store eight minutes before papa comes home.

When the products of Scotland were all exhausted except the rye bread the old man unwound me from the table leg and played me outside like a fisherman plays a salmon. Out there he took off my collar and threw it into the street.

'Poor doggie,' says he; 'good doggie. She shan't kiss you any more. 'Sa darned shame. Good doggie, go away and get run over by a street car and be happy.'

I refused to leave. I leaped and frisked around the old man's legs happy as a pug on a rug.

'You old flea-headed woodchuck-chaser,' I said to him—'you moon-baying, rabbit-pointing, egg-stealing old beagle, can't you see that I don't want to leave you? Can't you see that we're both Pups in the Wood and the missis is the cruel uncle after you with the dish towel and me with the flea liniment and a pink bow to tie on my tail. Why not cut that all out and be pards for ever more?'

Maybe you'll say he didn't understand—maybe he didn't. But he kind of got a grip on the Hot Scotches, and stood still for a minute, thinking.

'Doggie,' says he, finally, 'we don't live more than a dozen lives on this earth, and very few of us live to be more than 300. If I ever see that flat any more I'm a flat, and if you do you're flatter; and that's no flattery. I'm offering 60 to 1 that Westward Ho! wins out by the length of a dachshund.'

There was no string, but I frolicked along with my master to the Twenty-third Street ferry. And the cats on the route saw reason to give thanks that prehensile claws had been given them.

On the Jersey side my master said to a stranger who stood eating a currant bun:

'Me and my doggie, we are bound for the Rocky Mountains.'

But what pleased me most was when my old man pulled both of my ears until I howled, and said:

'You common, monkey-headed, rat-tailed, sulphur-coloured son of a door mat, do you know what I'm going to call you?'

I thought of 'Lovey', and I whined dolefully.

'I'm going to call you "Pete",' says my master; and if I'd had five tails I couldn't have done enough wagging to do justice to the occasion.

Tricki Woo

JAMES HERRIOT

AS autumn wore into winter and the high tops were streaked with the first snows, the discomforts of practice in the Dales began to make themselves felt.

Driving for hours with frozen feet, climbing to the high barns in biting winds which seared and flattened the wiry hill grass; the interminable stripping off in draughty buildings and the washing of hands and chest in buckets of cold water, using scrubbing soap and often a piece of sacking for a towel.

I really found out the meaning of chapped hands. When there was a rush of work, my hands were never quite dry, and the little red fissures crept up almost to my elbows.

This was when some small animal work came as a blessed relief. To step out of the rough, hard routine for a while; to walk into a warm drawing-room instead of a cow house and tackle something less formidable than a horse or a bull. And among all those comfortable drawing-rooms there was none so beguiling as Mrs Pumphrey's.

Mrs Pumphrey was an elderly widow. Her late husband, a beer baron whose breweries and pubs were scattered widely over the broad bosom of Yorkshire, had left her a vast fortune and a beautiful house on the outskirts of Darrowby. Here she lived with a large staff of servants, a gardener, a chauffeur, and Tricki Woo. Tricki Woo was a Pekinese and the apple of his mistress's eye.

Standing now in the magnificent doorway, I furtively rubbed the toes of my shoes on the backs of my trousers and blew on my cold hands. I could almost see the deep armchair drawn close to the leaping flames, the tray of cocktail biscuits, the bottle of excellent sherry. Because of the sherry, I was always careful to time my visits for half an hour before lunch.

A maid answered my ring, beaming on me as an honoured guest, and led me to the room, crammed with expensive furniture and littered with glossy magazines and the latest novels. Mrs Pumphrey, in the high-backed chair by the fire, put down her books with a cry of delight. 'Trick! Tricki! Here is your Uncle Herriot.' I had been made an uncle very early and, sensing the advantages of the relationship, had made no objection.

Tricki, as always, bounded from his cushion, leaped on to the back of a sofa and put his paws on my shoulders. He then licked my face thoroughly before retiring, exhausted. He was soon exhausted because he was given roughly twice the amount of food needed for a dog of his size. And it was the wrong kind of food.

'Oh, Mr Herriot,' Mrs Pumphrey said, looking at her pet anxiously, 'I'm so glad you've come. Tricki has gone flop-bott again.'

This ailment, not to be found in any text book, was her way of describing the symptoms of Tricki's impacted anal glands. When the glands filled up, he showed discomfort by sitting down suddenly in mid-walk and his mistress would rush to the phone in great agitation.

'Mr Herriot! Please come, he's going flop-bott again!'

I hoisted the little dog on to a table and, by pressure on the anus with a pad of cotton wool, I evacuated the glands.

It baffled me that the Peke was always so pleased to see me. Any dog who could still like a man who grabbed him and squeezed his bottom hard every time they met had to have an incredibly forgiving nature. But Tricki never showed any resentment; in fact he was an outstandingly equable little animal, bursting with intelligence, and I was genuinely attached to him. It was a pleasure to be his personal physician.

The squeezing over, I lifted my patient from the table, noticing the increased weight, the padding of extra flesh over the ribs. 'You know, Mrs Pumphrey, you're over-feeding him again. Didn't I tell you to cut out all those pieces of cake and give him more protein?'

'Oh yes, Mr Herriot,' Mrs Pumphrey wailed. 'But what can I do? He's so tired of chicken.'

I shrugged; it was hopeless. I allowed the maid to lead me

to the palatial bathroom where I always performed a ritual handwashing after the operation. It was a huge room with a fully stocked dressing table, massive green ware and rows of glass shelves laden with toilet preparations. My private guest towel was laid out next to the slab of expensive soap.

Then I returned to the drawing-room, my sherry glass was filled, and I settled down by the fire to listen to Mrs Pumphrey. It couldn't be called a conversation because she did all the talking, but I always found it rewarding.

Mrs Pumphrey was likeable, gave widely to charities and would help anybody in trouble. She was intelligent and amusing and had a lot of waffling charm; but most people have a blind spot and hers was Tricki Woo. The tales she told about her darling ranged far into the realms of fantasy, and I waited eagerly for the next instalment.

'Oh Mr Herriot, I have the most exciting news. Tricki has a pen pal! Yes, he wrote a letter to the editor of *Doggy World* enclosing a donation, and told him that even though he was

descended from a long line of Chinese emperors, he had decided to come down and mingle freely with the common dogs. He asked the editor to seek out a pen pal for him among the dogs he knew so that they could correspond to their mutual benefit. And for this purpose, Tricki said he would adopt the name of Mr Utterbunkum. And, do you know, he received the most beautiful letter from the editor' (I could imagine the sensible man leaping upon this potential gold mine) 'who said he would like to introduce Bonzo Fotheringham, a lonely Dalmatian who would be delighted to exchange letters with a new friend in Yorkshire.'

I sipped the sherry. Tricki snored on my lap. Mrs Pumphrey went on.

'But I'm so disappointed about the new summerhouse—you know I got it specially for Tricki so we could sit out together on warm afternoons. It's such a nice little rustic shelter, but he's taken a passionate dislike to it. Simply loathes it—absolutely refuses to go inside. You should see the dreadful expression on his face when he looks at it. And do you know what he called it yesterday? Oh, I hardly dare tell you.' She looked around the room before leaning over and whispering: 'He called it "the bloody hut"!'

The maid struck fresh life into the fire and refilled my glass. The wind hurled a handful of sleet against the window. This, I thought, was the life. I listened for more.

'And did I tell you, Mr Herriot, Tricki had another good win yesterday? You know, I'm sure he must study the racing columns, he's such a tremendous judge of form. Well, he told me to back Canny Lad in the three o'clock at Redcar yesterday and, as usual, it won. He put on a shilling each way and got back nine shillings.'

These bets were always placed in the name of Tricki Woo and I thought with compassion of the reactions of the local bookies. The Darrowby turf accountants were a harassed and fugitive body of men. A board would appear at the end of some alley urging the population to invest with Joe Downs and enjoy perfect security. Joe would live for a few months on a knife edge while he pitted his wits against the knowledgeable citizens, but the end was always the same: a few favourites would win in a row and Joe would be gone in the night, taking his board with him. Once I asked a local inhabitant about the sudden departure of one of these luckless nomads. He replied unemotionally: 'Oh, we brok 'im.'

Losing a regular flow of shillings to a dog must have been a heavy cross for these unfortunate men to bear.

'I had such a frightening experience last week,' Mrs Pumphrey continued. 'I was sure I would have to call you out. Poor little Tricki—he went completely crackerdog!'

I mentally lined this up with flop-bott among the new canine diseases and asked for more information.

'It was awful. I was terrified. The gardener was throwing rings for Tricki—you know he does this for half an hour every day.' I had witnessed this spectacle several times. Hodgkin, a dour, bent old Yorkshireman who looked as though he hated all dogs and Tricki in particular, had to go out on the lawn every day and throw little rubber rings over and over again. Tricki bounded after them and brought them back, barking madly till the process was repeated. The bitter lines on the old man's face deepened as the game progressed. His lips moved continually, but it was impossible to hear what he was saying.

Mrs Pumphrey went on: 'Well, he was playing his game, and he does adore it so, when suddenly, without warning, he went crackerdog. He forgot all about his rings and began to run around in circles, barking and yelping in such a strange way. Then he fell over on his side and lay like a little dead thing. Do you know, Mr Herriot, I really thought he was dead, he lay so perfectly still. And what hurt me most was that Hodgkin began to laugh. He has been with me for twenty-four years and I have never even seen him smile, and yet, when he looked down at that still form, he broke into a queer, high-pitched cackle. It was horrid. I was just going to rush to the telephone when Tricki got up and walked away—he seemed perfectly normal.'

Hysteria, I thought, brought on by wrong feeding and overexcitement. I put down my glass and fixed Mrs Pumphrey with a severe glare. 'Now look, this is just what I was talking about. If you persist in feeding all that fancy rubbish to Tricki you are going to ruin his health. You really must get him on to a sensible dog diet of one or, at the most, two small meals a day of meat and brown bread or a little biscuit. And nothing in between.'

Mrs Pumphrey shrank into her chair, a picture of abject guilt. 'Oh, please don't speak to me like that. I do try to give him the right things, but it is so difficult. When he begs for his little titbits, I can't refuse him.' She dabbed her eyes with a handkerchief.

But I was unrelenting. 'All right, Mrs Pumphrey, it's up to you, but I warn you that if you go on as you are doing, Tricki will go crackerdog more and more often.'

I left the cosy haven with reluctance, pausing on the gravelled drive to look back at Mrs Pumphrey waving and Tricki, as always, standing against the window, his wide-mouthed face apparently in the middle of a hearty laugh.

Driving home, I mused on the many advantages of being Tricki's uncle. When he went to the seaside he sent me boxes of oak-smoked kippers; and when the tomatoes ripened in his greenhouse, he sent a pound or two every week. Tins of tobacco arrived regularly, sometimes with a photograph carrying a loving inscription.

But it was when the Christmas hamper arrived from Fortnum and Mason's that I decided that I was on a really good thing which should be helped along a bit. Hitherto, I had merely rung up and thanked Mrs Pumphrey for the gifts, and she had been rather cool, pointing out that it was Tricki who had sent the things and he was the one who should be thanked.

With the arrival of the hamper it came to me, blindingly, that I had been guilty of a grave error of tactics. I set myself to compose a letter to Tricki. Avoiding Siegfried's sardonic eye, I thanked my doggy nephew for his Christmas gifts and for all his generosity in the past. I expressed my sincere hopes that the festive fare had not upset his delicate digestion and suggested that if he did experience any discomfort he should have recourse to the black powder his uncle always prescribed. A vague feeling of professional shame was easily swamped by floating visions of kippers, tomatoes and hampers. I addressed the envelope to Master Tricki Pumphrey, Barlby Grange, and slipped it into the post-box with only a slight feeling of guilt.

On my next visit, Mrs Pumphrey drew me to one side. 'Mr Herriot,' she whispered, 'Tricki adored your charming letter and he will keep it always, but he was very put out about one thing—you addressed it to Master Tricki and he does insist

30

upon Mister. He was dreadfully affronted at first, quite beside himself, but when he saw it was from you he soon recovered his good temper. I can't think why he should have these little prejudices. Perhaps it is because he is an only dog—I do think an only dog develops more prejudices than one from a large family.'

Entering Skeldale House was like returning to a colder world. Siegfried bumped into me in the passage. 'Ah, who have we here? Why I do believe it's dear Uncle Herriot. And what have you been doing, Uncle? Slaving away at Barlby Grange, I expect. Poor fellow, you must be tired out. Do you really think it's worth it, working your fingers to the bone for another hamper?'

*

Even in the most high-powered small-animal practice with a wide spectrum of clients, Mrs Pumphrey would have been remarkable, but to me, working daily with earthy farmers in rough conditions, she was almost unreal. Her drawing-room was a warm haven in my hard life and Tricki Woo a lovable patient. The little Peke with his eccentric ailments has captured the affection of people all over the world, and I have received countless letters about him. He lived to a great age, flop-botting but happy right to the end. Mrs Pumphrey was eighty-eight when she died. She was one of the few who recognised herself in my books, and I know she appreciated the fun because when I stopped writing about her she wrote to me, saying, 'There's nuffin' to larf at now.' I wonder if she had her tongue in her cheek all the time?

Having No Hearts

SIR HUGH WALPOLE

MR and Mrs William Thrush owned a very sweet little house in Benedict Canyon, Los Angeles. That is, the postal address was Los Angeles, but Benedict Canyon is a Hollywood district if ever there was one. The Thrushes liked it for that reason, among others, and it gave William Thrush a very real pleasure when he heard the big motor wagons, between seven and eight in the morning, thundering down the Canyon on their way to location. This was about as near as he ever got to Pictures. He didn't wish to get any nearer, because he had a certain pride; not very much, but enough to make him desire to live in a society where he would be valued. Every morning he read the columns of film-making gossip in his daily paper, and always remarked to Isabelle: 'Goodness! If they don't have a time!' Then they both felt happy and a little superior too.

Isabelle Thrush had more pride than William. In fact, she had a great deal, and she spent most of her time in feeding it or inducing other people to do so. Would you say they were a happy pair? If you didn't know all about them, certainly yes. If you did know all about them, you would probably be doubtful, as William often was. Thee was something wrong between Isabelle and himself, although they'd been married for ten years and very seldom squabbled about anything. They didn't quarrel, because William refused to. Isabelle had undoubtedly a shrill temper, especially when she didn't get what she wanted. Of course, she couldn't get all the things that she wanted because William, who was a clerk in one of the leading banks in Los Angeles, had but a moderate salary. It happened, however, that a wealthy aunt of his had died some three or four years before and left him a pretty little sum.

He invested this wisely, so that even through the depression it remained. But Isabelle had all of it and then a little more.

He asked himself sometimes, in the privacy of the night, whether she were greedy. He couldn't be sure, because he often read in American magazines about the tyranny of the American wife and how she eagerly bled her husband. Well, Isabelle wasn't as bad as that. Gosh! He'd see to it if she tried anything like that on him. And so, he decided comfortably, she was better than most American wives. Isabelle considered herself a really magnificent creature, filled with all the virtues — courage, wisdom, self-sacrifice, love and endurance. She thought that William was extremely lucky to be married to her. And this thought produced in her a kindly, motherly air when he was around, as though she were saying: 'Little man, I'll look after you. Don't be afraid.' And then: 'How lucky really you are!'

The Thrushes had no children. That was Isabelle's wish, because she said it was wicked to bring a child into the world when you weren't going to give it everything of the best. William, once when he was feeling peevish because of his indigestion, remarked to her that his aunt's money would look after the child all right. But Isabelle was indignant, indeed, and said that there was a cruel strain in his nature which he would have to watch or he'd be a real sadist.

Having no children, Isabelle thought that it would be pleasant to have a dog. Many of her lady friends had them. There were, in fact, far more hospitals for dogs in Beverly and Hollywood than for human beings. And everybody said that the dog hospitals were so perfectly run that it was worth having a dog just for that reason alone. Isabelle wanted a dog, but there were problems to be settled. She understood that unless you had it as a puppy, it never became really fond of you. On the other hand, puppies had to be trained, and one's beautiful rugs and carpets suffered in the process. Then, what kind of dog should she have? There were the darling Cockers, the adorable Scotch Terriers, the amusing Dachshunds and the great big splendid Setters and Airedales. Some very lonely women had Pekinese, and then there were French Bulldogs. She couldn't make up her mind, and used to ask William which sort he preferred. And William, while he

was trying to guess what she wanted him to say, would look at her with that slow, puzzling stare, which Isabelle always interpreted as a tribute of gratified recognition of her brilliance and beauty. In reality, what he was saying was: 'What is the matter with Isabelle? She has gone somewhere and I don't know quite where.'

They lived the social life of ladies and gentlemen of moderate means in Hollywood. That is, they went to previews of celebrated pictures; in the summer they sat in the Bowl and wiped the damp off their fingers as they listened confusedly to symphonies by Brahms and Beethoven; they occasionally, with great daring, went with a friend or two to a burlesque in Los Angeles; they played bridge quite badly and gave little dinner-parties at which the coloured maid was never quite satisfactory. On the whole, it was a happy life.

Then one day, William, sitting alone and doing a crossword puzzle in the patio of his little Spanish house, had a visitor. Isabelle was out playing bridge with some friends and he was enjoying the lovely tranquil sunset, which lay like a golden sheet let down from heaven protectingly over the Canyon. In another half-hour the light would be gone, the air would be chill and sharp and he would go indoors and read his evening newspaper, turn on the heat, and wonder why he wasn't as happy as he ought to be. Then he saw enter his little garden, through a hole in the hedge, a French bulldog.

This dog sniffed around, looked at him from a distance with a very nervous expression, and then slowly advanced towards him, twisting and bending his thick body as though it were made of some elastic substance. William Thrush looked at the dog and disliked him exceedingly. He'd never had a great passion for dogs, ever since, years and years ago, his mother in a real temper had shaken him and told him he was as silly as a terrier puppy. So he'd grown up disliking dogs. And being himself a short little man, with large glasses and rather bowed legs, short dogs were especially unpleasant to him.

In any case, this dog seemed to him the ugliest ever. The dog seemed to him to be so very ugly that he felt a sort of nausea. He said, 'Shoo! Go away!' But the dog was evidently accustomed to being disliked. On looking back over this first meeting, William reflected on the fact that the dog resembled himself, in that if anyone disliked him some kind of paralysis seized him and he simply stayed and stayed, although he knew that he ought to go away. So did the dog now. He didn't come up to William, but lay at full length on the grass at a short distance and looked at him with his bulging, ugly, and in some unpleasant way, very human eyes.

William went up to him that he might frighten him out of the garden. But instead of that, the dog lay over on his back, wriggling his stomach and waving his legs feebly in the air. 'You're horrible!' William said aloud. 'I don't like dogs and never have. For God's sake, get out of here!' and then had a dreadful sense of speaking to himself—telling himself to get out of the house and garden and go somewhere. The dog turned over, sat up, gave him a beseeching but intimate look, as though he said: 'I know you much better than you think I

35

do. Nothing could destroy our intimacy and then went quietly out of the garden.

His wife returned later, vexed because she had lost at bridge. 'Such cards, my dear, you would have thought there was a spell on me. I don't know what to do about it. The cards I've been having lately!' He told her about the dog, but she wasn't in the very least interested, and after her absent-minded 'Really? How revolting!' went on with a long story about a shop in Los Angeles, where you could get a mink coat, or if it wasn't mink it looked very like it, by paying so small a sum weekly that you really didn't know you were paying it.

'No, you wouldn't,' said William, who was most unexpectedly cross, 'because I should be paying it.'

This upset her very much indeed. She detested mean people, and suddenly, standing there in the garden, which the sun had left so that it was cold and dead, she realized that William *was* mean, and that she had been living with a mean man for years and years, and it was quite wonderful for her to endure it. William on his part felt, oddly enough, that she had behaved to him just as he had behaved to the dog. 'Damn that dog!' he thought to himself. 'I can't get it out of my mind.'

Next morning, however, Isabelle was in excellent temper again, and for this reason: Helena Peters rang her up on the telephone and informed her that she had the most enchanting Cocker puppy. In fact she had two, a male and a female. Which of them would Isabelle prefer? It seems that the breed was perfect and its price in any kind of market would be fifty dollars apiece, but Helena was giving this dog to Isabelle and it was an act of friendship, because she loved Isabelle so dearly.

'I don't know why she's doing it,' Isabelle said to William. 'She wants something or other. Helena never gives anything for nothing—but it sounds a perfect puppy. I'll go around for it myself this morning.'

William very feebly suggested the disadvantages of having puppies—the wear and tear, the unpleasant hidden smells, the certainty that the dog would have distemper and die and so on. Isabelle waved all these objections aside. She had cherished them herself until William mentioned them. But, as was so often the case, her brain, so superior to William's, insisted that

36

anything that he said must be foolish. So she went around and fetched the puppy.

Standing in the doorway at lunch-time, her face rosy with pleasure, the puppy lying in her arms against her dark green dress, its large amber eyes turned up to hers, its tongue suddenly licking her cheek, its soft brown body, its long silken ears, there was a picture so lovely that William, with a pang at his heart, wondered why it was that he didn't love her more dearly.

The puppy slowly turned its head towards William and looked at him. Was there in its eyes, even from the very first moment, a certain contempt? Had it hoped, young as it was, to find William someone quite different? Did its gaze wander to the incipient paunch, the bowed legs, and rise again to the round, rather pathetic face in which the eyes, William's best feature, were hidden behind the dull, gleaming glasses?

As they stood together in the cosy living-room, while the puppy wandered cautiously from table to chair, from chair to sofa, he was sure that Isabelle was above the puppy's social line, and that he, alas! was below it. The puppy sat down. 'Look out!' William cried. 'He had better be put in the garden.' Isabelle regarded him scornfully.

'*This* puppy is intelligent. Helena tells the most amazing stories about it. It isn't, technically, house-trained, of course, but it is wonderfully mature for a puppy. Helena says it avoids all the really valuable rugs.'

And the puppy did seem to be wonderfully sophisticated. Not that it wasn't a real puppy. It rushed about madly, it bit everything and everybody within sight, played with a string as though it had discovered the secret of perpetual motion at last, it went suddenly to sleep in your arms in the most adorable manner. It had everything that a puppy ought to have. The trouble was that it knew all about its charm. It was perfectly aware that when it lay on its side and grinned at you over its silken ear, it was entirely bewitching. And when it pretended to be angry, growling, showing its white little teeth and flashing its amber eyes, no-one in the world could resist it.

Isabelle insisted that it should be called Roosevelt.

'Why?' asked William.

'Well, I think he's the most wonderful man in the world, and now, when people are turning against him and saying horrid things about the New Deal and that he's a Socialist and everything of that sort, one has to stand up for him and come right out into the open.'

'I don't see,' said William, 'that calling the puppy Roosevelt is coming out into the open.'

'It's a kind of demonstration. After all, isn't the puppy the sweetest thing in the world?'

'I don't think,' said William, sulkily, 'that Roosevelt would like anyone to call him the sweetest thing in the world. He isn't at all that kind of man.'

She looked at him reflectively. What had happened to him? Was it, perhaps, that she was only now really beginning to discover him? And if she discovered him a little further, how would it be then? Would she be able to endure it?

There is no doubt that after the arrival of the puppy, they bickered a good deal. A happy marriage between two persons depends altogether on mutual charity, unless one of the two is so absolutely a sheep that he doesn't mind what is done to him. Isabelle was a woman who had charity for everyone and everybody, but it was charity of a kind. It never worked unless Isabelle's pride was properly fed first. William, unfortunately, continued increasingly to look at her with that puzzled bewildered expression that is so justly irritating to wives.

And then the puppy confirmed her in her growing sense of injustice. People love dogs because they are so flattering. If you are unjust to your friend and feel a certain shame, your dog swiftly restores your self-confidence. It never knows that you have been mean or jealous or grasping. It encourages you to be kindly to itself, and when you respond, it loves you.

The puppy, Roosevelt, must have been born a courtier; its tact was perfectly astonishing. For instance, when it arrived in the bedroom in the morning and greeted the twin beds with little yelps of ecstatic pleasure, it almost at once discriminated between Isabelle's bed and William's. It went to William first so that Isabelle, looking enchanting in her early-morning sleepy bewilderment, was given the opportunity to say: 'Isn't he coming to Mummy then?' and Isabelle's little smile of gratified pleasure when it rushed over to her, as though William never existed, was something delightful to witness.

When guests were present, as they often were, how

Roosevelt was adored! And how then he made it appear that it was really because of Isabelle that he seemed so charming. He bit delicately at a lady's dress, or chewed playfully at the corner of a handsome purse with a side glance at Isabelle, as though he were saying to the ladies: 'It is because I love her so. It is because she is such a perfect darling. It is because I'm so wonderfully happy with her that I'm behaving like this.' William had never greatly cared for Isabelle's lady friends and generally avoided occasions when they would be present. That was one of Isabelle's complaints. But now he simply could not bear to be there. Isabelle's patronage of him was one thing, but Isabelle and Roosevelt together were more than any man could endure. And so they had a quarrel.

'You're behaving ridiculously about that dog.'

'Ridiculously?' That was something that Isabelle never would forgive. 'You've hated it,' she asserted, her eyes flashing, 'ever since its arrival. And why? Why? Shall I tell you?'

'Please do,' said William, stony-faced.

'Because it prefers me to you, because it always has.'

'Oh, damn the dog!' said William.

Meanwhile, the French bulldog made frequent appearances, but never when Isabelle was about. Greatly though William disliked it, he began, very reluctantly, to be interested in its personality. It wanted so terribly to be loved, and it was a certainty nobody loved it. Building was in process near by. And William, after he shaved in the morning, looking out of the window, would watch its approach to the different workmen, wiggling its body and leaping heavily up and down, and all the workmen repulsed it. They were good, kindly men, no doubt, as most American workmen are, but they felt about it as William did, that it was too ugly to be borne. He christened it Ugly, and as soon as he had given it a name it seemed to have at once a closer relationship with him.

'Get away, Ugly, you beastly dog!' he would say. And the dog would be apparently in an ecstasy of enjoyment at being called anything at all. Once in a fit of abstraction, sitting there wondering why it was that he was so lonely, wondering why everything was going wrong with Isabelle and what it was that she really lacked, Ugly came close to him, and not knowing what he did, he stroked its back and tickled it behind the ear. He was aware then of a wave of affection that was almost terrifying.

As soon as William realized what he had done, he moved away with an irritated murmur. The dog did not follow him, but stayed there stretched out looking at him. How unpleasant is this naked sentimentality in this modern realistic world! How we run from sentiment and how right it is that we should do so! And yet William was sentimental too. Someone loved him, and although he detested the dog, he was not quite as lonely as he'd been before.

It happened, of course, that Roosevelt and Ugly had various encounters. Ugly would come across the path into the garden, and finding Roosevelt there, hoped that they might have a game. But Roosevelt, young as he was, played only with his social equals. He did not snarl at Ugly. He did nothing mean or common. He allowed Ugly supplicatingly to sniff him, to walk around him, even to cavort and prance a little, and then very quietly he strolled indoors. And then Isabelle realized that Ugly existed.

'William, do look at that hideous dog! What's it doing here? Shoo! Shoo! Get away, you horrible animal!' and Ugly went. William found himself, to his own surprise, defending Ugly.

'He isn't so bad,' he said. 'Not much to look at, of course, but friendly, obedient, rather a decent dog.'

'Oh, you would!' said Isabelle. 'It only needs the most hideous animal I've seen in my life to come your way for you to praise it. Really, William, I don't know what's happening to you.'

William smiled at her and said very gently: 'I don't know what's happening, either.' He made then, almost as though it were under Ugly's instructions, a serious attempt to persuade Isabelle to love him again. He was very patient, thoughtful, generous. A few people in the world knew that William Thrush had an extraordinary amount of charm—even a kind of penetrating wit when he liked. But William's charm was unconscious. It failed him when he tried to summon it. And now the more he tried, the more irritating to her he became.

The breach grew wider, and Isabelle confessed to her closer

friends that she didn't know whether she could stand it much longer. Then, as nothing ever stays where it is but always advances to its appointed climax, the catastrophe occurred.

One of the troubles between William and Isabelle had always been that William liked to read and Isabelle did not. William liked long, long novels, preferably about family life. Novels that went on and on for ever and ever, in which you could be completely lost. Novels that deceived you with so friendly and profuse a carelessness that it was like a personal compliment to yourself. Isabelle, on the other hand, could not bear to read. She looked at the social column of the daily paper and sometimes a film magazine or a fashion monthly. But for the most part, as she said, she adored to read, but 'just didn't have the time to open a book'.

This had once been very sad to William, who in his young glowing days had imagined sitting on one side of the fire reading aloud to his dear little wife, who was sewing things for the baby, but nevertheless able to take it all in and speculate about the characters. Well, on this particular day, he was deep in a novel by one of those English novelists who have so many characters in their family that they have to have a genealogical table at the end of the book. To this same table he would often refer with a pleasing sense that he was staying in the most delightful house with an enormous family of cousins. He read cosily and comfortably. The door leading on to the porch was open and the afternoon sun poured bountifully in. He was aware then that something had occurred. There had been no sound, no movement, but looking up, he beheld a very horrible sight.

Ugly was advancing towards him, and one of his eyes, a blood-red ball, was nearly torn from his head. The dog made no sound whatever. He simply came towards William, only once and again lifting a paw feebly, as though he were absurdly puzzled as to what had happened to him. When he got near to William, he crouched down, and, still without a sound, looked up into his face.

William's first feeling was of nausea. He hated the sight of blood. His sensitive soul was intensely distressed by any kind of physical suffering. This seemed to him quite horrible. Then almost at once he was overwhelmed with pity. He'd

never in his life before been so sorry for anything. Something in the distressed trusting patience of the dog won his heart completely and for ever. That the animal should be so silent, making no complaint, seemed to him himself as he ought to be. That was how he'd wish to behave had such a terrible thing happened to him. How, he was sure, he would *not* behave.

He said nothing, but arose from his chair, was about to take the dog in his arms and hasten at once with it to the nearest dog hospital, when Isabelle entered and Roosevelt scampered out from a room near by. She was smiling and happy. She greeted the cocker puppy with little cries of baby joy. 'Oh, the darling! The ickle, ickle darling! Wasn't he an angel to come and see his mummy?' And then she saw the other dog. Ugly had turned his head and was looking at her. She screamed. She put her hands in front of her face.

'Oh, William, how horrible! How frightful! It must be killed at once!'

William got up, took the heavy, bleeding dog in his arms, and without a word, passed her and went out.

He went into the garage, laid the dog on the old rug, got out his car, picked up the dog again, got into the car with him and drove off to the dog hospital. Here he talked to a very kindly plump little man and discussed whether Ugly should be destroyed or not. When the little man took Ugly in his arms to examine him, the dog very slowly turned his head, and, with his one eye, looked at William as much as to say: 'If you think this is the right thing for me to do, I'll suffer it.' William even nodded his head to the dog and a silent understanding seemed to pass between them.

'It seems to have no damage anywhere else,' the doctor said. 'It was done, of course, by another dog. They do that. They just take hold of one place and don't let go again. Poor old fellow!' The dog doctor caressed him. 'Not very handsome, anyway, is he?'

'Oh, I don't know,' said William; 'he's got a kind of character about him, I think.'

'Is he your dog?' asked the doctor.

'No. I don't think he belongs to anybody, but he comes to our garden sometimes. I've grown interested in him.'

'Well, I can tell you this,' the doctor said, 'I guess he'll be all right. We can sew it up so you'll hardly notice it. He won't exactly be a beauty, you know.'

'Yes, I know,' said William, who wasn't a beauty, either. He went home.

For some reason or another, Isabelle had been greatly excited by the incident. She sat there and gave William a terrific lecture, the total of which was that for ever so long now he'd been letting himself go. He was becoming soppy, almost a sissy, in fact.

'A sissy?' said William, indignantly.

'Oh, well, you know what I mean. You're getting dreadfully sentimental. You always had a tendency that way, but lately it's been terrible. All my friends notice it.'

I don't know why it is, but there is almost nothing so irritating in the world as to be told by someone that one's friends have been silently, mysteriously, observing one to one's disadvantage. William, for the first time in their married life, lost all control of himself. He stood up and raved. He said that it didn't matter whether he was getting sentimental or not, but anyway, perhaps sentiment wasn't a bad thing. What really mattered was that Isabelle was selfish, cold and unkind! That she hadn't any idea of the horrible woman she was becoming. Isabelle suitably replied. In fact, they both thoroughly lost their tempers. And while this was going on, Roosevelt sat in Isabelle's lap making little playful bites at Isabelle's dress and beautiful fingers. While he sat there, he looked at William with a really terrible sarcasm in his soft, amber eyes—sarcasm and scorn.

'I tell you what,' William cried in a last frenzy, 'I hate that dog! Puppies ought to be nice, gentle, loving creatures. Look at him! He's hard as iron and the most horrid snob.'

So then Isabelle burst into tears, went to her room and locked her door. There followed days of constrained silence, and after that William went down to the dog hospital.

'He's a patient dog, I must say,' the doctor remarked. 'Never a whine. Seems fond of you too.'

William was surprised at the pleasure that he felt at the tribute. The day came when Ugly's eye was gone, the empty space sewed up, and his whole air rather that of a drunken soldier who had been in the wars. What was to be done with him? William, realizing that the crisis in his life was upon him, decided that if Isabelle had her Roosevelt, he should have his Ugly. He went home and told her so. This was at breakfast. She said no word and he left for his work in the city.

When he returned in the late afternoon there was a strange silence about the house. He had been thinking and had decided that in some way or another this awful trouble with Isabelle must be stopped. After all, surely he loved her. Or if he didn't, they were at least man and wife. How miserable, how lost, he would be without her! Would he? At that appalling wonder, his whole soul shook. So he returned home with every intention of making everything all right again, although now he was to do that he didn't in the least know.

Ugly greeted him, coming in from the garden, rolling his body about, baring his teeth, showing an ecstasy of pleasure. But Isabelle was not there, nor Roosevelt. On his writing-table lay the note so essential to all dramatists and novelists who have learnt their job. What it said was that Isabelle had gone to her mother in Santa Barbara and would remain there. She wished that William would give her a divorce. She had been seeing for a long time how impossible things were. She had taken Roosevelt with her.

William read the note and felt a dreadful shame and despair. His impulse was to depart at once for Santa Barbara. And so he would have done if it had not been for Ugly. But he could not leave him just then. The dog was new to the house and the servants had no special affection for him. In a day or two he would go. But he did not. The days passed and he did not.

A quite terrible thing happened to him. He found that he liked the house better without Isabelle than with her. He found that he adored his freedom. That he could now have liberty of action and thought, that showed him what all these years he'd been missing. He discovered a number of other things. He took long walks up the Canyon with Ugly. He talked to the dog and it seemed to him that the dog answered him. Strangest of all, he was less lonely than he had been when Isabelle was there. It was as though for years there had been a padlock on his mind. Someone, something, had all the time inhibited his thought.

A letter came from Isabelle and he made his discovery. In her

45

letter she said she was now ready to return. Santa Barbara wasn't half the place it had once been, and her mother was in many ways unsympathetic, and, he would be glad to hear, she missed her dear old William. As he wrote his reply to her letter, he solved his problem. This was the letter he wrote.

Dear Isabelle,

I don't want you to come back. This sounds very unkind and rude on my part, but I've done a lot of thinking in the last few weeks and I know that I must be honest. For a long while I've been wondering what it was that was wrong between us. I admire you so much. You are far finer than I. You have been so good and so kind for so long, that it seems absurd to say that you are lacking in anything. But you are. You have no heart. That sounds like a thing you read in a novel, but I mean it just like that. I don't think you're any the worse for not having one—it is only that I have suddenly discovered while I've been alone here that that is the one real difference between human beings. Either you have a heart, or you haven't one. What I mean is, either the heart is the part of your body that functions more than any other or not. This is the one insuperable difference between people. Not whether you're a Fascist or Communist, American or French, teetotaller or a drunkard, clever or stupid. All those things can be got over quite easily. I'm not saying either that the people with hearts are preferable to those without. I think it is possibly just the opposite. The people with hearts are nearly always too sentimental, too emotional, prevent the work of the world being done, get in the way of the real thinkers. The people without hearts are, as the world is now going, the ones we really want. But the difference is there. I can't help feeling emotionally about things. You can't help the opposite. But we mustn't live together any more. This is a difference that nothing can get over.

Yours sincerely,

William.

PS—There is the same difference between Roosevelt and Ugly.

HAVING NO HEARTS

When he had posted the letter and was walking in a last cool flash of sunshine up the Canyon, Ugly ambling along beside him, he thought that possibly no one had ever written so silly a letter. And yet, he had this sense that he had made this marvellous discovery. He looked at all his friends, male and female, and saw the dividing line with absolute clearness. He looked beyond the other great figures in the world. Einstein had a heart—Hitler, even. On the other hand, Mussolini possibly not. And Simon Callahan, the manager of his bank in Los Angeles, most certainly not! Ugly, whose vision of course was now sadly dimmed, saw a golden leaf, one of the first signs of autumn, twirling through the air. He leapt rather foolishly, ran a little way and looked back at William. William smiled encouragement. Then he turned back home, Ugly delightedly following.

Comet

SAMUEL A. DERIEUX

NO puppy ever came into the world under more favourable conditions than Comet. He was descended from a famous family of pointers. Both his mother and father were champions. Before he opened his eyes, while he was still crawling about over his brothers and sisters, blind as puppies are at birth, Jim Thompson, Mr Devant's kennel master, picked him out.

'That's the best un in the bunch.'

When he was only three weeks old he pointed a butterfly that lit in the yard in front of his nose.

'Come here, Molly,' yelled Jim to his wife. 'Pointed—the little cuss!'

When Thompson started taking the growing pups out of the yard, into the fields to the side of the Devants' great southern winter home, Oak Knob, it was Comet who strayed farthest from the man's protecting care. And when Jim taught them all to follow when he said 'Heel,' to drop when he said 'Drop,' and to stand stock-still when he said 'Ho,' he learned far more quickly than the others.

At six months he set his first covey of quail, and remained perfectly staunch. 'He's goin' to make a great dog,' said Thompson. Everything—size, muscle, nose, intelligence, earnestness—pointed to the same conclusion. Comet was one of the favoured of the gods.

One day, after the leaves had tuned red and brown and the mornings grown chilly, a crowd of people, strangers to him, arrived at Oak Knob. Then out of the house with Thompson came a big man in tweed clothes, and the two walked straight to the curious young dogs, who were watching them with shining eyes and wagging tails.

'Well, Thompson,' said the big man, 'which is the future champion you've been writing me about?'

'Pick him out for yourself, sir,' said Thompson confidently.

After that they talked a long time planning for the future of Comet. His yard training was now over (Thompson was only yard trainer), and he must be sent to a man experienced in training and handling for field trials.

'Larsen's the man to bring him out,' said the big man in tweeds, who was George Devant himself. 'I saw his dogs work in the Canadian Derby.'

Thompson spoke hesitatingly, apologetically, as if he hated to bring the matter up. 'Mr Devant . . . you remember, sir, a long time ago Larsen sued us for old Ben.'

'Yes, Thompson; I remember, now that you speak of it.'

'Well, you remember the court decided against him, which was the only thing it could do, for Larsen didn't have any more right to that dog than the Sultan of Turkey. But, Mr Devant, I was there, and I saw Larsen's face when the case went against him.'

Devant looked keenly at Thompson.

'Another thing, Mr Devant,' Thompson went on, still hesitatingly; 'Larsen had a chance to get hold of this breed of pointers and lost out, because he dickered too long, and acted cheesy. Now they've turned out to be famous. Some men never forget a thing like that. Larsen's been talkin' these pointers down ever since, sir.'

'Go on,' said Devant.

'I know Larsen's a good trainer. But it'll mean a long trip for the young dog to where he lives. Now, there's an old trainer lives near here, Wade Swygert. There never was a straighter man than him. He used to train dogs in England.'

Devant smiled. 'Thompson, I admire your loyalty to your friends; but I don't think much of your business sense. We'll turn over some of the others to Swygert, if he wants 'em. Comet must have the best. I'll write Larsen to-night, Thompson. Tomorrow, crate Comet and send him off.'

Just as no dog ever came into the world under more favourable auspices, so no dog ever had a bigger 'send-off' than Comet. Even the ladies of the house came out to exclaim over him, and Marian Devant, pretty, eighteen, and a sportswoman, stooped down, caught his head between her hands, looked into his fine eyes, and wished him 'Good luck, old man'. In the living-room the men laughingly drank toasts to his future, and from the high-columned portico Marian Devant waved him good-bye, as in his clean padded crate he was driven off, a bewildered youngster, to the station.

Two days and two nights he travelled, and at noon of the third day, at a lonely railroad station in a prairie country that rolled like a heavy sea, he was lifted, crate and all, off the train. A lean, pale-eyed, sanctimonious-looking man came toward him.

'Some beauty that, Mr Larsen,' said the agent as he helped Larsen's man lift the crate on to a small truck.

'Yes,' drawled Larsen in a meditative voice, 'pretty enough to look at—but he looks scared—er—timid.'

'Of course he's scared,' said the agent; 'so would you be if they was to put you in some kind of a whale of a balloon an' ship you in a crate to Mars.'

The station agent poked his hands through the slats and patted the head. Comet was grateful for that, because everything was strange. He had not whined nor complained on the trip, but his heart had pounded fast, and he had been homesick.

And everything continued to be strange: the treeless country through which he was driven, the bald house and huge barns where he was lifted out, the dogs that crowded about him when he was turned into the kennel yard. These eyed him with enmity and walked round and round him. But he stood his ground staunchly for a youngster, returning fierce look for fierce look, growl for growl, until the man called him away and chained him to a kennel.

For days Comet remained chained, a stranger in a strange land. Each time at the click of the gate announcing Larsen's entrance he sprang to his feet from force of habit, and stared hungrily at the man for the light he was accustomed to see in human eyes. But with just a glance at him the man would turn one or more of the other dogs loose and ride off to train them.

But he was not without friends of his own kind. Now and then another young dog (he alone was chained up) would stroll his way with wagging tail, or lie down near by, in that strange bond of sympathy that is not confined to man. Then Comet would feel better and would want to play, for he was still half puppy. Sometimes he would pick up a stick and shake it, and his partner would catch the other end. They would tug and growl with mock ferocity, and then lie down and look at each other curiously.

If any attention had been paid him by Larsen, Comet would have quickly overcome his feeling of strangeness. He was no milksop. He was like an overgrown boy, off at college or in some foreign city. He was sensitive, and not sure of himself. Had Larsen gained his confidence, it would all have been different. And as for Larsen—he knew that perfectly well.

One fine sunny afternoon Larsen entered the yard, came straight to him, and turned him loose. In the exuberance of his spirits he ran round and round the yard, barking in the faces of his friends. Larsen let him out, mounted a horse, and commanded him to heel. He obeyed with wagging tail.

A mile or more down the road Larsen turned off into the fields. Across his saddle was something the young pointer had had no experience with—a gun. That part of his education Thompson had neglected, at least put off, for he had not expected that Comet would be sent away so soon. That was where Thompson had made a mistake.

At the command 'Hi on' the young pointer ran eagerly around the horse, and looked up into the man's face to be sure he had heard aright. At something he saw there the tail and ears drooped momentarily, and there came over him again a feeling of strangeness, almost of dismay. Larsen's eyes were mere slits of blue glass, and his mouth was set in a thin line.

At a second command, though, he galloped off swiftly, boldly. Round and round an extensive field of straw he circled, forgetting any feeling of strangeness now, every fibre of his being intent on the hunt, while Larsen, sitting on his horse, watched him with appraising eyes.

Suddenly there came to Comet's nose the smell of game birds, strong, pungent, compelling. He stiffened into an earnest, beautiful point. Heretofore in the little training he had had Thompson had come up behind him, flushed the birds, and made him drop. And now Larsen, having quickly dismounted and tied his horse, came up behind him, just as

51

Thompson had done, except that in Larsen's hand was the gun.

The old-fashioned black powder of a generation ago makes a loud explosion. It sounds like a cannon compared with the modern smokeless powder now used by all hunters. Perhaps it was only an accident that had caused Larsen before he left the house to load his pump gun with black powder shells.

As for Comet he only knew that the birds rose; then above his head burst an awful roar, almost splitting his tender eardrums, shocking every sensitive nerve, filling him with terror such as he had never felt before. Even then, in the confusion and horror of the surprise, he turned to the man, head ringing, eyes dilated. A single reassuring word, and he would have steadied. As for Larsen, though, he declared afterward (to others and to himself even) that he noticed no nervousness in the dog; that he was only intent on getting several birds for breakfast.

Twice, three times, four times, the pump gun bellowed in its cannon-like roar, piercing the eardrums, shattering the nerves. Comet turned; one more glance backward at a face, strange, exultant—and then the puppy in him conquered. Tail tucked, he ran away from that shattering noise.

Miles he ran. Now and then, stumbling over briars, he yelped. Not once did he look back. His tail was tucked, his eyes crazy with fear. Seeing a house, he made for that. It was the noon hour, and a group of farm hands was gathered in the yard. One of them, with a cry 'Mad dog!' ran into the house after a gun. When he came out, they told him the dog was under the porch. And so he was. Pressed against the wall, in the darkness, the magnificent young pointer with the quivering soul waited, panting, eyes gleaming, the horror still ringing in his ears.

Here Larsen found him that afternoon. A boy crawled underneath the porch and dragged him out. He, who had started life favoured of the gods, who that morning even had been full of high spirits, who had circled a field like a champion, was now a cringing, shaking creature, like a homeless cur.

And thus it happened that Comet came home, in disgrace—a gun-shy dog, a coward, expelled from college, not for some youthful prank, but because he was—yellow. And he knew he was disgraced. He saw it in the face of the big man, Devant, who looked at him in the yard where he had spent his happy puppyhood, then turned away. He knew it because of what he saw in the face of Jim Thompson.

In the house was a long and plausible letter, explaining how it happened:

I did everything I could. I never was as surprised in my life. The dog's hopeless.

As for the other inhabitants of the big house, their minds were full of the events of the season: de luxe hunting parties, more society events than hunts; lunches in the woods served by uniformed butlers; launch rides up the river; arriving and departing guests. Only one of them, except Devant himself, gave the gun-shy dog a thought. Marian Devant came out to visit him in his disgrace. She stooped before him as she had done on that other and happier day, and again caught his head between her hands. But his eyes did not meet hers, for in his dim way he knew he was not now what he had been.

'I don't believe he's yellow—inside!' she declared, looking up at Thompson, her cheeks flushed.

Thompson shook his head.

'I tried him with a gun, Miss Marian,' he declared. 'I just showed it to him, and he ran into his kennel.'

'I'll go get mine. He won't run from me.'

But at sight of her small gun it all came back. Again he seemed to hear the explosion that had shattered his nerves. The Terror had entered his very soul. In spite of her pleading, he made for his kennel. Even the girl turned away from him now. And as he lay panting in the shelter of his kennel he knew that never again would men look at him as they had looked, or life be sweet to him as it had been.

Then there came to Oak Knob an old man to see Thompson. He had been on many seas, he had fought in a dozen wars, and had settled at last on a little truck farm near by. Somewhere, in his life full of adventure and odd jobs, he had trained dogs and horses. His face was lined and seamed, his hair was white, his eyes piercing, blue and kind. Wade Swygert was his name.

'There's been dirty work,' he said, when he looked at the dog. 'I'll take him if you're goin' to give him away.'

Give him away—who had been Championship hope!

Marian Devant came out and looked into the face of the old man, shrewdly, understandingly.

'Can you cure him?' she demanded.

'I doubt it, miss,' was the sturdy answer.

'You will try?'

The blue eyes lighted up. 'Yes, I'll try.'

'Then you can have him. And—if there's any expense—'

'Come, Comet,' said the old man.

That night, in a neat, humble house, Comet ate supper, placed before him by a stout old woman, who had followed this old man to the ends of the world. That night he slept before their fire. Next day he followed the old man all about the place. Several days and nights passed this way, then, while he lay before the fire, old Swygert came in with a gun. At sight of it Comet sprang to his feet. He tried to rush out of the room, but the doors were closed. Finally, he crawled under the bed.

Every night after that Swygert got out the gun, until he crawled under the bed no more. Finally, one day the man fastened the dog to a tree in the yard, then came out with a gun. A sparrow lit in a tree, and he shot it. Comet tried to break the rope. All his panic had returned; but the report had not shattered him as that other did, for the gun was loaded light.

After that, frequently the old man shot a bird in his sight, loading the gun more and more heavily, and each time after the shot coming to him, showing him the bird, and speaking to him kindly, gently. But for all that the Terror remained in his heart.

One afternoon the girl, accompanied by a young man, rode over on horseback, dismounted, and came in. She always stopped when she was riding by.

'It's mighty slow business,' old Swygert reported; 'I don't know whether I'm makin' any headway or not.'

That night old Mrs Swygert told him she thought he had better give it up. It wasn't worth the time and worry. The dog was just yellow.

Swygert pondered a long time. 'When I was a kid,' he said at last, 'there came up a terrible thunderstorm. It was in South

America. I was water boy for a railroad gang, and the storm drove us in a shack. While lightnin' was hittin' all around, one of the grown men told me it always picked out boys with red hair. My hair was red, an' I was little and ignorant. For years I was skeered of lightnin'. I never have quite got over it. But no man ever said I was yellow.'

Again he was silent for a while. Then he went on: 'I don't seem to be makin' much headway, I admit that. I'm lettin' him run away as far as he can. Now I've got to shoot an' make him come toward the gun himself, right while I'm shootin' it.'

Next day Comet was tied up and fasted, and next, until he was gaunt and famished. Then, on the afternoon of the third day, Mrs Swygert, at her husband's direction, placed before him, within reach of his chain, some raw beefsteak. As he started for it, Swygert shot. He drew back, panting, then, hunger getting the better of him, started again. Again Swygert shot.

After that for days Comet 'Ate to music,' as Swygert expressed it. 'Now,' he said, 'he's got to come toward the gun when he's not even tied up.'

Not far from Swygert's house is a small pond and on one side the banks are perpendicular. Toward this pond the old man, with the gun under his arm, and the dog following, went. Here in the silence of the woods, with just the two of them together, was to be a final test.

On the shelving bank Swygert picked up a stick and tossed it into the middle of the pond with the command to 'fetch'. Comet sprang eagerly in and retrieved it. Twice this was repeated. But the third time, as the dog approached the shore, Swygert picked up the gun and fired.

Quickly the dog dropped the stick, then turned and swam toward the other shore. Here, so precipitous were the banks, he could not get a foothold. He turned once more and struck out diagonally across the pond. Swygert met him and fired.

Over and over it happened. Each time, after he fired, the old man stooped down with extended hand and begged him to come on. His face was grim now, and, though the day was cool, sweat stood out on his brow. 'You'll face the music,' he said, 'or you'll drown. Better be dead than called yellow.'

The dog was growing weary now. His head was barely above

water. His efforts to clamber up the opposite bank were feeble, frantic. Yet, each time as he drew near the shore Swygert fired.

He was not using light loads now. He was using the regular load of the bird hunter. Time had passed for temporizing. The sweat was standing out all over his face. The sternness in his eyes was terrible to see, for it was the sternness of a man who is suffering.

A dog can't swim a long time. The sun dropped over the trees. Still the firing went on, regularly, like a minute gun.

Just before the sun set an exhausted dog staggered toward an old man almost as exhausted as he. The dog had been too near death and was too faint to care now for the gun that was being fired over his head. On and on he came, toward the man, disregarding the noise of the gun. It would not hurt him, that he knew at last. He might have many enemies, but the gun, in the hands of this man, was not one of them. Suddenly old Swygert sank down and took the dripping dog in his arms.

'Old boy,' he said, 'old boy.'

That night Comet lay before the fire, and looked straight into the eyes of a man, as he used to look in the old days.

Next season Larsen, glancing over his sporting papers, was astonished to see that among promising Derbys the fall trials had called forth was a pointer named Comet. He would have thought it some other dog than the one who had disappointed him so by turning out gun-shy, in spite of all his efforts to prevent, had it not been for the fact that the entry was booked as: 'Comet; owner, Miss Marian Devant; handler, Wade Swygert.'

Next year he was still more astonished to see in the same paper that Comet, handled by Swygert, had won first place in a Western trial, and was prominently spoken of as a National Championship possibility. As for him, he had no young entries to offer, but was staking everything on the National Championship, where he was to enter Larsen's Peerless II.

It was strange how things fell out—but things have a habit of turning out strangely in field trials, as well as elsewhere. When Larsen reached the town where the National Championship was to be run, there on the street, straining at the leash held by old Swygert, whom he used to know, was a seasoned young pointer, with a white body, a brown head, and a brown saddle spot—the same pointer he had seen two years before turn tail and run in that terror a dog never quite overcomes.

But the strangest thing of all happened that night at the drawing, when, according to the slips taken at random from a hat, it was declared that on the following Wednesday Comet, the pointer, was to run with Peerless II.

It gave Larsen a strange thrill, this announcement. He left the meeting and went straightway to his room. There for a long time he sat pondering. Next day at a hardware store he bought some black powder and some shells.

The race was to be run next day, and that night in his room he loaded half-a-dozen shells. It would have been a study in faces to watch him as he bent over his work, on his lips a smile. Into the shells he packed all the powder they could stand, all the powder his trusted gun could stand, without bursting. It was a load big enough to kill a bear, to bring down a buffalo. It was a load that would echo and re-echo in the hills.

On the morning that Larsen walked out in front of the judges and the field, Peerless II at the leash, old Swygert, with Comet at his side, he glanced around at the 'field,' or spectators. Among them was a handsome young woman, and with her, to his amazement, George Devant. He could not help chuckling inside himself as he thought of what would happen that day, for once a gun-shy dog, always a gun-shy dog—that was *his* experience.

As for Comet, he faced the straw fields eagerly, confidently, already a veteran. Long ago fear of the gun had left him, for the most part. There were times when at a report above his head he still trembled, and the shocked nerves in his ear gave a twinge like that of a bad tooth. But always at the quiet voice of the old man, his god, he grew steady, and remained staunch.

Some disturbing memory did start within him to-day as he glanced at the man with the other dog. It seemed to him as if in another and an evil world he had seen that face. His heart began to pound fast, and his tail drooped for a moment. Within an hour it was all to come back to him—the terror, the panic, the agony of that far-away time.

He looked up at old Swygert, who was his god, and to whom his soul belonged, though he was booked as the property of Miss Marian Devant. Of the arrangements he could know

57

nothing, being a dog. Old Swygert, having cured him, could not meet the expenses of taking him to field trials. The girl had come to the old man's assistance, an assistance which he had accepted only under condition that the dog should be entered as hers, with himself as handler.

'Are you ready, gentlemen?' the judges asked.

'Ready,' said Larsen and old Swygert.

And Comet and Peerless II were speeding away across that field, and behind them came handlers, and judges and spectators, all mounted.

It was a race people still talk about, and for a reason, for strange things happened that day. At first there was nothing unusual. It was like any other field trial. Comet found birds, and Swygert, his handler, flushed them and shot. Comet remained steady. Then Peerless II found a covey, and Larsen flushed them and shot. And so for an hour it went.

Then Comet disappeared, and old Swygert, riding hard and looking for him, went out of sight over a hill. But Comet had not gone far. As a matter of fact, he was near by, hidden in some high straw, pointing a covey of birds. One of the spectators spied him, and called the judges' attention to him. Everybody, including Larsen, rode up to him, but still Swygert had not come back.

They called him, but the old man was a little deaf. Some of the men rode to the top of the hill but could not see him. In his zeal he had got a considerable distance away. Meanwhile, here was his dog, pointed.

If any one had looked at Larsen's face he would have seen the exultation there, for now his chance had come—the very chance he had been looking for. It's a courtesy one handler sometimes extends another who is absent from the spot, to go in and flush his dog's birds.

'I'll handle this covey for Mr Swygert,' said Larsen to the judges, his voice smooth and plausible, on his face a smile.

And thus it happened that Comet faced his supreme ordeal without the steadying voice of his god.

He only knew that ahead of him were birds, and that behind him a man was coming through the straw, and that behind the man a crowd of people on horseback were watching him. He had become used to that, but when, out of the corner of his eye, he saw the face of the advancing man, his soul began to tremble.

'Call your dog in, Mr Larsen,' directed the judge. 'Make him backstand.'

Only a moment was lost, while Peerless, a young dog himself, came running in and at a command from Larsen stopped in his tracks behind Comet, and pointed. Larsen's dogs always obeyed, quickly, mechanically. Without ever gaining their confidence, Larsen had a way of turning them into finished field-trial dogs. They obeyed, because they were afraid not to.

According to the rules the man handling the dog has to shoot as the birds rise. This is done in order to test the dog's steadiness when a gun is fired over him. No specification is made as to the size of the shotgun to be used. Usually, however, small-gauge guns are carried. The one in Larsen's hands was a twelve gauge, and consequently large.

All morning he had been using it over his own dog. Nobody had paid any attention to it, because he shot smokeless powder. But now, as he advanced, he reached into the left-hand pocket of his hunting coat, where six shells rattled as he hurried along. Two of these he took out and rammed into the barrels.

As for Comet, still standing rigid, statuesque, he heard, as has been said, the brush of steps through the straw, glimpsed a face, and trembled. But only for a moment. Then he steadied, head high, tail straight out. The birds rose with a whir—and then was repeated that horror of his youth. Above his ears, ears that would always be tender, broke a great roar. Either because of his excitement, or because of a sudden wave of revenge, or of a determination to make sure of the dog's flight, Larsen had pulled both triggers at once. The combined report shattered through the dog's eardrums, it shivered through his nerves, he sank in agony into the straw.

Then the old impulse to flee was upon him, and he sprang to his feet, and looked about wildly. But from somewhere in that crowd behind him came to his tingling ears a voice—clear, ringing, deep, the voice of a woman—a woman he knew— pleading as his master used to plead, calling on him not to run, but to stand.

'Steady,' it said. 'Steady, Comet!'

It called him to himself, it soothed him, it calmed him, and he turned and looked toward the crowd. With the roar of the shotgun the usual order observed in field trials was broken up. All rules seemed to have been suspended. Ordinarily, no one belonging to 'the field' is allowed to speak to a dog. Yet the girl had spoken to him. Ordinarily, the spectators must remain in the rear of the judges. Yet one of the judges had himself wheeled his horse about and was galloping off, and Marian Devant had pushed through the crowd and was riding toward the bewildered dog.

He stood staunch where he was, though in his ears was still a throbbing pain, and though all about him was this growing confusion he could not understand. The man he feared was running across the field yonder, in the direction taken by the judge. He was blowing his whistle as he ran. Through the crowd, his face terrible to see, his own master was coming. Both the old man and the girl had dismounted now, and were running toward him.

'I heard,' old Swygert was saying to her. 'I heard it! I might 'a' known! I might 'a' known!'

'He stood,' she panted, 'like a rock—oh, the brave, beautiful thing!'

'Where is that—' Swygert suddenly checked himself and looked around.

A man in the crowd (they had all gathered about now), laughed.

'He's gone after his dog,' he said. 'Peerless has run away!'

60

For the Love of a Man

JACK LONDON

WHEN John Thornton froze his feet in the previous December, his partners had made him comfortable and left him to get well, going on themselves up the river to get out a raft of saw-logs for Dawson. He was still limping slightly at the time he rescued Buck, but with the continued warm weather even the slight limp left him. And here, lying by the river bank through the long spring days, watching the running water, listening lazily to the songs of birds and the hum of nature, Buck slowly won back his strength.

A rest comes very good after one has travelled three thousand miles, and it must be confessed that Buck waxed lazy as his wounds healed, his muscles swelled out, and the flesh came back to cover his bones. For that matter, they were all loafing—Buck, John Thornton, and Skeet and Nig—waiting for the raft to come that was to carry them down to Dawson. Skeet was a little Irish setter who early made friends with Buck, who, in a dying condition, was unable to resent her first advances. She had the doctor trait which some dogs possess, and as a mother cat washes her kittens, so she washed and cleansed Buck's wounds. Regularly, each morning after he had finished his breakfast, she performed her self-appointed task, till he came to look for her ministrations as much as he did for Thornton's. Nig, equally friendly, though less demonstrative, was a huge black dog, half bloodhound and half deerhound, with eyes that laughed and a boundless good nature.

To Buck's surprise these dogs manifested no jealousy toward him. They seemed to share the kindliness and largeness of John Thornton. As Buck grew stronger they enticed him into all sorts of ridiculous games, in which Thornton himself could not forbear to join, and in this fashion Buck romped through his convalescence and into a new existence. Love, genuine passionate love, was his for the first time. This he had never experienced at Judge Miller's down in the sun-kissed Santa Clara Valley. With the Judge's sons, hunting and tramping, it had been a working partnership; with the Judge's grandsons, a sort of pompous guardianship; and with the Judge himself, a stately and dignified friendship. But love that was feverish and burning, that was adoration, that was madness, it had taken John Thornton to arouse.

This man had saved his life, which was something; but, further, he was the ideal master. Other men saw to the welfare of their dogs from a sense of duty and business expediency; he saw to the welfare of his as if they were his own children, because he could not help it. And he saw further. He never forgot a kindly greeting or a cheering word, and to sit down for a long talk with them ('gas' he called it) was as much his delight as theirs. He had a way of taking Buck's head roughly between his hands, and resting his own head upon Buck's, of shaking him back and forth, the while calling him ill names that to Buck were love names. Buck knew no greater joy than that rough embrace and the sound of murmured oaths, and at each jerk back and forth it seemed that his heart would be shaken out of his body so great was his ecstasy. And when, released, he sprang to his feet, his mouth laughing, his eyes eloquent, his throat vibrant with unuttered sound, and in that fashion remained without movement, John Thornton would reverently exclaim, 'God! you can all but speak!'

Buck had a trick of love expression that was akin to hurt. He would often seize Thornton's hand in his mouth and close so fiercely that the flesh bore the impress of his teeth for some time afterward. And as Buck understood the oaths to be love words, so the man understood this feigned bite for a caress.

For the most part, however, Buck's love was expressed in adoration. While he went wild with happiness when Thornton touched him or spoke to him, he did not seek these tokens. Unlike Skeet, who was wont to shove her nose under Thornton's hand and nudge and nudge till petted, or Nig, who would stalk up and rest his great head on Thornton's knee, Buck was content to adore at a distance. He would lie by the hour, eager, alert, at Thornton's feet, looking up into his face, dwelling upon it, studying it, following with keenest interest each fleeting expression, every movement or change of feature. Or, as chance might have it, he would lie farther away, to the side or rear, watching the outlines of the man and the occasional movements of his body. And often, such was the communion in which they lived, the strength of Buck's gaze would draw John Thornton's head around, and he would return the gaze, without speech, his heart shining out of his eyes as Buck's heart shone out.

For a long time after his rescue, Buck did not like Thornton to get out of his sight. From the moment he left the tent to when he entered it again, Buck would follow at his heels. His transient masters since he had come into the Northland had bred in him a fear that no master could be permanent. He was afraid that Thornton would pass out of his life as Perrault and François and the Scotch half-breed had passed out. Even in the night, in his dreams, he was haunted by this fear. At such times he would shake off sleep and creep through the chill to the flap of the tent, where he would stand and listen to the sound of his master's breathing.

But in spite of this great love he bore John Thornton, which seemed to bespeak the soft civilizing influence, the strain of the primitive, which the Northland had aroused in him, remained alive and active. Faithfulness and devotion, things born of fire and roof, were his; yet he retained his wildness and wiliness. He was a thing of the wild, come in from the wild to sit by John Thornton's fire, rather than a dog of the soft Southland stamped with the marks of generations of civilization. Because of his very great love, he could not steal from this man, but from any other man, in any other camp, he did not hesitate an instant; while the cunning with which he stole enabled him to escape detection.

His face and body were scored by the teeth of many dogs, and he fought as fiercely as ever and more shrewdly. Skeet and Nig were too good-natured for quarrelling—besides, they belonged to John Thornton; but the strange dog, no matter what the breed or valour, swiftly acknowledged Buck's supremacy or found himself struggling for life with a terrible antagonist. And Buck was merciless. He had learned well the law of club and fang, and he never forewent an advantage or drew back from a foe he had started on the way to Death. He had lessoned from Spitz, and from the chief fighting dogs of the police and mail, and knew there was no middle course. He must master or be mastered; while to show mercy was a weakness. Mercy did not exist in the primordial life. It was misunderstood for fear, and such misunderstandings made for death. Kill or be killed, eat or be eaten, was the law; and this mandate, down out of the depths of Time, he obeyed.

He was older than the days he had seen and the breaths he had drawn. He linked the past with the present, and the eternity behind him throbbed through him in a mighty rhythm to which he swayed as the tides and seasons swayed. He sat by John Thornton's fire, a broad-breasted dog, white-fanged and long-furred; but behind him were the shades of all manner of dogs, half-wolves and wild wolves, urgent and prompting, tasting the savour of the meat he ate, thirsting for the water he drank, scenting the wind with him, listening with him and telling him the sounds made by the wild life in the forest, dictating his moods, directing his actions, lying down to sleep with him when he lay down, and dreaming with him and beyond him and becoming themselves the stuff of his dreams.

So peremptorily did these shades beckon him that each day mankind and the claims of mankind slipped farther from him. Deep in the forest a call was sounding, and as often as he heard this call, mysteriously thrilling and luring, he felt compelled to turn his back upon the fire and the beaten earth around it, and to plunge into the forest, and on and on, he knew not where or why; nor did he wonder where or why, the call sounding imperiously, deep in the forest. But as often as he gained the soft unbroken earth and the green shade, the love for John Thornton drew him back to the fire again.

Thornton alone held him. The rest of mankind was as nothing. Chance travellers might praise or pet him; but he was cold under it all, and from a too demonstrative man he would get up and walk away. When Thornton's partners, Hans and Pete, arrived on the long-expected raft, Buck refused to notice them till he learned they were close to Thornton; after that he tolerated them in a passive sort of way, accepting favours from them as though he favoured them by accepting. They were of the same large type as Thornton, living close to the earth, thinking simply and seeing clearly; and ere they swung the raft into the big eddy by the saw-mill at Dawson, they understood Buck and his ways, and did not insist upon an intimacy such as obtained with Skeet and Nig.

For Thornton, however, his love seemed to grow and grow. He, alone among men, could put a pack upon Buck's back in the summer travelling. Nothing was too great for Buck to do, when Thornton commanded. One day (they had grub-staked themselves from the proceeds of the raft and left Dawson for the head-waters of the Tanana) the men and dogs were sitting on the crest of a cliff which fell away, straight down, to naked bed-rock three hundred feet below. John Thornton was sitting near the edge, Buck at his shoulder. A thoughtless whim seized Thornton, and he drew the attention of Hans and Pete to the experiment he had in mind. 'Jump, Buck!' he commanded, sweeping his arm out and over the chasm. The next instant he was grappling with Buck on the extreme edge, while Hans and Pete were dragging them back into safety.

'It's uncanny,' Pete said, after it was over and they had caught their speech.

Thornton shook his head. 'No, it is splendid, and it is terrible, too. Do you know, it sometimes makes me afraid.'

'I'm not hankering to be the man that lays hands on you while he's around,' Pete announced conclusively, nodding his head toward Buck.

'Py jingo!' was Hans' contribution. 'Not mineself either.'

It was at Circle City, ere the year was out, that Pete's apprehensions were realized. 'Black' Burton, a man evil-tempered and malicious, had been picking a quarrel with a tenderfoot at the bar, when Thornton stepped good-naturedly between. Buck, as was his custom, was lying in a corner, head on paws, watching his master's every action. Burton struck out, without warning, straight from the shoulder. Thornton was sent spinning, and saved himself from falling only by clutching the rail of the bar.

Those who were looking on heard what was neither bark nor yelp, but a something which is best described as a roar, and they saw Buck's body rise up in the air as he left the floor for Burton's throat. The man saved his life by instinctively throwing out his arm, but was hurled backward to the floor with Buck on top of him. Buck loosed his teeth from the flesh of the arm and drove in again for the throat. This time the man succeeded only in partly blocking, and his throat was torn open. Then the crowd was upon Buck, and he was driven off; but while a surgeon checked the bleeding, he prowled up and down, growling furiously, attempting to rush in, and being forced back by an array of hostile clubs. A 'miners' meeting', called on the spot, decided that the dog had sufficient provocation, and Buck was discharged. But his reputation was made, and from that day his name spread through every camp in Alaska.

Later on, in the fall of the year, he saved John Thornton's life in quite another fashion. The three partners were lining a long and narrow poling-boat down a bad stretch of rapids on the Forty-Mile Creek. Hans and Pete moved along the bank, snubbing with a thin Manila rope from tree to tree, while Thornton remained in the boat, helping its descent by means of a pole, and shouting directions to the shore. Buck, on the bank, worried and anxious, kept abreast of the boat, his eyes never off his master.

At a particularly bad spot, where a ledge of barely submerged rocks jutted out into the river, Hans cast off the rope, and, while Thornton poled the boat out into the stream, ran down the bank with the end in his hand to snub the boat when it had cleared the ledge. This it did, and was flying downstream in a current as swift as a mill-race, when Hans checked it with the rope and checked too suddenly. The boat flirted over and snubbed in to the bank bottom up, while Thornton, flung sheer out of it, was carried down-stream toward the worst part of the rapids, a stretch of wild water in which no swimmer could live.

Buck had sprung in on the instant, and at the end of three hundred yards, amid a mad swirl of water, he overhauled Thornton. When he felt him grasp his tail, Buck headed for the bank, swimming with all his splendid strength. But the progress shoreward was slow; the progress down-stream amazingly rapid. From below came the fatal roaring where the wild current went wilder and was rent in shreds and spray by the rocks which thrust through like the teeth of an enormous comb. The suck of the water as it took the beginning of the last steep pitch was frightful, and Thornton knew that the shore was impossible. He scraped furiously over a rock, bruised across a second, and struck a third with crushing force. He clutched its slippery top with both hands, releasing Buck, and above the roar of the churning water shouted: 'Go, Buck! Go!'

Buck could not hold his own, and swept on down-stream, struggling desperately, but unable to win back. When he heard Thornton's command repeated, he partly reared out of the water, throwing his head high, as though for a last look, then turned obediently toward the bank. He swam powerfully and was dragged ashore by Pete and Hans at the very point where swimming ceased to be possible and destruction began.

They knew that the time a man could cling to a slippery rock in the face of that driving current was a matter of minutes, and they ran as fast as they could up the bank to a point far above where Thornton was hanging on. They attached the line with which they had been snubbing the boat to Buck's neck and shoulders, being careful that it should neither strangle him nor impede his swimming, and launched him into the stream. He struck out boldly, but not straight enough into the stream. He discovered the mistake too late, when Thornton was abreast of him and a bare half-dozen strokes away while he was being carried helplessly past.

Hans promptly snubbed with the rope, as though Buck were a boat. The rope thus tightening on him in the sweep of the current, he was jerked under the surface, and under the surface he remained till his body struck against the bank and he was hauled out. He was half drowned, and Hans and Pete threw themselves upon him, pounding the breath into him and the water out of him. He staggered to his feet and fell down. The faint sound of Thornton's voice came to them, and though they could not make out the words of it, they knew that he was in his extremity. His master's voice acted on Buck like an electric shock. He sprang to his feet and ran up the bank ahead of the men to the point of his previous departure.

Again the rope was attached and he was launched, and again he struck out, but this time straight into the stream. He had miscalculated once, but he would not be guilty of it a second time. Hans paid out the rope, permitting no slack while Pete kept it clear of coils. Buck held on till he was on a line straight above Thornton; then he turned, and with the speed of an express train headed down upon him. Thornton saw him coming, and, as Buck struck him like a battering ram, with the whole force of the current behind him, he reached up and closed with both arms around the shaggy neck. Hans snubbed the rope around the tree, and Buck and Thornton were jerked under the water. Strangling, suffocating, sometimes one uppermost and sometimes the other, dragging over the jagged bottom, smashing against rocks and snags, they veered in to the bank.

Thornton came to, belly downward and being violently propelled back and forth across a drift log by Hans and Pete. His first glance was for Buck, over whose limp and apparently lifeless body Nig was setting up a howl, while Skeet was licking the wet face and closed eyes. Thornton was himself bruised and battered, and he went carefully over Buck's body, when he had been brought around, finding three broken ribs.

'That settles it,' he announced. 'We camp right here.' And camp they did, till Buck's ribs knitted and he was able to travel.

That winter, at Dawson, Buck performed another exploit, not so heroic, perhaps, but one that put his name many notches higher on the totem-pole of Alaskan fame. This exploit was particularly gratifying to the three men; for they stood in need of the outfit which it furnished, and were enabled to make a long-desired trip into the virgin East, where miners had not yet appeared. It was brought about by a conversation in the Eldorado Saloon, in which men waxed boastful of their favourite dogs. Buck, because of his record, was the target for these men, and Thornton was driven stoutly to defend him. At the end of half an hour one man stated that his dog could start a sled with five hundred pounds and walk off with it; a second bragged six hundred for his dog; and a third seven hundred.

'Pooh! pooh!' said John Thornton. 'Buck can start a thousand pounds.'

'And break it out? and walk off with it for a hundred yards?' demanded Matthewson, a Bonanza King, he of the seven hundred vaunt.

'And break it out, and walk off with it for a hundred yards,' John Thornton said coolly.

'Well,' Matthewson said, slowly and deliberately, so that all could hear, 'I've got a thousand dollars that says he can't. And there it is.' So saying, he slammed a sack of gold dust of the size of a bologna sausage down upon the bar.

Nobody spoke. Thornton's bluff, if bluff it was, had been called. He could feel a flush of warm blood creeping up his face. His tongue had tricked him. He did not know whether Buck could start a thousand pounds. Half a ton! The enormousness of it appalled him. He had great faith in Buck's strength and had often thought him capable of starting such a load; but never, as now, had he faced the possibility of it, the eyes of a dozen men fixed upon him, silent and waiting. Further, he had no thousand dollars; nor had Hans or Pete.

'I've got a sled standing outside now, with twenty fifty-pound sacks of flour on it,' Matthewson went on with brutal directness, 'so don't let that hinder you.'

Thornton did not reply. He did not know what to say. He glanced from face to face in the absent way of a man who has lost the power of thought and is seeking somewhere to find the thing that will start it going again. The face of Jim O'Brien, a Mastodon King and old-time comrade, caught his eyes. It was as a cue to him, seeming to rouse him to do what he would never have dreamed of doing.

'Can you lend me a thousand?' he asked, almost in a whisper.

'Sure,' answered O'Brien, thumping down a plethoric sack by the side of Matthewson's. 'Though it's little faith I'm having, John, that the beast can do the trick.'

The Eldorado emptied its occupants into the street to see the test. The tables were deserted, and the dealers and game-keepers came forth to see the outcome of the wager and to lay odds. Several hundred men, furred and mittened, banked around the sled within easy distance. Matthewson's sled, loaded with a thousand pounds of flour, had been standing for a couple of hours, and in the intense cold (it was sixty below zero) the runners had frozen fast to the hard-packed snow. Men offered odds of two to one that Buck could not budge the sled. A quibble arose concerning the phrase 'break out.' O'Brien contended it was Thornton's privilege to knock the runners loose, leaving Buck to 'break it out' from a dead standstill. Matthewson insisted that the phrase included breaking the runners from the frozen grip of the snow. A majority of the men who had witnessed the making of the bet decided in his favour, whereat the odds went up to three to one against Buck.

There were no takers. Not a man believed him capable of the feat. Thornton had been hurried into the wager, heavy with doubt; and now that he looked at the sled itself, the concrete fact, with the regular team of ten dogs curled up in the snow before it, the more impossible the task appeared. Matthewson waxed jubilant.

'Three to one!' he proclaimed. 'I'll lay you another thousand at that figure, Thornton. What d'ye say?'

Thornton's doubt was strong in his face, but his fighting spirit was aroused—the fighting spirit that soars above odds, fails to recognize the impossible, and is deaf to all save the clamor for battle. He called Hans and Pete to him. Their sacks were slim, and with his own the three partners could rake together only two hundred dollars. In the ebb of their fortunes, this sum was their total capital; yet they laid it unhesitatingly against Matthewson's six hundred.

The team of ten dogs was unhitched, and Buck, with his own harness, was put into the sled. He had caught the contagion of the excitement, and he felt that in some way he must do a great thing for John Thornton. Murmurs of admiration at his splendid appearance went up. He was in perfect condition, without an ounce of superfluous flesh, and the one hundred and fifty pounds that he weighed were so many pounds of grit and virility. His furry coat shone with the sheen of silk. Down the neck and across the shoulders, his mane, in repose as it was, half bristled and seemed to lift with every movement, as though excess of vigour made each particular hair alive and active. The great breast and heavy fore legs were no more than in proportion with the rest of the body, where the muscles showed in tight rolls underneath the skin. Men felt these muscles and proclaimed them hard as iron, and the odds went down to two to one.

'Gad, sir! Gad, sir!' stuttered a member of the latest dynasty, a king of the Skookum Benches. 'I offer you eight hundred for him, sir, before the test, sir; eight hundred just as he stands.'

Thornton shook his head and stepped to Buck's side.

'You must stand off from him,' Matthewson protested. 'Free play and plenty of room.'

The crowd fell silent; only could be heard the voices of the gamblers vainly offering two to one. Everybody acknowledged Buck a magnificent animal, but twenty fifty-pound sacks of flour bulked too large in their eyes for them to loosen their pouch-strings.

Thornton knelt down by Buck's side. He took his head in his two hands and rested cheek on cheek. He did not playfully shake him, as was his wont, or murmur soft love curses; but he whispered in his ear. 'As you love me, Buck. As you love me,' was what he whispered. Buck whined with suppressed eagerness.

The crowd was watching curiously. The affair was growing mysterious. It seemed like a conjuration. As Thornton got to his feet, Buck seized his mittened hand between his jaws, pressing in with his teeth and releasing slowly, half-reluctantly. It was the answer, in terms not of speech, but of love. Thornton stepped well back.

'Now, Buck,' he said.

Buck tightened the traces, then slacked them for a matter of several inches. It was the way he had learned.

'Gee!' Thornton's voice rang out, sharp in the tense silence.

Buck swung to the right, ending the movement in a plunge that took up the slack and with a sudden jerk arrested his one hundred and fifty pounds. The load quivered, and from under the runners arose a crisp crackling.

'Haw!' Thornton commanded.

Buck duplicated the manoeuvre, this time to the left. The crackling turned into a snapping, the sled pivoting and the runners slipping and grating several inches to the side. The sled was broken out. Men were holding their breaths, intensely unconscious of the fact.

'Now, MUSH!'

Thornton's command cracked out like a pistol-shot. Buck threw himself forward, tightening the traces with a jarring lunge. His whole body was gathered compactly together in the tremendous effort, the muscles writhing and knotting like live things under the silky fur. His great chest was low to the ground, his head forward and down, while his feet were flying like mad, the claws scarring the hard-packed snow in parallel grooves. The sled swayed and trembled, half-started forward. One of his feet slipped, and one man groaned aloud. Then the sled lurched ahead in what appeared a rapid succession of jerks though it never really came to a dead stop again . . . half an inch . . . an inch . . . two inches. . . . The jerks perceptibly diminished; as the sled gained momentum, he caught them up, till it was moving steadily along.

Men gasped and began to breathe again, unaware that for a moment they had ceased to breathe. Thornton was running behind, encouraging Buck with short, cheery words. The distance had been measured off, and as he neared the pile of firewood which marked the end of the hundred yards, a cheer began to grow and grow, which burst into a roar as he passed the firewood and halted at command. Every man was tearing himself loose, even Matthewson. Hats and mittens were flying in the air. Men were shaking hands, it did not matter with whom, and bubbling over in a general incoherent babel.

But Thornton fell on his knees beside Buck. Head was against head, and he was shaking him back and forth. Those who hurried up heard him cursing Buck, and he cursed him long and fervently, and softly and lovingly.

'Gad, sir! Gad, sir!' spluttered the Skookum Bench king. 'I'll give you a thousand for him, sir, a thousand, sir—twelve hundred, sir.'

Thornton rose to his feet. His eyes were wet. The tears were streaming frankly down his cheeks. 'Sir,' he said to the Skookum Bench king, 'no, sir. You can go to hell, sir. It's the best I can do for you, sir.'

Buck seized Thornton's hand in his teeth. Thornton shook him back and forth. As though animated by a common impulse, the onlookers drew back to a respectful distance; nor were they again indiscreet enough to interrupt.

The Coming of Riquet

ANATOLE FRANCE

SEATED at his table one morning in front of the window, against which the leaves of the plane-tree quivered, M. Bergeret, who was trying to discover how the ships of Aeneas had been changed into nymphs, heard a tap at the door, and forthwith his servant entered, carrying in front of her, opossum-like, a tiny creature whose black head peeped out from the folds of her apron, which she had turned up to form a pocket. With a look of anxiety and hope upon her face, she remained motionless for a moment, then she placed the little thing upon the carpet at her master's feet.

'What's that?' asked M. Bergeret.

It was a little dog of doubtful breed, having something of the terrier in him, and a well-set head, a short, smooth coat of a dark tan colour, and a tiny little stump of a tail. His body retained its puppy-like softness, and he went sniffing at the carpet.

'Angélique,' said M. Bergeret, 'take this animal back to its owner.'

'It has no owner, Monsieur.'

M. Bergeret looked silently at the little creature, who had come to examine his slippers, and was giving little sniffs of approval. M. Bergeret was a philologist, which perhaps explains why at this juncture he asked a vain question.

'What is he called?'

'Monsieur,' replied Angélique, 'he has no name.'

M. Bergeret seemed put out at this answer: he looked at the dog sadly, with a disheartened air.

Then the little animal placed its two front paws on M. Bergeret's slipper, and, holding it thus, began innocently to nibble at it. With a sudden access of compassion M. Bergeret took the tiny nameless creature upon his knee. The dog looked at him intently, and M. Bergeret was pleased at his confiding expression.

'What beautiful eyes!' he cried.

The dog's eyes were indeed beautiful, the pupils of a golden-flecked chestnut set in warm white. And his gaze spoke of simple, mysterious thoughts, common alike to the thoughtful beasts and simple men of the earth.

Tired, perhaps, with the intellectual effort he had made for the purpose of entering into communication with a human being, he closed his beautiful eyes, and, yawning widely, revealed his pink mouth, his curled-up tongue, and his array of dazzling teeth.

M. Bergeret put his hand into the dog's mouth, and allowed him to lick it, at which old Angélique gave a smile of relief.

'A more affectionate little creature doesn't breathe,' she said.

'The dog,' said M. Bergeret, 'is a religious animal. In his savage state he worships the moon and the lights that float upon the waters. These are his gods, to whom he appeals at night with long-drawn howls. In the domesticated state he seeks by his caresses to conciliate those powerful genii who dispense the good things of this world—to wit, men. He worships and honours men by the accomplishment of the rites passed down to him by his ancestors: he licks their hands, jumps against their legs, and when they show signs of anger towards him he approaches them crawling on his belly as a sign of humility, to appease their wrath.'

'All dogs are not the friends of man,' remarked Angélique. 'Some of them bite the hand that feeds them.'

'Those are the ungodly, blasphemous dogs,' returned M. Bergeret, 'insensate creatures like Ajax, the son of Telamon, who wounded the hand of the golden Aphrodite. These sacrilegious creatures die a dreadful death, or lead wandering and miserable lives. They are not to be confounded with those dogs who, espousing the quarrel of their own particular god, wage war upon his enemy, the neighbouring god. They are heroes. Such, for example, is the dog of Lafolie, the butcher, who fixed his sharp teeth into the leg of the tramp Pied-d'Alouette. For it is a fact that dogs fight among themselves like men, and Turk, with his snub nose, serves his god Lafolie against the robber gods, in the same way that Israel helped Jehovah to destroy Chamos and Moloch.'

The puppy, however, having decided that M. Bergeret's remarks were the reverse of interesting, curled up his feet and stretched out his head, ready to go to sleep upon the knees that harboured him.

'Where did you find him?' asked M. Bergeret.

'Well, Monsieur, it was M. Dellion's *chef* gave him to me.'

'With the result,' continued M. Bergeret, 'that we now have this soul to care for.'

'What soul?' asked Angélique.

'This canine soul. An animal is, properly speaking, a soul; I do not say an immortal soul. And yet, when I come to consider the positions this poor little beast and I myself occupy in the scheme of things, I recognize in both exactly the same right to immortality.'

After considerable hesitation, old Angélique, with a painful effort that made her upper lip curl up and reveal her two remaining teeth, said:

'If Monsieur does not want a dog, I will return him to M. Dellion's *chef*; but you may safely keep him, I assure you. You won't see or hear him.'

She had hardly finished her sentence when the puppy, hearing a heavy van rolling down the street, sat bolt upright on M. Bergeret's knees, and began to bark both loud and long, so that the window-panes resounded with the noise.

M. Bergeret smiled.

'He's a watch-dog,' said Angélique, by way of excuse. 'They are by far the most faithful.'

'Have you given him anything to eat?' asked M. Bergeret.

'Of course,' returned Angélique.

'What does he eat?'

'Monsieur must be aware that dogs eat bread and meat.'

Somewhat piqued, M. Bergeret retorted that in her eagerness she might very likely have taken him away from his mother before he was old enough to leave her, upon which he was lifted up again and re-examined, only to make sure of the fact that he was at least six months old.

M. Bergeret put him down on the carpet, and regarded him with interest.

'Isn't he pretty?' said the servant.

'No, he is not pretty,' replied M. Bergeret. 'But he is engaging, and has beautiful eyes. That is what people used to say about me,' added the professor. 'when I was three times as old, and not half as intelligent. Since then I have no doubt acquired an outlook upon the universe which he will never attain. But, in comparison with the Absolute, I may say that my knowledge equals his in the smallness of its extent. Like his, it is a geometrical point in the infinite.' Then, addressing the little creature who was sniffing the waste-paper basket, he went on: 'Smell it out, sniff it well, take from the outside world all the knowledge that can reach your simple brain through the medium of that black truffle-like nose of yours. And what though I at the same time observe, and compare, and study? We shall never know, neither the one nor the other of us, why we have been put into this world, and what we are doing in it. What are we here for, eh?'

As he had spoken rather loudly, the puppy looked at him anxiously, and M. Bergeret, returning to the thought which had first filled his mind, said to the servant:

'We must give him a name.'

With her hands folded in front of her she replied laughingly that that would not be a difficult matter.

Upon which M. Bergeret made the private reflection that to

the simple all things are simple, but that clear-sighted souls, who look upon things from many and divers aspects, invisible to the vulgar mind, experience the greatest difficulty in coming to a decision about even the most trivial matters. And he cudgelled his brains, trying to hit upon a name for the little living thing that was busily engaged in nibbling the fringe of the carpet.

'All the names of dogs,' thought he, 'preserved in the ancient treatises of the huntsmen of old, such as Fouilloux, and in the verses of our sylvan poets such as La Fontaine—Finaud, Miraut, Briffaut, Ravaud, and such-like names, are given to sporting dogs, who are the aristocracy of the kennel, the chivalry of the canine race. The dog of Ulysses was called Argos, and he was a hunter too, so Homer tells us. 'In his youth he hunted the little hares of Ithaca, but now he was old and hunted no more.' What we require is something quite different. The names given by old maids to their lap-dogs would be more suitable, were they not usually pretentious and absurd. Azor, for instance, is ridiculous!'

So M. Bergeret ruminated, calling to memory many a dog name, without being able to decide, however, on one that pleased him. He would have liked to invent a name, but lacked the imagination.

'What day is it?' he asked at last.

'The ninth,' replied Angélique. 'Thursday, the ninth.'

'Well, then!' said M. Bergeret, 'can't we call the dog Thursday, like Robinson Crusoe who called his man Friday, for the same reason?'

'As Monsieur pleases,' said Angélique. 'But it isn't very pretty.'

'Very well,' said M. Bergeret, 'find a name for the creature yourself, for, after all, you brought him here.'

'Oh, no,' said the servant. 'I couldn't find a name for him; I'm not clever enough. When I saw him lying on the straw in the kitchen, I called him Riquet, and he came up and played about under my skirts.'

'You called him Riquet, did you?' cried M. Bergeret. 'Why didn't you say so before? Riquet he is and Riquet he shall remain; that's settled. Now be off with you, and take Riquet with you. I want to work.'

'Monseiur,' returned Angélique, 'I am going to leave the puppy with you; I will come for him when I get back from market.'

'You could quite well take him to market with you,' retorted M. Bergeret.

'Monsieur, I am going to church as well.'

It was quite true that she really was going to church at Saint-Exupère, to ask for a Mass to be said for the repose of her husband's soul. She did that regularly once a year, not that she had even been informed of the decease of Borniche, who had never communicated with her since his desertion, but it was a settled thing in the good woman's mind that Borniche was dead. She had therefore no fear of his coming to rob her of the little she had, and did her best to fix things up to his advantage in the other world, so long as he left her in peace in this one.

'Eh!' ejaculated M. Bergeret. 'Shut him up in the kitchen or some other convenient place, and do not wor—'

He did not finish his sentence, for Angélique had vanished, purposely pretending not to hear, that she might leave Riquet with his master. She wanted them to grow used to one another, and she also wanted to give poor, friendless M. Bergeret a companion. Having closed the door behind her, she went along the corridor and down the steps.

M. Bergeret set to work again and plunged head foremost into his *Virgilius nauticus*. He loved the work; it rested his thoughts, and became a kind of game that suited him, for he played it all by himself. On the table beside him were several boxes filled with pegs, which he fixed into little squares of cardboard to represent the fleet of Aeneas. Now while he was thus occupied he felt something like tiny fists tapping at his legs. Riquet, whom he had quite forgotten, was standing on his hind legs patting his master's knees, and wagging his little stump of a tail. When he tired of this, he let his paws slide down the trouser leg, then got up and began his coaxing over again. And M. Bergeret, turning away from the printed lore before him, saw two brown eyes gazing up at him lovingly.

'What gives a human beauty to the gaze of this dog,' he thought, 'is probably that it varies unceasingly, being by turns bright and vivacious, or serious and sorrowful; because through these eyes his little dumb soul finds expression for

78

thought that lacks nothing in depth nor sequence. My father was very fond of cats, and, consequently, I liked them too. He used to declare that cats are the wise man's best companions, for they respect his studious hours. Bajazet, his Persian cat, would sit at night for hours at a stretch, motionless and majestic, perched on a corner of his table. I still remember the agate eyes of Bajazet, but those jewel-like orbs concealed all thought, that owl-like stare was cold, and hard, and wicked. How much do I prefer the melting gaze of the dog!'

Riquet, however, was agitating his paws in frantic fashion, and M. Bergeret, who was anxious to return to his philological amusements, said kindly, but shortly:

'Lie down, Riquet!'

Upon which Riquet went and thrust his nose against the door through which Angélique had passed out. And there he remained, uttering from time to time plaintive, meek little cries. After a while he began to scratch, making a gentle rasping noise on the polished floor with his nails. Then the whining began again followed by more scratching. Disturbed by these sounds, M. Bergeret sternly bade him keep still.

Riquet peered at him sorrowfully with his brown eyes, then, sitting down, he looked at M. Bergeret again, rose, returned to the door, sniffed underneath it, and wailed afresh.

'Do you want to go out?'

Putting down his pen, he went to the door, which he held a few inches open. After making sure that he was running no risk of hurting himself on the way out, Riquet slipped through the doorway and marched off with a composure that was scarcely polite. On returning to his table, M. Bergeret, sensitive man that he was, pondered over the dog's action. He said to himself:

'I was on the point of reproaching the animal for going without saying either good-bye or thank you, and expecting him to apologize for leaving me. It was the beautiful human expression of his eyes that made me so foolish. I was beginning to look upon him as one of my own kind.'

After making this reflection M. Bergeret applied himself anew to the metamorphosis of the ships of Aeneas, a legend both pretty and popular, but perhaps a trifle too simple in itself for expression in such noble language. M. Bergeret, however, saw nothing incongruous in it. He knew that the nursery tales have furnished material for nearly all epics, and that Virgil had carefully collected together in his poem the riddles, the puns, the uncouth stories, and the puerile imaginings of his fore-fathers; that Homer, his master and the master of all the bards, had done little more than tell over again what the good wives of Ionia and the fishermen of the islands had been narrating for more than a thousand years before him. Besides, for the time being, this was the least of his worries; he had another far more important preoccupation. An expression, met with in the course of the charming story of the metamorphosis, did not appear sufficiently plain to him. That was what was worrying him.

'Bergeret, my friend,' he said to himself, 'this is where you must open your eyes and show your sense. Remember that Virgil always expresses himself with extreme precision when writing on the technique of the arts; remember that he went yachting at Baiae, that he was an expert in naval construction, and that therefore his language, in this passage, must have a precise and definite signification.'

And M. Bergeret carefully consulted a great number of texts, in order to throw a light upon the word which he could not understand, and which he had to explain. He was almost on the point of grasping the solution, or, at any rate, he had caught a glimpse of it, when he heard a noise like the rattling of chains at his door, a noise which, although not alarming, struck him as curious. The disturbance was presently accompanied by a shrill whining, and M. Bergeret, interrupted in his philological investigations, immediately concluded that these importunate wails must emanate from Riquet.

As a matter of fact, after having looked vainly all over the house for Angélique, Riquet had been seized with a desire to see M. Bergeret again. Solitude was as painful to him as human society was dear. In order to put an end to the noise, and also because he had a secret desire to see Riquet again, M. Bergeret got up from his armchair and opened the door, and Riquet re-entered the study with the same coolness with which he had quitted it, but as soon as he saw the door close behind him he assumed a melancholy expression, and began to wander up and down the room like a soul in torment.

He had a sudden way of appearing to find something of interest beneath the chairs and tables, and would sniff long and noisily; then he would walk aimlessly about or sit down in a corner with an air of great humility, like the beggars who are to be seen in church porches. Finally he began to bark at a cast of Hermes which stood upon the mantelshelf, whereupon M. Bergeret addressed him in words full of just reproach.

'Riquet! such vain agitation, such sniffing and barking were better suited to a stable than to the study of a professor, and they lead one to suppose that your ancestors lived with horses whose straw litters they shared. I do not reproach you with that. It is only natural you should have inherited their habits, manners, and tendencies as well as their close-cropped coat, their sausage-like body, and their long, thin nose. I do not speak of your beautiful eyes, for there are few men, few dogs even, who can open such beauties to the light of day. But, leaving all that aside, you are a mongrel, my friend, a mongrel from your short, bandy legs to your head. Again I am far from despising you for that. What I want you to understand is that if you desire to live with me, you will have to drop your mongrel manners and behave like a *scholar*, in other words, to remain silent and quiet, to respect work, after the manner of Bajazet, who of a night would sit for four hours without stirring, and watch my father's pen skimming over the paper.

He was a silent and tactful creature. How different is your own character, my friend! Since you came into this chamber of study your hoarse voice, your unseemly snufflings and your whines, that sound like steam whistles, have constantly confused my thoughts and interrupted my reflections. And now you have made me lost the drift of an important passage in Servius, referring to the construction of one of the ships of Aeneas. Know then, Riquet, my friend, that this is the house of silence and the abode of meditation, and that if you are anxious to stay here you must become literary. Be quiet!'

Thus spoke M. Bergeret. Riquet, who had listened to him with mute astonishment, approached his master, and with suppliant gesture placed a timid paw upon the knee, which he seemed to revere in a fashion that savoured of long ago. Then a kind thought struck M. Bergeret. He picked him up by the scruff of his neck, and put him upon the cushions of the ample easy chair in which he was sitting. Turning himself round three times, Riquet lay down, and then remained perfectly still and silent. He was quite happy. M. Bergeret was grateful to him, and as he ran through Servius he occasionally stroked the close-cropped coat, which, without being soft, was smooth and very pleasant to the touch. Riquet fell into a gentle doze, and communicated to his master the generous warmth of his body, the subtle, gentle heat of a living, breathing thing. And from that moment M. Bergeret found more pleasure in his *Virgilius nauticus*.

From floor to ceiling his study was lined with deal shelves, bearing books arranged in methodical order. One glance, and all that remains to us of Latin thought was ready to his hand. The Greeks lay half-way up. In a quiet corner, easy to access, were Rabelais, the excellent story-tellers of the *Cent nouvelles nouvelles*, Bonaventure des Périers, Guillaume Bouchet, and all the old French 'conteurs,' whom M. Bergeret considered better adapted to humanity than writings in the more heroic style, and who were the favourite reading of his leisure. He possessed them in cheap modern editions only, but he had discovered a poor bookbinder in the town who covered his volumes with leaves from a book of anthems, and it gave M. Bergeret the keenest pleasure to see these free-spoken gentlemen thus clad in Requiems and Misereres. This was the sole luxury and the only peculiarity of his austere library. The other books were paɣ ʳbacked or bound in poor and worn-out bindings. The gentle friendly manner in which they were handled by their owner gave them the look of tools set out in a busy man's workshop. The books of archæology and art found a resting-place on the highest shelves, not by any means out of contempt, but because they were not so often used.

Now, while M. Bergeret worked at his *Virgilius nauticus* and shared his chair with Riquet, he found, as chance would have it, that it was necessary to consult Ottfried Müller's little *Manual*, which happened to be on one of the topmost shelves.

There was no need of one of those tall ladders on wheels topped by railings and a shelf, to enable him to reach the book; there were ladders of this description in the town library, and they had been used by all the great book-lovers of the eighteenth and nineteenth centuries; indeed, several of the latter had fallen from them, and thus died honourable deaths, in the manner spoken of in the pamphlet entitled: *Des bibliophiles qui moururent en tombant de leur échelle*. No, indeed! M. Bergeret had no need of anything of the sort. A small pair of folding steps would have served his purpose excellently well, and he had once seen some in the shop of Clérambaut, the cabinet-maker, in the Rue de Josde. They folded up, and looked just the thing, with their bevelled uprights each pierced with a trefoil as a grip for the hand. M. Bergeret would have given anything to possess them, but the state of his finances, which were somewhat involved, forced him to abandon the idea. No one knew better than he did that financial ills are not mortal, but, for all that, he had no steps in his study.

In place of such a pair of steps he used an old cane-bottomed chair, the back of which had been broken, leaving only two horns or antennæ, which had shown themselves to be more dangerous than useful. So they had been cut to the level of the seat, and the chair had become a stool. There were two reasons why this stool was ill-fitted to the use to which M. Bergeret was wont to put it. In the first place the woven-cane set had grown slack with long use, and now contained a large hollow, making one's foothold precarious. In the second place the stool was too low, and it was hardly possible when standing upon it to reach the books on the highest shelf, even with the finger-tips. What generally happened was that in the endeavour to grasp one book, several others fell out; and it depended upon their being bound or paper-covered whether they lay with broken corners, or sprawled with leaves spread like a fan or a concertina.

Now, with the intention of getting down the *Manual* of Ottfried Müller, M. Bergeret quitted the chair he was sharing with Riquet, who, rolled into a ball with his head tight pressed to his body, lay in warm comfort, opening one voluptuous eye, which he re-closed as quickly. Then M. Bergeret drew the stool from the dark corner where it was hidden and placed it where it was required, hoisted himself upon it, and managed, by making his arm as long as possible, and straining upon tiptoe, to touch, first with one, then with two fingers, the back of a book which he judged to be the one he was needing. As for the thumb, it remained below the shelf and rendered no assistance whatever. M. Bergeret, who found it therefore exceedingly difficult to draw out the book, made the reflection that the reason why the hand is a precious implement is on account of the position of the thumb, and that no being could rise to be an artist who had four feet and no hands.

'It is to the hand,' he reflected, 'that men owe their power of becoming engineers, painters, writers, and manipulators of all kinds of things. If they had not a thumb as well as their other fingers, they would be as incapable as I am at this moment, and they could never have changed the face of the earth as they have done. Beyond a doubt it is the shape of the hand that has assured to man the conquest of the world.'

Then, almost simultaneously, M. Bergeret remembered that monkeys, who possess four hands, have not, for all that, created the arts, nor disposed that earth to their use, and he erased from his mind the theory upon which he had just embarked. However, he did the best he could with his four fingers. It must be known that Ottfried Müller's *Manual* is composed of three volumes and an atlas. M. Bergeret wanted volume one. He pulled out first the second volume, then the atlas, then volume three, and finally the book that he required. At last he held it in his hands. All that now remained for him to do was to descend, and this he was about to do when the cane seat gave way beneath his foot, which passed through it. He lost his balance and fell to the ground, not as heavily as might have been feared, for he broke his fall by grasping at one of the uprights of the bookshelf.

He was on the ground, however, full of astonishment, and wearing on one leg the broken chair; his whole body was permeated and as though constricted by a pain that spread all over it, and that presently settled itself more particularly in the region of the left elbow and hip upon which he had fallen. But, as his anatomy was not seriously damaged, he gathered his wits together; he had got so far as to realize that he must draw his right leg out of the stool in which it had so unfortunately become entangled, and that he must be careful to raise himself up on his right side, which was unhurt. He was even trying to put this into execution when he felt a warm breath upon his cheek, and turning his eyes, which fright and pain had for the moment fixed, he saw close to his cheek Riquet's little face.

At the sound of the fall Riquet had jumped down from the chair and run to his unfortunate master; he was now standing near him in a state of great excitement; then he commenced to run round him. First he came near out of sympathy, then he retreated out of fear of some mysterious danger. He understood perfectly well that a misfortune had taken place, but he was neither thoughtful nor clever enough to discover what it was; hence his anxiety. His fidelity drew him to his suffering friend, and his prudence stopped him on the very brink of the fatal spot. Encouraged at length by the calm and silence which eventually reigned, he licked M. Bergeret's neck and looked at him with eyes of fear and of love. The fallen master smiled, and the dog licked the end of his nose. It was a great comfort to M. Bergeret, who freed his right leg, stood erect, and limped good-humouredly back to his chair.

Riquet was there before him. All that could be seen of his eyes was a gleam between the narrow slit of the half-closed lids. He seemed to have forgotten all about the adventure that a moment before had so stirred them both. The little creature lived in the present, with no thought of time that had run its course; not that he was wanting in memory, inasmuch as he could remember, not his own past alone, but the faraway past of his ancestors, and his little head was a rich store-house of useful knowledge; but he took no pleasure in remembrance, and memory was not for him, as it was for M. Bergeret, a divine muse.

Gently stroking the short, smooth coat of his companion, M. Bergeret addressed him in the following affectionate terms:

'Dog! at the price of the repose which is dear to your heart, you came to me when I was dismayed and brought low. You did not laugh, as any young person of my own species would have done. It is true that however joyous or terrible nature may appear to you at times, she never inspires you with a sense of the ridiculous. And it is for that very reason, because of your innocent gravity, that you are the surest friend a man can have. In the first instance I inspired confidence and admiration in you, and now you show me pity.

'Dog! when we first met on the highway of life, we came from the two poles of creation; we belong to different species. I refer to this with no desire to take advantage of it, but rather with a strong sense of universal brotherhood. We have hardly been acquainted two hours, and my hand has never yet fed you. What can be the meaning of the obscure love for me that has sprung up in your little heart? The sympathy you bestow on me is a charming mystery, and I accept it. Sleep, friend, in the place that you have chosen!'

Having thus spoken, M. Bergeret turned over the leaves of Ottfried Müller's *Manual*, which with marvellous instinct he had kept in his hand both during and after his fall. He turned over the pages, and could not find what he sought.

Every moment, however, seemed to increase the pain he was feeling.

'I believe,' he thought, 'that the whole of my left side is bruised and my hip swollen. I have a suspicion that my right leg is grazed all over and my left elbow aches and burns, but shall I cavil at pain that has led me to the discovery of a friend?

His reflections were running thus when old Angélique, breathless and perspiring, entered the study. She first opened the door, and then she knocked, for she never permitted herself to enter without knocking. If she had not done so before she opened the door, she did it after, for she had good manners, and knew what was expected of her. She went in therefore, knocked, and said:

'Monsieur, I have come to relieve you of the dog.'

M. Bergeret heard these words with decided annoyance. He had not as yet inquired into his claims to Riquet, and now realized that he had none. The thought that Madame Borniche might take the animal away from him filled him with sadness, yet, after all, Riquet did belong to her. Affecting indifference, he replied:

'He's asleep; let him sleep!'

'Where is he? I don't see him,' remarked old Angélique.

'Here he is,' answered M. Bergeret. 'In my chair.'

With her two hands clasped over her portly figure, old Angélique smiled, and, in a tone of gentle mockery, ventured:

'I wonder what pleasure the creature can find in sleeping there behind Monsieur!'

'That,' retorted M. Bergeret, 'is his business.'

Then, as he was of inquiring mind, he immediately sought of Riquet his reasons for the selection of his resting-place, and lighting on them, replied with his accustomed candour:

'I keep him warm, and my presence affords a sense of security; my comrade is a chilly and homely little animal.' Then he added: 'Do you know, Angélique? I will go out presently and buy him a collar.'

Jimmy,
The Dog in My Life

ARTHUR BRYANT

JIMMY was a rough-haired English terrier. He had a snow-white coat which, when brushed and washed, was almost dazzlingly white; large and well-proportioned brown and black spots, a short, stuggy brown-tipped tail that usually, like his aspiring spirit, pointed perkily upwards; long, graceful legs that with his stout heart could carry him swiftly as any deer or racehorse; two satiny bown ears that sometimes lay in repose and at others pointed upwards like the pavilions of a mediaeval army; and the most beautiful brown eyes I have ever seen. He may not have conformed to the pedantic requirements of any Breeding Society but, viewed purely as dog, he had everything proper about him.

He entered my life on a Cornish cliff eighteen years ago. It was at the darkest moment of the war soon after our defeat at Knightsbridge and when the victorious Germans were hammering on the gates of Alexandria and Stalingrad, when the position at sea was more grave than at any time of the war and when the Japanese tide in the Pacific and South-East Asia had still to be turned. I had just been given a fortnight's respite from work which I was doing for the Services, and had taken the opportunity of spending ten days in a farmhouse on the North Cornish cliffs. It was my one wartime holiday and during the afternoons my wife and I made the most of it; sometimes picnicking on the beach and at other times taking long tramps over the cliffs. On one of these we walked to Boscastle, about six or seven miles from the farmhouse where we were staying. And there we encountered the waif who for the next fourteen years was to dominate our lives. In a backwater of immeasurable quiet—the quiet of long rollers and surge and heather cliffs—the dog in our lives found us.

We were eating sandwiches at the time on a small promontory overlooking the west side of the harbour, and I had thrown a few crumbs to some gulls who were obviously old *habitués* of the place and who, voraciously soaring and diving, were taking their customary toll of the picnicking few—honeymoon couples, old people and Service men and women on leave who were scattered about the cliff.

Suddenly I became aware that my wife and I were no longer alone. Sitting very silent and intent by our side was a white, shaggy terrier with brown cap and ears and a stump of a tail, gazing at my sandwiches with a look of infinite reproach and longing; he was obviously grieved that such largesse should be distributed among undeserving seagulls. Though food in those days was not plentiful and I was hungry, I was unable to resist the look in those large brown eyes, and my last two sandwiches, bit by bit, were handed over to this obviously expert and, as it turned out, professional beggar. What was so remarkable was that, though, as we subsequently came to realize, he must have been half starving, he made not the slightest attempt to snatch the proffered food and took it so gently that it seemed to leave one's hand by an imperceptible process of suction. Never in all my experience had I known a dog with such a soft mouth or with more gentle winning manners—not even the great-hearted, graceful, deep-ruffed Alsatian who for seven years formed the background to my life and after his death left it, for many months, desolate. This soft mouth was one of the dog's distinguishing traits and always remained so. A connoisseur of food, especially as we discovered later, of the rarer and more expensive kinds, he was never greedy. He merely showed, as only he could, that he needed it, and then waited patiently for his need to be satisfied.

Owing to his half-starved condition, he seemed at the time to be an old dog: thin, matted, mangy, with a pink hairless underneath on which black spots showed like skin eruptions. We took him to be the property of some poor family who could afford him little food or attention. Yet before he had been with us many minutes he gave us a taste of his quality. A hundred feet or so beneath us was an estuary, with scores of gulls resting on the sand. These the dog obviously regarded as enemies, for he suddenly jumped up, dashed down the precipitous rocks and, barking wildly, drove them, squalling and wheeling, out to sea. Then he raced up the cliff to us, wagged his little stern ecstatically as he approached, and sat down again by our side, intently and wistfully surveying the sandwich-box. The whole exercise was carried out in double-quick time and evinced the highest degree of alertness, zest and *savoir-faire*. And yet, as I have said, he seemed an old, rugged, undernourished dog, and was unquestionably very mangy.

It was only after we had sat there for an hour that we realized with a shock that he had no collar and that he belonged to none of the picnicking parties who had been sharing the promontory with us. And when, now alone, we rose to leave, the dog rose and followed us. Or, to be precise, he preceded us, for from the start of our association he took the initiative. He did so in a manner that made it perfectly clear that there was now a bond between us and that he regarded us as his property. Whenever we paused he paused, and when we sat down—which we deliberately did to see what would happen—he sat down too, and regarded us with a look of deep interest and affection. He seemed, indeed, for all his shaggy and disreputable appearance, the soul of amiability, for we noted particularly the friendliness with which he greeted the dogs in the outskirts of the little town through which we had to pass, wagging his tail in a frenzy of welcome at their approach and lavishing upon them those attentions which seem to endear dogs to one another. There was never the faintest hint of a fight in his manner; he positively loved his fellow-dogs, all of them, the motion of his quivering tail seemed to say. Not even the churliest cur could have picked a quarrel with a creature so imbued with the spirit of universal charity.

After that, passing through the town, we lost him—or rather, he lost us. We were relieved, for the prospect of a stray dog on our hands so far from home, and at such a time, naturally dismayed us. But some days later, just before my brief holiday ended, we walked over the cliffs again to pay our last visit to the storm-battered estuary where we had encountered the little creature. In the intervening days we had sometimes spoken of him and his inexplicable charm, and had half-wondered whether we should ever see him again. But we were not thinking of him at all when, just as we were finishing our tea in the local hostelry, we found him once more sitting quietly by our side.

It was inevitable, I suppose, that we should have offered him cake, and inevitable, too—though we were not expecting it— that he should again have followed us. This time, as we climbed the steep hill out of the town, it became clear that he was following us in earnest. Remembering that we had a six or seven miles' walk over the cliffs before us, and that we should have to retrace our steps next day—our last before I returned to my labours—if we were not either heartlessly to abandon him or adopt him for life, we were greatly distressed. We were still on a main road, and to all the people we met walking towards the town we explained our plight and asked them to take the dog back to where he belonged. But from them we also learned what we had guessed—that he belonged to nowhere; that he was an inveterate runaway for whom the police were seeking a home and who had been eking out a summer's existence rabbiting on the cliffs and begging largesse from picnic parties. And though two or three of them did their best to lure him back to the town, he refused to be caught and persisted in following us.

A mile or so out of the town our way left the main road and struck across the cliffs. After that, we knew, we should meet no other travellers. We accordingly did our best to persuade the dog to return. But he appeared to regard our gestures and pointings as a species of game, cocked up his ears and watched us for a time, then lost interest and sat down, awaiting our pleasure. In the end I was reduced to threatening him with a stone, which I threw, miserably and feebly, in his direction. When the dog realized that what I was doing was no game, but a deliberate attempt to get rid of him, the confidence in his bearing vanished in a moment and he became a broken, forlorn, abject creature, with drooping tail and tragic eyes. He slunk away, and we hurriedly resumed our path towards the cliff; daring neither to speak nor look at one another. I felt as though I was a murderer.

But we had not done with the dog; that loving heart was to redeem us. For suddenly my wife gripped my arm and said, 'Look,' and, turning, I saw him following, miserably, far back from the underside of the hedge. That was the end or, so far as we were concerned, the beginning. We let him come up and thereafter he took charge of us, trotting on ahead of us as though everything was now arranged, as indeed—though we did not know it—it was. But, as we discussed him, I agreed that, if the farmer and his wife with whom we were lodging would let him stay for the next two nights—our last in Cornwall—I would telephone the police in the morning and offer him a home.

At the farm we were successful in obtaining permission for the dog to stay with us. When, after eating our supper, we returned to the room where we had left him on the floor, we found him, to our horror, curled up on one of our landlady's armchairs. It was symptomatic of what was to come: the quiet assurance of it, the luxurious comfort, the air of full proprietorship. Consigned for the night to a barn into which he was inveigled with a bowl of bread and milk—a dish for which, for all his recent hunger, he showed considerable contempt—he was waiting at the door to be let out when early next morning my wife went to release him. I can still see that eager, slightly offended, little white figure emerging like a bullet from his place of confinement and greeting his rescuer on the top of the stone steps that led to it.

During that day the dog was constantly disappearing and reappearing, as befitted the incorrigible rover he so clearly was. And yet the curious thing was that, just as he took food so gently and with such irreproachable manners, he was perfectly house-trained. In all the fourteen years he was with us, only once did he misbehave himself in a house, and then in the staircase hall of an immense nineteenth-century Gothic edifice whose pillars he not unnaturally confused with lamp-posts. A good home he must have had at some time, and now he apparently wanted another. And yet in all other ways he was a wild dog, used to complete liberty and impatient of the slightest restraint. In the course of the morning, while we were bathing, he attached himself to at least half a dozen other parties, and there seemed no reason to expect that he would remain with us. When I telephoned the police to offer him a home he had already vanished, only to reappear unexpectedly soon after the permission to take him had been granted.

Yet when that afternoon, after we had toiled up the cliff from the beach after his twentieth disappearance and my wife and I had agreed that if he rejoined us, as at that moment he did, I should walk him back to Boscastle and return him there if he would follow me—since it scarcely seemed a kindness to deprive one of his liberty who valued it so much—he turned his back firmly on me and persisted in following his mistress to the farm and a life of domesticity. He had chosen.

Next morning, when the car called to take us to the station, he had again disappeared—rabbiting—and it seemed certain we should have to depart without him. But just as the luggage was being put in, he reappeared. My wife had made him a collar of string, and with this round his neck—a symbol of his changed status—he accompanied us to the station. When he saw the train and realized he was to go with us he went mad with joy. And through all the long, crowded journey to London he remained quiet and gentle, curled up at our feet or in the corridor, patiently awaiting his future. Even Waterloo, with its to him bewildering turmoil and clatter, did not daunt that staunch little heart, though when a little later his mistress left the taxi and disappeared into a shop he became wildly agitated. And when, late at night, we arrived after further train and car journeys at the old North Buckinghamshire house that for the next three years was to be his home, he trotted into the garden as though he had lived there all his life. By every muscle of his taut, alert body he made it clear that he regarded it as his own.

*

From an existence of rabbit-hunting on wind-blown cliffs, cadging scraps out of paper bags from picnic parties and periodic sojourns in village police stations, Jimmy, as we christened him, passed into the possession of nearly all that a stray dog can ask—a fireside, regular meals, regular petting, soft sitting and lying and the devotion of two human beings. Within twenty-four hours of his arrival, despite some foolish talk by his new owners about housing him in an outhouse, he had established himself on his mistress's bed, which remained his sleeping place until he died fourteen years later. It was astonishing how quickly he changed from the gentle, almost barkless creature we had found into an animal almost embarrassingly vocal, with the lordliest airs and a pugnacity towards every creature bigger than himself that would have done credit to a Red Indian on the warpath. He became, at once, a boss dog, and let the world know it. Never was terrier more a terrier—more challenging, inquiring, restless—than this white, brown-capped, black-spotted, stuggy-tailed piece of fur and spirit that had so unexpectedly invaded and now so ruthlessly dominated our lives. If he felt his authority and superiority to the rest of his species to be challenged in even the smallest particular, he gave loud and authoritative tongue and prepared to fight. No Tammany Hall boss, no European dictator could be more insistent and menacingly urgent about his rights and powers. In his own esteem, he was the first dog in any place into which he entered and, regardless of questions of size and dogpower, was ready to force any posible challenger to admit it. Nor did he wait for challengers. He looked round for them and joyfully invited them.

Yet—and this was the pathos of him—a harsh word, a stick raised to chasten, a suitcase packed for a journey he might not share, and all the confidence went out of him like water drained from a cup. His tail went down, his head hung, and a look of unutterable sadness came into his big, brown eyes. Even chocolate, which in some mysterious way—and most inconveniently, seeing it was stringently rationed—he made it clear he loved above all other foods, would remain untouched at his feet if his mistress went out without him. To her, for all his fiery challenge to a world which had tragically misused him and which he had now so triumphantly overcome, he gave a love as single-hearted and unquestioning as I have ever witnessed in any creature, human or animal.

Jimmy's first three years of domesticity were wartime years. They must have seemed to him strangely static. His master, doing work for all three Services, was often away, travelling by rail, road and sometimes by air, while Jimmy remained with his mistress in the heavy clay Buckinghamshire uplands. I think he regarded this as a real deprivation, for all his life he was essentially a dog who wanted to be off somewhere. It mattered little to him where, so long as he went, and up to the end any journey, even the shortest—for a shopping expedition or merely to take the car a hundred yards to the garage at the back of the house—was heralded by excited, imperious barking.

Having no outlet for his roving instincts at a time when unnecessary journeys were frowned on, not only for little dogs but for non-combatant humans, he at this period of his life frequently, and not unnaturally, ran away. It was not that he wanted to leave us; on the contrary, from the start he was clearly as devoted to us as we were to him and always returned to us with every manifestation of passionate devotion and contrition for having left us. But he could not resist his longing for adventure. We had only to leave a window or the garden gate open and he would be through it and, though at first he might intend to go no further than the neighbouring smallholder's manure heap—our village dogs' club—or to pick a bone, in more senses than one, with his great enemy and rival, Farmer Hinton's dog down the road, unless speedily detected and recalled he would as likely as not attach himself to some passing soldier or follow a scent across the fields and, travelling at his usual remarkable speed—for he could outdistance a bicycle coasting down the steepest hill—soon be far beyond recall or, in those petrol-less days, discovery. There would then follow hours of agonized searching the neighbouring fields and woods and, when the searching proved vain, as it almost invariably did, much telephoning to distant police-stations, whence, usually long after nightfall, he would be retrieved by his long-suffering mistress on a bicycle.

On one of his odysseys, I remember, he had followed a W.A.A.F. on a bicycle to a nearby town. Here he spent some hours in the typists' room at the Headquarters of the local Group of Bomber Operational Training Command, being petted and fed on sweet biscuits and other favourite and, at that time, rare foods. Then, feeling the call of the road again or possibly being ejected by outraged higher authority, he transferred himself to an airfield a few miles distant, where, apparently rabbiting, he was caught in the slipstream of a departing Wellington and was subsequently, dazed and much shaken by his aeronautical experience, all but run over by a car. At this point—it was about tea-time and he had been absent since breakfast—we succeeded in picking up his trail as a result of telephoning the entire neighbourhood, including our most august neighbour, the Air Vice-Marshal himself, who, as a result of a kindly search signal, was able to give us a report of his adventures. But he had by then again vanished and it was not till nine o'clock that a police station seven miles away telephoned to inform us that he was once more among his old friends, the constabulary. When collected, at the expense of a week's precious petrol ration, he was found in a circle of solemn policemen beside the station fire, sitting there with an expression of great intelligence and listening to a lecture on gas, though his contentment may have arisen less from his enjoyment of this intellectual fare than from a justly founded association of uniforms with meals and titbits. Yet, as usual, he greeted his rescuers with frantic delight, and returned home, barking, as though reunion with us had been his only thought all day. On this occasion we were so relieved to get him back safe and sound that we had not even the heart to reproach him.

More usually he was punished for his escapades. This usually took the form of a horrible penance called 'Black Hole', in which he was banished, amid minatory noises, to a wood-shed or cupboard and left there for ten minutes, half an hour or even longer, according to the heinousness of his crime and the degree of exasperation aroused by his misbehaviour. This was a very real punishment for a dog who lived every moment of his time with so great an intensity of feeling. I can still see the look of dejection and shame with which, at the dread words, 'Black Hole!' he would creep to his place of captivity. Nor, once there—for he was the manliest of beasts—did he ever howl or try to escape, but remained, a picture of inconsolable dejection, with his head on the ground or pressed miserably against the door until his cruel punishment was over. Meanwhile his jailers suffered quite as acutely as he, as they reflected on his misery and loneliness, until even his inexorable master could bear the thought of his imprisonment and the reproaches of the dog's tender-hearted mistress no longer, and hurried, with ill-concealed eagerness, to let him out. Usually it took several minutes of petting before the dog's self-confidence could be restored and he became once more his eager, assured self.

For under the self-confidence and even arrogance that the possession of a home had given him was the remembrance of what it was to be unloved and homeless. The fierceness and arrogance of his challenge to his fellow-dogs derived, I am sure, from the time when he slunk, a sad, bedraggled little outcast, past farms the savour of whose good things was guarded by a proud, angry housedog and utterly forbidden to the likes of him. To his dying day I do not believe Jimmy ever lost this deep-seated realization. It made the bond between him and those who had given him a home stronger than the usual bond between dog and man, and anything that seemed to threaten it struck at the roots of his being. I shall never forget the look of terror that came over him once when, hunting on a roadside heath during a halt on a car journey far from his home and familiar haunts, he had to be recalled by the sound

97

of the horn: the fear that we would go without him and condemn him once more to a life of solitary wandering made him suddenly forget, in that agonized moment, even the presence of imminent rabbits. And on another occasion, when he had been taken to a London dog-shop to be clipped and had been left, perhaps injudiciously, to be called for, he was found two hours later as if shell-shocked, unable for a while to take his bearings or know where he was.

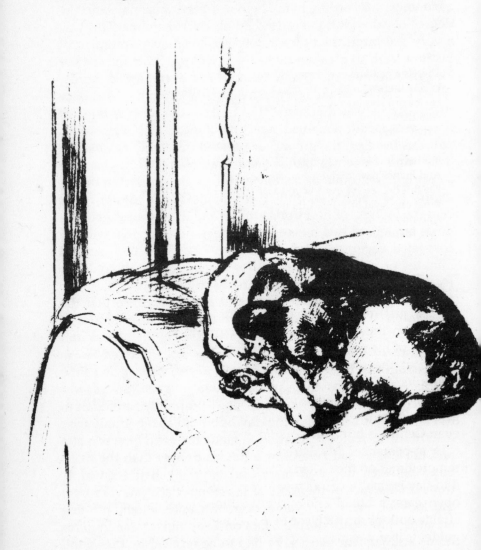

'Teem':
a Treasure-Hunter

RUDYARD KIPLING

There's a gentleman of France—better met by choice than chance,
Where there's time to turn aside and space to flee—
He is born and bred and made for the cattle-droving trade,
And they call him Monsieur Bouvier de Brie.
'What—Brie?' 'Yes, Brie.' 'Where those funny cheeses come from?'
  'Oui! Oui! Oui!
But his name is great through Gaul as the wisest dog of all,
And France pays high for Bouvier de Brie.'
'De Brie?' 'C'est lui. And, if you read my story,—you will see
What one loyal little heart thought of Life and Love and Art,
And notably of Bouvier de Brie—
"My friend the Vicomte Bouvier de Brie." '

NOTHING could prevent my adored Mother from demanding at once the piece of sugar which was her just reward for every Truffle she found. My revered Father, on the other hand, contented himself with the strict practice of his Art. So soon as that Pierre, our Master, stooped to dig at the spot indicated, my Father moved on to fresh triumphs.

From my Father I inherit my nose, and, perhaps, a touch of genius. From my Mother a practical philosophy without which even Genius is but a bird of one wing.

In appearance? My Parents come of a race built up from remote times on the Gifted of various strains. The fine flower of it to-day is small—of a rich gold, touched with red; pricked and open ears; a broad and receptive brow; eyes of intense but affable outlook, and a Nose in itself an inspiration and unerring guide. Is it any wonder, then, that my Parents stood apart from

99

the generality? Yet I would not make light of those worthy artisans who have to be trained by Persons to the pursuit of Truffles. They are of many stocks and possess many virtues, but not the Nose—that gift which is incommunicable.

Myself? I am not large. At birth, indeed, I was known as The Dwarf; but my achievements early won me the title of The Abbé. It was easy. I do not recall that I was ever trained by any Person. I watched, imitated, and, at need, improved upon, the technique of my Parents among the little thin oaks of my country where the best Truffles are found; and that which to the world seemed a chain of miracles was, for me, as easy as to roll in the dust.

My small feet could walk the sun up and down across the stony hill-crests where we worked. My well-set coat turned wet, wind, and cold, and my size enabled me to be carried, on occasion, in my Master's useful outside pocket.

My companions of those days? At first Pluton and Dis—the solemn, dewlapped, black, mated pair who drew the little wooden cart whence my master dispensed our Truffles at the white Château near our village, and to certain shopkeepers in the Street of the Fountain where the women talk. Those Two of Us were peasants in grain. They made clear to me the significance of the flat round white Pieces, and the Thin Papers, which my Master and his Mate buried beneath the stone of their fireplace. Not only Truffles but all other things, Pluton told me, turn into Pieces or Thin Papers at last.

But my friend of friends; my preceptor, my protector, my life-long admiration; was Monsieur le Vicomte Bouvier de Brie—a Marshal of Bulls whom he controlled in the stony pastures near the cottage. There were many sheep also, with whom neither the Vicomte nor I was concerned. Mutton is bad for the Nose, and, as I have reason to know, for the disposition.

He was of race, too—'born' as I was—and so accepted me when, with the rash abandon of puppyhood, I attached myself to his ear. In place of abolishing me, which he could have done with one of his fore-paws, he lowered me gently between both of them, so that I lay blinking up the gaunt cliff of his chest into his unfathomable eyes, and 'Little bad one!' he said. 'But I prophesy thou wilt go far!'

Here, fenced by those paws, I would repair for my slumbers, to avoid my enemies or to plague him with questions. And, when he went to the Railway Station to receive or despatch more Bulls, I would march beneath his belly, hurling infantile insults at the craven doggerie of the Street of the Fountain. After I was expert in my Art, he would talk to me of his own, breaking off with some thunder of command to a young Bull who presumed to venture too near the woods where our Truffles grow, or descending upon him like hail across walls which his feet scorned to touch.

His strength, his audacity, overwhelmed me. He, on his side, was frankly bewildered by my attainments. 'But how— *how*, little one, is it done, your business?' I could not convey to him, nor he to me, the mystery of our several Arts. Yet always unweariedly he gave me the fruits of his experience and philosophy.

I recall a day when I had chased a chicken which, for the moment, represented to me a sufficiently gross Bull of Salers. There seemed a possibility of chastisement at the hands of the owner, and I refuged me beneath my friend's neck where he watched in the sun. He listened to my foolish tale, and said, as to himself, 'These Bulls of mine are but beef fitted with noses and tails by which one regulates them. But these black hidden lumps of yours which only such as you can unearth—*that* is a business beyond me! I should like to add it to my repertoire.'

'And I,' I cried (my second teeth were just pushing), 'I will be a Driver of Bulls!'

'Little one,' he responded with infinite tenderness, 'here is one thing for us both to remember. Outside his Art, an Artist must never dream.'

About my fifteenth month I found myself brother to four who wearied me. At the same time there was a change in my Master's behaviour. Never having had any regard for him, I was the quicker to notice his lack of attention. My Mother, as always, said, 'If it is not something, it is sure to be something else.' My Father simply, 'At all hazards follow your Art. That can never lead to a false scent.'

There came a Person of abominable odours to our cottage, not once but many times. One day my Master worked me in his presence. I demonstrated, through a long day of changing airs, with faultless precision. After supper, my Master's Mate said to him, 'We are sure of at least two good workers for next season—and with a dwarf one never knows. It is far off, that England the man talks of. Finish the affair, Pierril.'

Some Thin Papers passed from hand to hand. The Person then thrust me into his coat-pocket (Ours is not a breed to be shown to all) and there followed for me alternations of light and dark in stink-carts: a period when my world rose and rolled till I was sick; a silence beside lapping water under stars; transfer to another Person whose scent and speech were unintelligible; another flight by stink-cart; a burst of sunrise between hedges; a scent of sheep; violent outcries and rockings: finally, a dissolution of the universe which projected me through a hedge from which I saw my captor lying beneath the stink-cart where a large black-and-white She bit him with devotion.

A ditch led me to the shelter of a culvert. I composed myself within till the light was suddenly blocked out by the head of that very She, who abused me savagely in *Lingua canina*. (My Father often recommended me never to reply to a strange She.) I was glad when her Master's voice recalled this one to her duties, and I heard the clickety of her flock's feet above my head.

In due time I issued forth to acquaint myself with this world into which I had been launched. It was new in odour and aspect, but with points of likeness to my old one. Clumps of trees fringed close woods and smooth green pastures; and, at the bottom of a shallow basin crowned with woodland, stood a white Château even larger than the one to which Pluton and Dis used to pull their cart.

I kept me among the trees, and was congratulating my Nose on its recovery from the outrageous assaults it had suffered during my journeys, when there came to it the unmistakable aroma of Truffles—not, indeed, the strawberry-scented ones of my lost world, but like enough to throw me into my working-pose.

I took wind, and followed up my line. I was not deceived. There were Truffles of different sorts in their proper places under those thick trees. My Mother's maxim had proved its truth. This was evidently the 'something else' of which she had spoken; and I felt myself again my own equal. As I worked amid the almost familiar odours it seemed to me that all that had overtaken me had not happened, and that at any moment I should meet Pluton and Dis with our cart. But they came not. Though I called they did not come.

A far-off voice interrupted me, with menace. I recognised it for that of the boisterous She of my culvert, and was still.

After cautious circuits I heard the sound of a spade, and in a wooded hollow saw a Person flattening earth round a pile of wood, heaped to make charcoal. It was a business I had seen often.

My Nose assured me that the Person was authentically a peasant and (I recalled the memory later) had not handled One of Us within the time that such a scent would hang on him. My Nose, further, recorded that he was imbued with the aromas proper to his work and was, also, kind, gentle, and equable in temperament. (You Persons wonder that All of Us know your moods before you yourselves realise them? Be well sure that every shade of his or her character, habit, or feeling cries itself aloud in a Person's scent. No more than We All can deceive Each Other can You Persons deceive Us—though We pretend—We pretend—to believe!)

His coat lay on a bank. When he drew from it bread and cheese, I produced myself. But I had been so long at gaze, that my shoulder, bruised in transit through the hedge, made me fall. He was upon me at once and, with strength equal to his gentleness, located my trouble. Evidently—though the knowledge even then displeased me—he knew how We should be handled.

I submitted to his care, ate the food he offered, and, reposing in the crook of his mighty arm, was borne to a small cottage where he bathed my hurt, set water beside me and returned to his charcoal. I slept, lulled by the cadence of his spade and the bouquet of natural scents in the cottage which included all those I was used to, except garlic and, strangely, Truffles.

I was roused by the entry of a She-Person who moved slowly and coughed. There was on her (I speak now as We speak) the Taint of *the* Fear—of that Black Fear which bids Us throw up our noses and lament. She laid out food. The Person of the Spade entered. I fled to his knee. He showed me to the Girl-

Person's dull eyes. She caressed my head, but the chill of her hand increased the Fear. He set me on his knees, and they talked in the twilight.

Presently, their talk nosed round hidden flat Pieces and Thin Papers. The tone was so exactly that of my Master and his Mate that I expected they would lift up the hearthstone. But *theirs* was in the chimney, whence the Person drew several white Pieces, which he gave to the Girl. I argued from this they had admitted me to their utmost intimacy and—I confess it— I danced like a puppy. My reward was their mirth—his specially. When the Girl laughed she coughed. But *his* voice warmed and possessed me before I knew it.

After night was well fallen, they went out and prepared a bed on a cot in the open, sheltered only by a large faggot-stack. The Girl disposed herself to sleep there, which astonished me. (In my lost world out-sleeping is not done, except when Persons wish to avoid Forest Guards.) The Person of the Spade then set a jug of water by the bed and, turning to re-enter the house, delivered a long whistle. It was answered across the woods by the unforgettable voice of the old She of my culvert. I inserted myself at once between, and a little beneath, some of the more robust faggots.

On her silent arrival the She greeted the Girl with extravagant affection and fawned beneath her hand, till the coughings closed in uneasy slumber. Then, with no more noise than the moths of the night, she quested for me in order, she said, to tear out my throat. 'Ma Tante,' I replied placidly from within my fortress, 'I do not doubt you could save yourself the trouble by swallowing me alive. But, first, tell me what I have done.' 'That there is *My* Bone,' was the reply. It was enough! (Once in my life I had seen poor honest Pluton stand like a raging wolf between his Pierril, whom he loved, and a Forest Guard.) *We* use that word seldom and never lightly. Therefore, I answered, 'I assure you she is not mine. She gives me the Black Fear.'

You know how We cannot deceive Each Other? The She accepted my statement; at the same rime reviling me for my lack of appreciation—a crookedness of mind not uncommon among elderly Shes.

To distract her, I invited her to tell me her history. It appeared that the Girl had nursed her through some early distemper. Since then, the She had divided her life between her duties among sheep by day and watching, from the First Star till Break of Light, over the Girl, who, she said, also suffered from a slight distemper. This had been her existence, her joy and her devotion long before I was born. Demanding nothing more, she was prepared to back her single demand by slaughter.

Once, in my second month, when I would have run away from a very fierce frog, my friend the Vicomte told me that, at crises, it is best to go forward. On a sudden impulse I emerged from my shelter and sat beside her. There was a pause of life and death during which I had leisure to contemplate all her teeth. Fortunately, the Girl waked to drink. The She crawled to caress the hand that set down the jug, and waited till the breathing resumed. She came back to me—I had not stirred— with blazing eyes. 'How can you *dare* this?' she said. 'But why not?' I answered. 'If it is not something, it is sure to be something else.' Her fire and fury passed. 'To whom do you say it!' she assented. 'There is always something else to fear— not for myself but for My Bone yonder.'

Then began a conversation unique, I should imagine, even among Ourselves. My old, unlovely, savage Aunt, as I shall henceforth call her, was eaten alive with fears for the Girl—not so much on account of her distemper, but because of Two She-Persons-Enemies—whom she described to me minutely by Eye and Nose—one like a Ferret, the other like a Goose.

These, she said, meditated some evil to the Girl against which my Aunt and the Girl's Father, the Person of the Spade, were helpless. The Two Enemies carried about with them certain papers, by virtue of which the Girl could be taken away from the cottage and my Aunt's care, precisely as she had seen sheep taken out of her pasture by Persons with papers, and driven none knew whither.

The Enemies would come at intervals to the cottage in daytime (when my Aunt's duty held her with the sheep) and always they left behind them the Taint of misery and anxiety. It was not that she feared the Enemies personally. She feared nothing except a certain Monsieur The-Law who, I understood later, cowed even her.

Naturally I sympathised. I did not know this *gentilhommier* de

Loire, but I knew Fear. Also, the Girl was of the same stock as He who had fed and welcomed me and Whose voice had reassured. My Aunt suddenly demanded if I purposed to take up my residence with them. I would have detailed to her my adventures. She was acutely uninterested in them all except so far as they served her purposes, which she explained. She would allow me to live on condition that I reported to her, nightly beside the faggot-stack, all I had seen or heard or suspected of every action and mood of the Girl during the day; any arrival of the Enemies, as she called them; and whatever I might gather from their gestures and tones. In other words I was to spy for her as Those of Us who accompany the Forest Guards spy for their detestable Masters.

I was not disturbed. (I had had experience of the Forest Guard.) Still there remained my dignity and something which I suddenly felt was even more precious to me. 'Ma Tante,' I said, 'what I do depends not on you but on *My* Bone in the cottage there.' She understood. 'What is there on *Him*,' she said, 'to draw you?' 'Such things are like Truffles,' was my answer. 'They are there or they are not there.' 'I do not know what "Truffles" may be,' she snapped. 'He has nothing useful to me except that He, too, fears for my Girl. At any rate your infatuation for Him makes you more useful as an aid to my plans.' 'We shall see,' said I. 'But—to talk of affairs of importance—do you seriously mean that you have no knowledge of Truffles?' She was convinced that I mocked her. 'Is it,' she demanded, 'some lapdog's trick?' She said this of Truffles—of my Truffles!

The impasse was total. Outside of the Girl on the cot and her sheep (for I can testify that, with them, she was an artist) the square box of my Aunt's head held not one single thought. My patience forsook me, but not my politeness. 'Cheer-up, old one!' I said. 'An honest heart outweighs many disadvantages of ignorance and low birth.' . . .

And She? I thought she would have devoured me in my hair! When she could speak, she made clear that she was 'born'— entirely so—of a breed mated and trained since the days of the First Shepherd. In return I explained that I was a specialist in the discovery of delicacies which the genius of my ancestors had revealed to Persons since the First Person first scratched in the first dirt.

She did not believe me—nor do I pretend that I had been entirely accurate in my genealogy—but she addressed me henceforth as 'My Nephew.'

Thus that wonderful night passed, with the moths, the bats, the owls, the sinking moon, and the varied respirations of the Girl. At sunrise a call broke out from beyond the woods. My Aunt vanished to her day's office. I went into the house and found Him lacing one gigantic boot. Its companion lay beside the hearth. I brought it to Him (I had seen my Father do as much for that Pierrounet my Master).

He was loudly pleased. He patted my head, and when the Girl entered, told her of my exploit. She called me to be caressed, and, though the Black Taint upon her made me cringe, I came. She belonged to Him—as at that moment I realised that I did.

Here began my new life. By day I accompanied Him to His charcoal—sole guardian of His coat and the bread and cheese on the bank, or, remembering my Aunt's infatuation, fluctuated between the charcoal-mound and the house to spy upon the Girl, when she was not with Him. He was all that I desired—in the sound of His solid tread; His deep but gentle voice; the sympathetic texture and scent of His clothes; the safe hold of His hand when He would slide me into His great outer pocket and carry me through the far woods where He dealt secretly with rabbits. Like peasants, who are alone more than most Persons, He talked aloud to himself, and presently to me, asking my opinion of the height of a wire from the ground.

My devotion He accepted and repaid from the first. My Art he could by no means comprehend. For, naturally, I followed my Art as every Artist must, even when it is misunderstood. If not, he comes to preoccupy himself mournfully with his proper fleas.

My new surroundings; the larger size and closer spacing of the oaks; the heavier nature of the soils; the habits of the lazy wet winds—a hundred considerations which the expert takes into account—demanded changes and adjustments of my technique. . . . My reward? I found and brought Him Truffles of the best. I nosed them into His hand. I laid them on the threshold of the cottage and they filled it with their fragrance. He and the Girl thought that I amused myself, and would

throw—throw!—them for me to retrieve, as though they had been stones and I a puppy! What more could I do? The scent over that ground was lost.

But the rest was happiness, tempered with vivid fears when we were apart lest, if the wind blew beyond moderation, a tree might fall and crush Him; lest when He worked late He might disappear into one of those terrible riverpits so common in the world whence I had come, and be lost without trace. There was no peril I did not imagine for Him till I could hear His feet walking securely on sound earth long before the Girl had even suspected. Thus my heart was light in spite of the nightly conferences with my formidable Aunt, who linked her own dismal apprehensions to every account that I rendered of the

Girl's day-life and actions. For some cause or other, the Two
Enemies had not appeared since my Aunt had warned me
against them, and there was less of Fear in the house. Perhaps,
as I once hinted to my Aunt, owing to my presence.

It was an unfortunate remark. I should have remembered her
gender. She attacked me, that night, on a new scent, bidding
me observe that she herself was decorated with a Collar of
Office which established her position before all the world.
I was about to compliment her, when she observed, in the low
even tone of detachment peculiar to Shes of age, that, unless
I were so decorated, not only was I outside the Law (that
Person of whom, I might remember, she had often spoken) but
could not be formally accepted into any household.

How, then, I demanded, might I come by this protection? In
her own case, she said, the Collar was hers by right as a
Preceptress of Sheep. To procure a Collar for me would be a
matter of Pieces or even of Thin Papers, from His chimney.
(I recalled poor Pluton's warning that everything changes
at last into such things.) If He chose to give of His Pieces for my
Collar, my civil status would be impregnable. Otherwise,
having no business or occupation, I lived, said my Aunt, like
the rabbits—by favour and accident.

'But, ma Tante,' I cried, 'I have the secret of an Art beyond all
others.'

'That is not understood in these parts,' she replied. 'You
have told me of it many times, but I do not believe. What a pity
it is not rabbits! You are small enough to creep down their
burrows. But these precious things of yours under the ground
which no one but you can find—it is absurd.'

'It is an absurdity, then, which fills Persons' chimney-places
with Pieces and Thin Papers. Listen, ma Tante!' I all but
howled. 'The world I came from was stuffed with things
underground which all Persons desired. This world here is also
rich in them, but I—I alone—can bring them to light!'

She repeated acridly, 'Here is not there. It should have been
rabbits.'

I turned to go. I was at the end of my forces.

'You talk too much of the world whence you came,' my Aunt
sneered. 'Where is that world?'

'I do not know,' I answered miserably and crawled under my

faggots. As a matter of routine, when my report had been made to my Aunt, I would take post on the foot of His bed where I should be available in case of bandits. But my Aunt's words had barred that ever-open door.

My suspicions worked like worms in my system. If He chose, He could kick me off on to the floor—beyond sound of His desired voice—into the rabid procession of fears and flights whence He had delivered me. Whither, then, should I go? . . . There remained only my lost world where Persons knew the value of Truffles and of Those of Us who could find them. I would seek that world!

With this intention, and a bitterness in my belly as though I had mouthed a toad, I came out after dawn and fled to the edge of the woods through which He and I had wandered so often. They were bounded by a tall stone wall, along which I quested for an opening. I found none till I reached a small house beside shut gates. Here an officious One of Us advanced upon me with threats. I was in no case to argue or even to expostulate. I hastened away and attacked the wall again at another point.

But after a while, I found myself back at the house of the Officious One. I recommenced my circuit, but—there was no end to that Wall. I remembered crying aloud to it in hope it might fall down and pass me through. I remember appealing to the Vicomte to come to my aid. I remember a flight of big black birds, calling the very name of my lost world—'Aa—or' [1]—above my head. But soon they scattered in all directions. Only the Wall continued to continue, and I blindly at its foot. Once a She-Person stretched out her hand towards me. I fled—as I fled from an amazed rabbit who, like myself, existed by favour and accident.

Another Person coming upon me threw stones. This turned me away from the Wall and so broke its attraction. I subsided into an aimless limp of hours, until some woods that seemed familiar received me into their shades. . . .

I found me at the back of the large white Château in the hollow, which I had seen only once, far off, on the first day of my arrival in this world. I looked down through bushes on to ground divided by strips of still water and stone. Here were

---

[1] Cahors?

birds, bigger than turkeys, with enormous voices and tails which they raised one against the other, while a white-haired She-Person dispensed them food from a pan she held between sparkling hands. My Nose told me that she was unquestionably of race—descended from champion strains. I would have crawled nearer, but the greedy birds forbade. I retreated uphill into the woods, and, moved by I know not what agonies of frustration and bewilderment, threw up my head and lamented.

The harsh imperative call of my Aunt cut through my self-pity. I found her on duty in pastures still bounded by that Wall which encircled my world. She charged me at once with having some disreputable affair, and, for its sake, deserting my post with the Girl. I could but pant. Seeing, at last, my distress, she said, 'Have you been seeking that lost world of yours?' Shame closed my mouth. She continued, in softer tones, 'Except when it concerns My Bone, do not take all that I say at full-fang. There are others as foolish as you. Wait my return.'

She left me with an affectation, almost a coquetry, of extreme fatigue. To her charge had been added a new detachment of sheep who wished to escape. They had scattered into separate crowds, each with a different objective and a different speed. My Aunt, keeping the high ground, allowed them to disperse, till her terrible voice, thrice lifted, brought them to halt. Then, in one long loop of flight, my Aunt, a dumb fury lying wide on their flank, swept down with a certainty, a speed, and a calculation which almost reminded me of my friend the Vicomte. Those diffuse and errant imbeciles reunited and inclined away from her in a mob of mixed smells and outcries— to find themselves exquisitely penned in an angle of the fence, my Aunt, laid flat at full length, facing them! One after another their heads dropped and they resumed their eternal business of mutton-making.

My Aunt came back, her affectation of decrepitude heightened to heighten her performance. And who was I, an Artist also, to mock her?

'You wonder why my temper is not of the bluntest?' she said. 'You could not have done that!'

'But at least I can appreciate it,' I cried. 'It was superb! It was unequalled! It was faultless! You did not even nip one of them.'

'With sheep that is to confess failure,' she said. 'Do *you*, then, gnaw your Truffles?' It was the first time that she had ever admitted their existence! My genuine admiration, none the worse for a little flattery, opened her heart. She spoke of her youthful triumphs at sheep-herding expositions; of rescues of lost lambs, or incapable mothers found reversed in ditches. Oh, she was all an Artist, my thin-flanked, haggard-eyed Aunt by enforced adoption. She even let me talk of the Vicomte!

Suddenly (the shadows had stretched) she leaped, with a grace I should never have suspected, on to a stone wall and stood long at far gaze. 'Enough of this nonsense,' she said brutally. 'You are rested now. Get to your work. If you could see, my Nephew, you would observe the Ferret and the Goose walking there, three fields distant. They have come again for My Bone. They will keep to the path made for Persons. Go at once to the cottage before they arrive and—do what you can to harass them. Run—run—mountebank of a yellow imbecile that you are!'

I turned on my tail, as We say, and took the direct line through my well-known woods at my utmost speed since her orders dispatched me without loss of dignity towards my heart's one desire. And I was received by Him, and by the Girl with unfeigned rapture. They passed me, from one to the other like the rarest of Truffles; rebuked me, not too severely, for my long absence; felt me for possible injuries from traps; brought me bread and milk, which I sorely needed; and by a hundred delicate attentions showed me the secure place I occupied in their hearts. I gave my dignity to the cats, and it is not too much to say that we were all engaged in a veritable *pas de trois* when a shadow fell across our threshold and the Two Enemies most rudely entered!

I conceived, and gave vent to, instant detestation which, for a while, delayed their attack. When it came, He and the Girl accepted it as yoked oxen receive the lash across the eyes—with the piteous dignity which Earth, having so little to give them, bestows upon her humbles. Like oxen, too, they backed side by side and pressed closer together. I renewed my comminations from every angle as I saw how these distracted my adversaries. They then pointed passionately to me and my pan of bread and milk which joy had prevented me from altogether emptying. Their tongues I felt were foul with reproach.

At last He spoke. He mentioned my name more than once, but always (I could tell) in my defence. The Girl backed His point. I assisted with—and it was something—all that I had ever heard in my lost world from the *sans-kennailerie* of the Street of the Fountain. The Enemies renewed the charge. Evidently my Aunt was right. Their plan was to take the Girl away in exchange for pieces of paper. I saw the Ferret wave a paper beneath His nose. He shook His head and launched that peasant's 'No,' which is one in all languages.

Here I applauded vehemently, continuously, monotonously, on a key which, also, I had learned in the Street of the Fountain. Nothing could have lived against it. The Enemies threatened, I could feel, some prodigious action or another; but at last they marched out of our presence. I escorted them to the charcoal-heap—the limit of our private domain—in a silence charged with possibilities for their thick ankles.

I returned to find my Two sunk in distress, but upon my account. I think they feared I might run away again, for they shut the door. They frequently and tenderly repeated my name, which, with them, was *'Teem.'* Finally He took a Thin Paper from the chimney-piece, slid me into His outside pocket and walked swiftly to the Village, which I had never smelt before.

In a place where a She-Person was caged behind bars, He exchanged the Thin Paper for one which he laid under my nose, saying 'Teem! Look! This is Licence-and-Law all-right!' In yet another place, I was set down before a Person who exhaled a grateful flavour of dried skins. My neck was then encircled by a Collar bearing a bright badge of office. All Persons round me expressed admiration and said 'Lor!' many times. On our return through the Village I stretched my decorated neck out of His pocket, like one of the gaudy birds at th Château, to impress Those of Us who might be abroad that I was now under full protection of Monsieur Le Law (whoever he might be), and thus the equal of my exacting Aunt.

That night, by the Girl's bed, my Aunt was at her most difficult. She cut short my history of my campaign, and cross-examined me coldly as to what had actually passed. Her interpretations were not cheering. She prophesied our Enemies would return, more savage for having been checked. She said that when they mentioned my name (as I have told you) it was to rebuke Him for feeding me, a vagabond, on good bread and milk, when I did not, according to Monsieur Law, belong to Him. (She herself, she added, had often been shocked by His extravagance in this regard.) I pointed out that my Collar now disposed of inconvenient questions. So much she ungraciously conceded, but—I had described the scene to her—argued that He had taken the Thin Paper out of its hiding-place because I had cajoled Him with my 'lapdog's tricks,' and that, in default of that Paper, He would go without food, as well as without what he burned under His nose, which to Him would be equally serious.

I was aghast. 'But, Ma Tante,' I pleaded, 'show me—make me any way to teach Him that the earth on which He walks so loftily can fill His chimneys with Thin Papers, and I promise you that *She* shall eat chicken!' My evident sincerity—perhaps, too, the finesse of my final appeal—shook her. She mouthed a paw in thought.

'You have shown Him those wonderful underground-things of yours?' she resumed.

'But often. And to your Girl also. They thought they were stones to throw. It is because of my size that I am not taken seriously.' I would have lamented, but she struck me down. Her Girl was coughing.

'Be silent, unlucky that you are! Have you shown your Truffles, as you call them, to anyone else?'

'Those Two are all I have ever met in this world, my Aunt.'

'That was true till yesterday,' she replied. 'But at the back of the Château—this afternoon—eh?' (My friend the Vicomte was right when he warned me that all elderly Shes have six ears and ten noses. And the older the more!)

'I saw that Person only from a distance. You know her, then, my Aunt?'

'If I know Her! She met me once when I was lamed by thorns under my left heel-pad. She stopped me. She took them out. She also put her hand on my head.'

'Alas, *I* have not your charms!' I riposted.

'Listen, before my temper snaps, my Nephew. She has

114

returned to her Château. Lay one of those things that you say you find, at her feet. *I* do not credit your tales about them, but it is possible that *She* may. She is of race. She knows all. She may make you that way for which you ask so loudly. It is only a chance. But, if it succeeds, and My Bone does *not* eat the chickens you have promised her, I will, for sure, tear out your throat.'

'My Aunt,' I replied, 'I am infinitely obliged. You have, at least, shown me a way. What a pity you were born with so many thorns under your tongue!' And I fled to take post at the foot of His bed, where I slept vigorously—for I had lived that day!—till time to bring Him His morning boots.

We then went to our charcoal. As official Guardian of the Coat I permitted myself no excursions till He was busied stopping the vents of little flames on the flanks of the mound. Then I moved towards a patch of ground which I had noted long ago. On my way, a chance of the air told me that the Born One of the Château was walking on the verge of the wood. I fled to my patch, which was even more fruitful than I had thought. I had unearthed several Truffles when the sound of her tread hardened on the bare ground beneath the trees. Selecting my largest and ripest, I bore it reverently towards her, dropped it in her path, and took a pose of humble devotion. Her Nose informed her before her eyes. I saw it wrinkle and sniff deliciously. She stooped and with sparkling hands lifted my gift to smell. Her sympathetic appreciation emboldened me to pull the fringe of her clothes in the direction of my little store exposed beneath the oak. She knelt and, rapturously inhaling their aroma, transferred them to a small basket on her arm. (All Born Ones bear such baskets when they walk upon their own earths.)

Here He called my name. I replied at once that I was coming, but that matters of the utmost importance held me for the moment. We moved on together, the Born One and I, and found Him beside His coat setting apart for me my own bread and cheese. We lived, we two, each always in the other's life!

I had often seen that Pierrounet my Master, who delivered me to strangers, uncover and bend at the side-door of the Château in my lost world over yonder. At no time was he beautiful. But He—My Own Bone to me!—though He too was uncovered, stood beautifully erect and as a peasant of race should bear himself when He and His are not being tortured by Ferrets or Geese. For a short time, He and the Born One did not concern themselves with me. They were obviously of old acquaintance. She spoke; she waved her sparkling hands; she laughed. He responded gravely, at dignified ease, like my friend the Vicomte. Then I heard my name many times. I fancy He may have told her something of my appearance in this world. (We peasants do not tell all to *any* one.) To prove to her my character, as He conceived it, He threw a stone. With as much emphasis as my love for Him allowed, I signified that this game of lapdogs was not mine. She commanded us to return to the woods. There He said to me as though it were some question of His magnificent boots, 'Seek, Teem! Find, Teem!' and waved His arms at random. He did not know! Even then, My Bone did not know!

But I—I was equal to the occasion! Without unnecessary gesture; stifling the squeaks of rapture that rose in my throat; coldly, almost, as my Father, I made point after point, picked up my lines and worked them (His attendant spade saving me the trouble of digging) till the basket was full. At this juncture the Girl—they were seldom far apart—appeared with all the old miseries on her face, and, behind her (I had been too occupied with my Art, or I should have yelled on their scent) walked the Two Enemies!

They had not spied us up there among the trees, for they rated her all the way to the charcoal-heap. Our Born One descended upon them softly as a mist through which shine the stars, and greeted them in the voice of a dove out of summer foliage. I held me still. She needed no aid, that one! They grew louder and more loud; she increasingly more suave. They flourished at her one of their detestable papers which she received as though it had been all the Truffles in the world. They talked of Monsieur Le Law. From her renewed smiles I understood that he, too, had the honour of her friendship. They continued to talk of him. . . . Then . . . she abolished them! How? Speaking with the utmost reverence of both, she reminded me of my friend the Vicomte disentangling an agglomeration of distracted, and therefore dangerous, beefs at the Railway Station. There was the same sage turn of the head, the same almost invisible stiffening of the shoulders, the very same small voice out of the side of the mouth, saying 'I charge myself with this.' And then—and then—those insupportable offspring of a jumped-up *gentilhommier* were transformed into amiable and impressed members of their proper class, giving ground slowly at first, but finally evaporating—yes, evaporating—like bad smells—in the direction of the world whence they had intruded.

During the relief that followed, the Girl wept and wept and wept. Our Born One led her to the cottage and consoled. We showed her our bed beside the faggots and all our other small dispositions, including a bottle out of which the Girl was used to drink. (I tasted once some that had been spilt. It was like unfresh fish—fit only for cats.) She saw, she heard, she considered all. Calm came at her every word. She would have given Him some Pieces, in exchange, I suppose, for her filled basket. He pointed to me to show that it was my work. She repeated most of the words she had employed before—my name among them—because one must explain many times to a peasant who desires *not* to comprehend. At last He took the Pieces.

Then my Born One stooped down to me beside His foot and said, in the language of my lost world, 'Knowest thou, Teem, that this is all *thy* work? Without thee we can do nothing. Knowest thou, my little dear Teem?' If I knew! Had He listened to me at the first the situation would have been regularised half a season before. Now I could fill his chimney-places as my Father had filled that of that disgusting Pierrounet. Logically, of course, I should have begun a fresh demonstration of my Art in proof of my zeal for the interests of my famille. But I did not. Instead, I ran—I rolled—I leaped—I cried aloud—I fawned at their knees! What would you? It was hairless, toothless sentiment, but it had the success of a hurricane! They accepted me as though I had been a Person—and He more unreservedly than any of them. It was my supreme moment!

*

I have at last reduced my famille to the Routine which is indispensable to the right-minded among Us. For example: At intervals He and I descend to the Château with our basket of Truffles for our Born One. If she is there she caresses me. If elsewhere, her basket pursues her in a stink-cart. So does, also, her Chef, a well-scented Person and, I can testify, an Artist. This, I understand, is our exchange for the right to exploit for ourselves all other Truffles that I may find inside the Great Wall. These we dispense to another stink-cart, filled with delightful comestibles, which waits for us regularly on the stink-cart-road by the House of the Gate where the Officious One pursued me. We are paid into the hand (trust us peasants!) in Pieces or Papers, while I stand guard against bandits.

As a result, the Girl has now a wooden-roofed house of her own—open at one side and capable of being turned round against winds by His strong one hand. Here she arranges the bottles from which she drinks, and here comes—but less and less often—a dry Person of mixed odours, who applies his ear at the end of a stick, to her thin back. Thus, and owing to the chickens which, as I promised my Aunt, she eats, the Taint of her distemper diminishes. My Aunt denies that it ever existed, but her infatuation—have I told you?—has no bounds! She has been given honourable demission from her duties with sheep and has frankly installed herself in the Girl's outside bed-house, which she does not encourage me to enter. I can support that. I too have My Bone. . . .

Only it comes to me, as it does to most of Us who live so swiftly, to dream in my sleep. Then I return to my lost world—to the whistling, dry-leaved, thin oaks that are not these giant ones—to the stony little hillsides and treacherous river-pits that are not these secure pastures—to the sharp scents that are not these scents—to the companionship of poor Pluton and Dis—to the Street of the Fountain up which marches to meet me, as when I was a rude little puppy, my friend, my protector, my earliest adoration, Monsieur le Vicomte Bouvier de Brie.

At this point always, I wake; and not till I feel His foot beneath the bedderie, and hear His comfortable breathing, does my lost world cease to bite. . . .

Oh, wise and well-beloved guardian and playmate of my youth—it is true—it is true, as thou didst warn me—Outside his Art an Artist must never dream!

Gone Wrong

P. G. WODEHOUSE

HOLLYWOOD is a good place for dogs. At least, when I say Hollywood, I mean Beverly Hills. Hollywood itself is a noisome spot, where no self-respecting dog would live, but Beverly Hills is different. It is an oasis in a rather depressing countryside, consisting of a series of parallel roads with nice houses dotted along at intervals. Each house has a lawn in front of it, running unfenced down to the pavement, and on each lawn sits a dog. And, as you pass, each dog comes down to the edge of its lawn and chats with you.

Stiffy, when I first saw him, was not on his lawn. He was out in the road, dodging a motor and laughing his head off. Presently he came trotting back, took a sniff at me, decided that I smelled all right, and became friendly.

Stiffy was a sort of bull-terrier, with variations. His hind legs were pure black, his body white with a few black stripes. He looked like a member of some football club, and he was as charming and unaffected a dog as I have ever met. As nobody in this motor-ridden place ever takes a dog for a walk, for nobody ever goes for a walk, he was delighted to meet a genuine pedestrian. He came with me all the way to Wilshire Boulevard, which involved my carrying him across three crowded streets, and from that day there were no reserves between us.

He was a mine of gossip about the neighbours. It was Stiffy who, by telling me the secret in the life of the Peke at 1005 Benedict Canyon Drive, enabled me to get the goods on the latter and force him to treat me as an equal. It seems that this Peke, though outwardly a tough egg and standing no nonsense from postmen, tradesmen and the like, is not really the terror he appears on the surface.

A week or so ago, the Peke's mistress went away for a holiday, and the Peke, as usual, slept in her room. At seven the next morning it occurred to the master of the house to go in and see how he was getting on. It is the habit of the master of the house, on going to bed, to tie a black bandage over his eyes in order to keep the light from them. This bandage he omitted to remove, with the result that the Peke, seeing a masked stranger entering, uttered one panic-stricken howl and shot under the bed, from which it required all the persuasion of the entire household to remove him.

'Gave me a good laugh, that did,' said Stiffy.

It was he, too, who told me of the Sealyham at No. 415 rolling in the box of toffee and getting it all over the curtains. In short, if there was one dog of my acquaintance on whom I

felt I could rely for real companionship, it was Stiffy. Always absolutely himself. Never an ounce of side about him.

And then one morning the tragedy burst upon me. Without warning, too, which made it all the worse.

I was on my way down to the village for tobacco; and, passing Stiffy's lawn and seeing him curled up on it, I yoo-hooed to him without a second thought. I was particularly anxious to pass the time of day, for I had seen nothing of him for some weeks. For some reason, his lawn had always been empty when I had come by.

So I shouted to him, and then a strange thing happened. Usually, on these occasions, he would leap across the lawn in two bounds and be licking my face before you could say 'What ho!' But now he scarcely moved. As he heard my voice, he raised his head slowly, opened his eyes very wide, turned his head so that his profile was exposed to an imaginary camera, and, having held the position for a moment, relaxed again. Finally he rose, and, walking in an abominably affected way, came mincing towards me.

'Hullo, Stiffy,' I said.

His manner was cold.

'*Mister* Stiffy, I prefer to be called,' he replied. 'That,' he went on with an ill-assumed carelessness, 'is how Izzy always addresses me.'

'Izzy?'

'Isadore Wertheimer, the production manager of the Bigger and Better.'

'Bigger and Better what?' I asked, perplexed.

'Studio, of course, you poor chump,' he snapped, in a rather more natural tone. 'I'm with the B. and B. now.'

'You are?' I said weakly.

He yawned.

'Yes,' he said. 'Doing a picture with Clarry.'

'Clarry?'

'Clara Svelte. A nice little thing. I could wish no better support. I see no reason why I should not use her in my next, unless this girl Garbo is as good as they say. I am having Greta watched closely, with a view to taking her on. That Swedish accent is a bit of a drawback, of course, but I could carry her. And now, my dear fellow,' said Stiffy, 'I know you will excuse me. I have to save my voice. And my man will be along in a moment wih the car to take me to the lot. So glad to have seen you.'

He nodded distantly and curled up in a ball. And I walked on.

I started this article by saying that Hollywood is a good place for dogs. I have changed my mind. As far as the climate and surroundings go, it may be excellent, but there are always

GONE WRONG

those fatal studios in the background; and, since that wire-haired terrier made such a hit in Ronald Colman's last picture, the executives are beginning to consider a canine interest essential to a film. They have spoiled Stiffy. It is perfectly sickening to see that dog now. A few days ago I was present when a friendly Aberdeen trotted up to fraternize with him, and I have never witnessed anything more repulsive than the way in which he registered Aristocratic Disdain.

However, I am told that his contract runs out next month. If it is not renewed, the old Stiffy may return.

The Great Lad

JOYCE STRANGER

IT had been a wicked day. Snow lay deep in crack and crevice and gully, drifted against the drystone walls, and hid the shape of the land beneath it. A wind whipped across the steeps, whining as it came, and the trees were heavy laden, branches cracking under the sullen weight.

The dog had been uneasy all day. Restless as they quartered the ground, digging out the ewes, and trying to guide them back to the farm through snow that came tail high, so that the beasts plunged miserably, each step a struggle.

He could not tell his master his fears. The snowfilled sky lay dark and leaden, sulphur yellow on the far horizon, eerie with light that made the dog shiver. The hill grumbled to itself, too softly for the shepherd to hear, but loud enough to panic the sheep and make the dog unbiddable.

Twice he crouched and whined, refusing to move on, and the man shouted at him, hating the weather and annoyed that his dog should choose such a day to play him up. He wanted to get back to the farmhouse, to scalding tea and a blazing fire. He cursed the sheep.

Once he used his crook to drag a beast down from a rocky plateau where it stood stupefied, having never seen such weather before in its short life. Once he had to use it to help the dog out of a drift that covered a deep gully, and into which the animal plunged with a yelp of terror.

A moment later, the dog was clear. The man used his crook to judge the depth of the snow and found a way to the other side. Before he reached it the hill shuddered and a weight of snow and rock and earth came tumbling from the heights, gathering momentum, rushing faster and faster, straight at the shepherd.

The dog barked and ran. Wyn followed, clumsy in his thick

clothing. He missed the main tide but a rock struck his shoulder, and another, hurling itself downwards, trapped his arm as he fell. Try as he would he could not move, but lay helpless as an insect pinned on a collector's board.

He whistled the dog and Moss came doubtfully, tail moving slowly, not in greeting, but in bewilderment. He was too young to have seen snow before, but he was well drilled. He knew he must never move without his master's command.

Now Wyn Jones cursed the gruelling training he had given the dog. Training that ensured that if told to sit he would sit for days if not given a counter order, training that ensured he would watch other dogs herd sheep and never interfere. Training that ensured he would rely on his master's brains and never on his own.

'Home, lad,' the shepherd said.

He could think of no other command. If the dog reached home alone they would come out and look for him. If it did not snow again they might be able to follow his tracks. If it did snow. . . . Wyn closed his eyes and prayed to his Maker, sweat darkening his skin in spite of the cold that seeped through his clothes and the damp that soaked him.

The dog was puzzled. 'Home' was a command meant for unruly pups, not for a grown dog out with his master on the hill. He crept forward, whining.

'Home, you fool.'

The voice was testy, but not yet a shout. The dog looked at the sheep, grey against the dazzling white, huddled in misery, woolly fleeces close packed, as they waited patiently for the dog to herd them. They knew about dogs and were used to the collie.

Wyn Jones cursed to himself, for one of the ewes was due to lamb and any lamb born in the snow and the cold was doomed unless he could get them all to safety.

'Home, dog,' he yelled, with all the strength he could muster, and watched anxiously as Moss's tail went between his legs, and crouching, hangdog, punished unknowingly, the dog turned away.

Moss still could not believe his ears. There was work to be done and his master had no right to lie in the snow. He ran back and tried to dig at the rock that pinioned the man and held

him prisoner. Wyn sighed. The poor beast was trying his best but help must come from men.

'No,' the shepherd said sharply, pain adding to his irritation. The dog backed away, head on one side, ears half cocked, puzzled.

'Home,' Wyn roared.

This time the dog started along the trail that lay to safety and to rescue, but kept looking back, eyes anxious, as if hoping to see his master stand and follow him. Soon, persuaded that this was not going to happen, he gave his whole mind to following the trail back to the farm.

He knew the way by scent and sight, and by the feel of the ground, but scent was masked, landmarks had vanished and the unbroken snow lay all around him. He plunged and floundered, afraid of the quietness, of being alone, of the absence of birds and the dimming light and the sultry glow in the sky.

Much was hidden because he was so small. Each crest was a mountain to be traversed with difficulty. Once he fell into a small drift and struggled out again, panting. Once he dropped to the ground to rest, but the command given him was too powerful. His duty was to obey and he had to go home.

The shepherd, lying where he had fallen, wiped tears of cold away from his eyes with gloved fingers and looked at the sheep.

They stood listlessly, heads hanging, tails into the wind.

When he moved one of them turned towards him and perhaps seeking shelter under the lee of the snow that partly covered him now, came and stood beside him.

The other sheep followed, acting as windbreaks, not knowing that their coming offered the shepherd a longer grip on life. The man was known to them, was familiar, brought them feed when the grazing was scarce, handled them daily to make sure all was well, and had brought most of their lambs into the world. They came to him when he fed them hay, and they came to him now, needing familiarity in a world that had suddenly grown very strange.

He pulled at the nearest fleece and the ewe lay in the snow against him, the presence of the man giving her comfort. These sheep were hand-tame and this one had been bottle reared, a pet lamb with her own way of belonging in a human world. She butted people asking for titbits and for affection and would raid the kitchen if the door were open. She came and went in the farmyard as she pleased, and had only recently been introduced into the flock. As a youngster she had followed the man, close as his shadow. Now she cradled against him, doglike, giving him warmth.

He pushed his free hand into her rank-smelling wool and dozed, dreaming uneasily of scalding coffee and steak and kidney pudding, rich with hot gravy, and the warmth and comfort of the farmhouse.

Each waking was a small agony. Each sleeping brought death a little closer, so that he knew, with a vague foreboding, that within an hour or so he would close his eyes for the last time and they would find him stiff and cold among the huddled sheep.

Numbness was overtaking his brain. He had forgotten the dog. He was trapped, and no-one would ever come to help him. The sulphur glow swallowed the night and new snow threatened. The first thin flakes chilled his cheeks and melted against the rough fleece beside his hand.

The sheepdog was halfway home. The wind caused his eyes to water, stung his eyeballs and froze his muzzle so that there was ice clinging to the fur around his lips. His paws were frozen. He had never known such cold.

He hungered more for men than for food. A pack animal, he

dreaded aloneness. It was a punishment beyond any that man could wish on him. Denied the company of dogs, he needed man. Men encouraged him and brought him comfort and gave him warmth. He could not bear the dismal landscape where nothing moved, and he was too low on the ground to see the faraway plume of welcoming smoke from the farmhouse chimneys.

He struck the track, worn by the passing of sheep and humans. Here a path had been cleared in the deep snow that formed solid walls on either side where the plough had passed over the ground. He ran jauntily, the freer movement bringing warmth.

When he paused, weary, his breath plumed on the air and he shook his head, not liking this sudden manifestation of something he could not understand.

The track ended as the snowplough had turned away to a farm further down the valley. His own farm, the sheep still on the hill, caught by the sudden unexpected snowfall, lay islanded and white, the only path there cleared round the yard so that the cows could be brought for milking and the chickens and pigs be fed.

The dog was almost home when the blizzard struck, coming, for him, without any warning. One moment he was plunging, able to see, through hard-packed snow on which were the tracks of fox and stoat and pheasant and weasel. The next, blindness came on him as the great flakes swirled on the wind and fell on eyes and muzzle, on shoulder and back, and on his head and neck. He shook himself repeatedly and then sat in the clammy snow using first one paw and then another to try and clear the clinging uncanny stuff that prevented sight and movement.

It was useless to go on. He crouched where he lay, listening to the wind keening from the North and the now close and familiar sounds. The clank of a bucket, oddly muffled, the low of a cow as she was led to shelter, the yelp of a dog.

That gave him his clue. He barked, sharp and loud, calling to the dog below and Rex heard his companion and answered, a welcoming bark that went on even after the farmer had shouted at him.

When Rex stopped for breath Moss barked again.

'Dammit, that's Wyn's dog out there,' the farmer called to his wife, and he stood in the doorway, staring at the swirling flakes. 'What's happened to shepherd, then? The dog'd never leave him. Too well trained.'

Mair Thomas could only stare at her husband, white faced. The dog had never come home alone before. Not since he was a pup. Wyn would never have needed to send him home now for disobedience. Nor would he send any animal home alone on a night like this.

'What can we do?' she asked Dai Thomas, almost whispering, fear taking away her voice. Death lurked in the hills, striking the unwary, and even an experienced man could die only yards from safety in a whiteout like this.

The farmer was already huddled into his coat, dialling at the telephone that was the only link with neighbours too far away to see or call on casually.

'Damme, the line's dead,' he said, after futile jerkings at the receiver rest.

'You can't go out in this.' Mair pushed her dark hair back with her hands, a gesture of extreme worry that Dai recognised. He halted at the door and called.

'Moss. Here, Moss. Come then, good dog.'

The dog barked and, given the guidance of a voice, crawled over the ridge, slipping on ice that had formed on top of a trickle of water coming out of the spring.

'It is Moss,' Dai said.

He stared out into the night. The snow had eased but the wild wind whipped down the hill and stung his cheeks, making his eyes water. Gathering darkness hid the world. A tree, normally winter stark, was a blurred outline, soft with snow, fairylike by day, but now inimical, a symbol of the weather that paralysed all movement on the hill.

The dog barked again. He was in the dark, too far away as yet to see the farmhouse lights, which for him were hidden behind the low wall that lay under snow, humped and unrecognisable, blocking his view.

'Moss. Good lad. Here then.'

The familiar voice was welcome, offering warmth and friendship. He plunged towards it and came to grief, with a yelp of fright, in the ditch, which was hidden and deep. He tried to claw his way out but the soft snow was loose and fell away, leaving him beyond the wall, whimpering.

Dai Thomas brought the big torch that he used in the byre at calving time. It threw a feeble circle of light on the packed snow, beaten by the hooves of the cows into a flat and sodden mush that had thawed and frozen again. Now it was glacier-like, threatening a man with sudden disaster if he failed to watch his step.

The dog whined again and Dai walked cautiously towards the sound, his voice reassuring.

He leaned over the wall, feeling it hard beneath the snow that gave under his weight. He moved, looked down and saw the dog, a dark patch against the glitter. He gripped the loose scruff and heaved and Moss, wild with pleasure at being once more with men, whined and wagged his tail and licked the man's hand in an ecstacy of welcome.

'Don't usually do that,' Dai said, as he brought the dog into the warmth. He set food before it. Moss stared at him, whimpered and refused to eat.

'Well then, you'd best be eating. We can't find shepherd now,' the man said, looking out of the window into the darkness where flakes swirled again, feather light, drifting and clinging to barn and byre and stable. Beyond the patch of light one of the ponies yikkered a complaint, afraid of the weather as the snow drifted in through his half-open stable door. The day had been long and over busy, and half the chores were still to do.

Dai went out to shut the stable door, which he had forgotten. He slid and he cursed. He returned in time to see the dog, half a leg of lamb in his mouth, streak out into the night.

'Dammed little thief,' he shouted in fury. 'Wouldn't touch his own food. Had to take mine.'

'Are you going out on the hill?' Mair asked, busy at the sink.

Dai moved restlessly, looking into the darkness. The snow came thickly now, swirling towards him, eddying upwards as the wind blew. He listened unhappily to the scream of the gale and the bluster in the chimney.

'Be two of us lost out there,' he said at last, unwilling to face the truth, yet aware of his responsibility to his wife and the three little lads safely asleep upstairs.

'First light,' he said. 'I'll get help from the Williams. Can't even track the dog in the snow in this. All traces will be covered.'

He was too restless for sleep. The thought of the shepherd irked him. Perhaps the man was dead, but more likely buried in some drift, or fallen on the ice, to die by creeping inches in the wicked cold. He felt useless, and went down in the hour of mourning to brew tea and sit staring at the blank window and think of his man out there in the doomlike dark.

Death comes in the little hours, he remembered his grandfather saying. Creeping up like a trespasser, hovering unseen when the spirits are low and the life stream is at the ebb, and God passes over us and breathes upon us, and we go out on the tide. The old man had a good death, falling asleep in his warm bed when he was ninety-five and never waking on the world again.

Shepherd's deathbed would be wicked cold and his last hours a torment and no man to help him or heed him or hold his hand as he went. Dai knew it would be many days before he forgave himself for not trying to brave the storm, for putting his family first, for letting a life slip away.

He thought of his wife and the bairns asleep and sat by the new-banked fire, warming himself, for the cold seemed to have crept into his bones as he thought of his shepherd. He watched the kittens, wakeful in the light, playing with a straw brought in on somebody's shoe. He thought of the wildness beyond the windows and wished he had a warm job in town, not tied to the cattle and the sheep and the bitter bleak hills. Not working for a pittance grubbed from the ground with raw hands while other men fattened on the food he grew and played with their money, earned so much more easily than his.

He forgot about Moss and the stolen meat though his wife had had to cook bacon and eggs instead for his meal.

The dog was trying to retrace his path, back to the hill and the man who meant more to him than food and warmth. The meat held in his jaws made his mouth slaver, but he did not take a single bite. He picked his way carefully out of the farmyard and back onto the hill. This time he crawled between the bars of the big gate and did not attempt his usual leap of the wall. He remembered the deep snow and the ditch that had betrayed him.

The wind was behind him and in spite of the snow the going was easier. A faint trace of scent lay on the ground and he tracked back, with difficulty because the smell of the mutton was strong in his nose. It did not mask his own familiar trail, nor the rankness of the fox that caught a whiff of dog and meat and came running, only to find disaster as it met a drift that covered it completely and left it hungry and tantalised, buried until the thaw released it, thinner and wiser, not to be caught that way a second time.

The snow stopped. The moon broke through a layer of laced cloud, and shone on whiteness that covered all tracks, that hid the shepherd and the sheep that sheltered him, and hid the path.

Moss floundered on. In places he struggled, neck deep, dragging each leg from the snow, jumping and bounding on, more and more weary. Once he rested by a hump that hid a tree stump, and the meat tempted him but he left it alone. It made his jaws ache but he went on.

He came to the patch where the shepherd lay, and stopped and looked in surprise at the unbroken snow. Carefully, he put the meat down and then began to dig. He found man and sheep in a hollow made by their breath, and the man, glad of fresh air, felt overwhelming disappointment when he saw the dog.

'Moss, Moss. You damned old fool. We'll both die out here now,' he said, and the dog wagged a forlorn tail, unable to understand why he was not greeted with fervour.

He went back for the meat.

This time, he approached more cautiously, afraid of a cuff for his trouble. The shepherd, watching him with dull eyes, saw the half leg of lamb and stared at it, unbelieving.

'You durned old fool. You been back? I hope they saw you,' he said and reached out a hand to pat the wet coat. The dog dropped beside him, and licked his face. The sheep, too exhausted by snow and cold, were apathetic and did not move. They watched Moss warily, but he ignored them, his eyes on his master.

The lambing ewe was struggling to give birth. The shepherd heard her and could do nothing but pray that all would be well and the adventure end safely.

Wyn Jones took the meat. It was slimed and snowy but he dragged at it with his teeth and spat the outer parts to the dog, who took his reward greedily, while his master gnawed at the bone, too hungry to care what he ate.

The farmer, tracking the dog through the snow at first light, with the men from the farm in the hollow, found the pair asleep, the lamb cuddled between them, the ewe under the shepherd's head, acting as a pillow, her own head stretched to lick her son.

Dai Thomas stared at them, at the dog which came to greet them, and at the bone that lay, gnawed clean, beside them.

'Moss brought me some dinner, kept me warm and saved my life,' the shepherd said, his eyes proud on the dog as they dug the rock and snow away from his arm and helped him to stand, then rolled him in blankets to lie on the stretcher that a second farmer had provided.

Hot coffee with a shot of rum soon restored him, and the damage to his arm, apart from bruising, was not bad.

That night he was bedded in the warm farmhouse on Mair Thomas's settee, which she thought a better bed than his own above the cow byre until he was well and rested. Wyn watched his dog eat a meal fit for a king.

'Eh, Moss, you're a great lad,' he said, and the dog turned and looked at him, and his tail beat a steady thunder on the wooden floor before he returned to the dish of roast chicken that Mair had given him as his right.

Bunch

JAMES DOUGLAS

I AM a very fond and very foolish inhabitant of the Royal Borough of Kensington, for here I sit in my book-lined library, with all my heavy curtains drawn to shut out the howling winds, with my electric lamp shining obediently at my left elbow, with my anthracite coals ardently glowing in my grate, with my oldest and foulest pipe in my mouth, with the muted and muffled roar of London sounding far and faint six floors below my feet, and with a ridiculously nebulous purpose humming in my head; the said purpose being to hew and hammer out of the said head the biography of a dog.

I am, for all the world, like a forked radish, with a head fantastically carved upon it with a knife, and if you doubt the propriety of Sir John Falstaff's image I invite you to inspect me in my bath, for there I am fully as farcical, ridiculous, and ludicrous in my peeled and pink absurdity as the greatest and grandest grandee in Christendom, who, for all I know, may be your honour's self.

It teases, tickles, and arrides me to contemplate the imaginary spectacle of the nude and naked magnates, mandarins, majesties, excellencies, serenities, and swollen panjandrums of mankind as they creep, crawl, reel, and totter down the aisles and alleys of history. It pleases me to unclothe and undress them all, be they ancients or moderns, and whatsoever may be or may have been the shape of their head or their nose, or the colour of their skin.

And while I am stripping all the multicoloured giants I amuse myself by stripping all the pigmies too. I march them all into battle in their buff to gratify my taste for universal buffoonery. It does not take me a second to denude all the soldiers and civilians who have been, who are, and who will be, and to compel them to prance and dance in the folly and fantasy of their birthday and deathday pelt.

Nay, in half a trice I disrobe the whole human race from the first to the last, as an ironical and satirical prelude and exordium for these my meditations on my dog. Pray observe that there is no breath of indecency in any of my denudations, for my sole aim is to compare the naked human animal with the naked canine animal at this moment sleeping before my fire with one eye and one ear open.

I refuse to grant my beloved human tribe any advantage over his beloved canine tribe. I throw away every whim and caprice of the everlasting tailor. I choose to see myself and my fellow-creatures as stark naked as any fish or any worm, and I beg them to believe that they run no risk of blushing or catching cold while I am smiling at their predicament and my own.

Shakespeare, Swift, Sterne, and Carlyle have not exhausted the spiritual comedy of caricature. Swift sees man as 'a forked straddling animal with bandy legs.' Sterne envisages our human faction or sect or species of life as a flock of 'turkeys driven with a stick and red clout to the market, or if some drivers, as they do in Norfolk, take a dried bladder and put peas in it, the rattle thereof terrifies the boldest.'

Gentle critic, do not accuse me of making a vile to-do and pother about my dog Bunch, for I plead that he is only to me and mine what your dog is to you and yours, and not a whit, particle, jot, or tittle more lovable and beloved, and, by your leave, not a whit, particle, jot, or tittle less.

I do not thrust him upon your reverence as a rival of the dog that is for you the one and only dog in the world of dogs. I do not pretend that he is more worthy of my love than your dog is worthy of your love, or that I am more worthy of his love than you are worthy of your dog's love. Let us agree that your dog is for you superior in every way to every other dog in dogdom, and that mine is for me superior in every way to every other dog in dogdom.

Let us admit that any dog may love any man and that any man may love any dog. And when I say man I include woman, for the love of a man for a dog is not greater than the love of a woman for a dog. Nor is the love of a dog for a man greater than the love of a dog for a woman. Let us have no ambiguity.

When I say Man and Woman I include boys and girls, children of all ages.

There is no age-limit in this matter of loving a dog or being loved by a dog. No one is too young or too old to love a dog or to be loved by a dog. A dog is capable of loving any man, woman, or child, and any man, woman, or child is capable of loving a dog.

You may be so unloving and so unlovable that you cannot love or be loved by anybody of your own kind, but you can love and be loved by a dog, any dog, he being a mongrel or a cur, and you being an outcast, an exile, a scallywag, a thief, a forger, a liar, a murderer, or any kind of villain, rascal, ragamuffin, and enemy of society.

Therefore I hold that my dog Bunch is Everydog and that I am Everyman in my capacity of biographer, dogographer, or Bunchographer. I am only doing for my dog what you could do for your dog if your worship chose to do it. If the history of all the dogs who have loved and been loved by the race of man could be written, each history of a dog would resemble all the other histories. It would be a love story.

Let us begin at the beginning, for a dog has a beginning as well as a man, and if the whole truth were known he begins in the same way. That is to say, he is born, he has a birthplace, and he has a father and a mother. What more can the most ingenious biographer say about the beginning of the greatest and most glorious human beings who ever made history, or wrote prose or poetry, or hewed marble, or painted paintings, or composed music, or governed and misgoverned nations, or invented inventions, or made money?

I do not care how tall his family-tree may be or how many branches it may have, his birth is the proper beginning of a man, and all his ancestors, back to Adam, have mighty little to do with him and he has mighty little to do with them, for there are far too many of them to matter if you push his pedigree back far enough. Indeed, it is absurd to fix your gaze on the handful of progenitors who are nearer to him than they are to Adam, for those who are nearer Adam than they are to him may be fully as important and may be more important.

My dog Bunch, then, was brought forth into this scurvy and

disastrous world of ours in the year of our Lord one thousand nineteen hundred and twenty-four. I know not the hour of the day of the month, and therefore I cannot cast his horoscope by calculating the degree of the ecliptic on the eastern horizon and the disposition of the heavens, or the posture and place of the planets.

All I can tell you is that he was born in the month of July, and I wish I knew his birthday, not to gratify my idle curiosity, but to enable me to celebrate it as human birthdays are celebrated. I would not give him an iced birthday cake with candles on it, but I would at least present him with a birthday bone.

And now it is right to record his birthplace, although he does not care a doit or a dump where he was born. He was born in the good county of Essex at a pretty little town called Frinton-on-Sea. If he had not been born there I am afraid that he and I might never have fallen in love with each other. Our orbits

might never have intersected. He might have gone his way through his little life and I might have gone my way through my little life without any personal impact or impingement upon each other.

It is strange that a dog's life, like a man's, is ruled and regulated by the whims and caprices of chance and circumstance. Consider the number of things which coincided and concatenated (or condoginated) in order to interweave and intertwine the life of Bunch with my life.

It was necessary for two human families, or households, or homes, or domesticities to select Frinton-on-Sea out of all other seaside towns for their annual August holiday. In order to produce or evolve that simultaneous choice it was necessary to create Frinton-on-Sea out of a bare and desolate beach. It was necessary to make its natural ugliness beautiful by making lovely avenues and building lovely houses with lovely rose gardens. In fine, a miracle of town-planning had to be wrought by the landlord or lord of the land.

All the shops had to be violently shoved into a shopping street, and ruthlessly shepherded away from the sea-front. There had to be no pier and no pierrots, no hawkers or buskers, no band, no noisy trippers, and no noisy lures for trippers, no public-houses or saloons, no speak-easies, and no noises of any sort or kind.

The place had to be a paradise for children, with silver sands for spade and pail, and safe bathing. It had also to be-a playground for their elders, and so it was necessary to build a sea-wall and drain a marsh and turn it into a golf course seamed with ditches or fletes, and to make tennis courts. All this and more was done in order to bring Bunch and me together, and if it had not been done we might have lost each other for all eternity.

I do not say that the owner and architect of Frinton consciously worked for this delectable end and aim. They may have been inspired by meaner and lower motives. I am none the less grateful to them for not creating another Clacton-on-Sea or another Walton-on-the-Naze. Like many other great artists, they builded better than they knew.

I tremble when I think that I might never have seen Bunch if I had not been afflicted late in life with an incurable and loathsome disease known all over the world by the hideous and horrible name of golf, a word which sounds like gulf, which indeed it is, as every wight knows who flounders into it.

Bunch is the only good and righteous thing I have ever got out of golf, but he is well worth all the anguish and agony I so long have so impatiently endured. If I had been a good golfer I might have haled and hauled my helpless wife and my godforsaken daughter to some benighted hell where there is golf and nothing but golf. Being a blighted and misbegotten golfer I had mercy on them. I did not drag my innocent wife and my guiltless child to eat out their bitter hearts in some joyless Westward Ho! or laughterless Dornoch, or lugubrious Gullane, or sorrowful Sandwich, or melancholy North Berwick, or surly St Andrews, where the greens are watered by the tears of the golf widow and the golf orphan.

The chapter of accidents is not yet filled to the brim. If I had not possessed a maiden aunt I might never have heard of William Powell, who wrote *The Marrow of Methodism*. If William Powell had not been an eloquent Methodist divine, my maiden aunt might not have persuaded me to escort her to the ornate Carlisle Memorial Church in Carlisle Circus, Belfast, one fine Sunday morning in the eighties. I bless Mr Carlisle.

If my maiden aunt's pew had not been situated in the proper and predestined southern aisle, and if I had not been plumped or dumped down at the aisle end of the said pew, I should not

have been favoured with a clear and unobstructed view of the said aisle, and I should not have seen with these mortal eyes the most beautiful girl in Ireland, walking as only an Irish girl can walk, with her lovely head held high among the golden stars sprinkled over the roof, on her way to the celestial choir, from which her angelical voice vibrated down to the bottom of my youthful and hitherto unenchanted heart.

'What has this romantic rigmarole to do with Bunch?' cries Sir Petulance. 'Why do you turn a dog story into a love story? Nine-tenths of the people who like dogs and dog stories have been crossed in love or robbed of love, and may never again fall in love. Some of them love dogs because they hate men, women, and children. I pray you to regale us with undiluted and unadulterated dog, and deliver us from the weariness of wading through the syrup and treacle and molasses of erotic flimflam.'

Farewell, sir or madam. Read no more. A dog story must be a love story, and I warn you than I am resolved to pour all the love I can collect or concoct into the biography of Bunch. If you desire a reprieve or amnesty from the decretals, ukases, edicts and firmans of love, I say good-bye to you cheerfully and joyfully. Go hence; comfort and console yourself with the aromantic plays and prefaces of Georgius Bernardus Shavius, with the synthetic philosophy of Herbert Spencer, with the bleak and dismal geometry of Bertrand Russell, or with the splenetic and atrabilious grimaces of Aldous Huxley. And may the Lord have mercy upon what you are pleased to call your soul!

I say, then, that if I had not fallen in love at first sight with the Lady of the Aisle, I might never have heard of Bunch, for I might have become a mouldy and mildewed celibate. In that case I might have yawned myself into my grave before Bunch was born. Marriage lengthens life and shortens folly.

Even if I had lived I doubt whether I would have chosen Frinton for my bachelor holiday. I should have found myself boring myself into bed and out of it in some outlandish place where Bunch could not possibly have been born.

But it was not enough to marry the Lady of the Aisle in the hottest of hot haste, and to keep her in a state of rebellious resignation to her fate for heaven only knows how many hours, days, weeks, months, and years. No. It was also necessary to possess or be possessed by another variety of angel, to wit, a daughter, and this daughter at this precise moment must be persistently persuading her mother to persuade her father to beg, buy, borrow, or steal a dog for her.

Thus it came to pass that I was gently prepared by the hand of fate, manipulating me and mine with patient foresight, for the fore-ordained meeting with Bunch. A dog was in my imagination. Almost any dog of almost any breed or no breed at all could have walked into my heart. The odds against Bunch were incalculable, but he won.

It so chanced that I was carelessly strolling past a bathing hut on the beach and I heard a voice calling my name. As I turned on my heel I deflected the whole course of my life, my wife's life, my daughter's life, and Bunch's life. Now what did the beautiful lady in the cabin desire to say to a man she had met only once at a tea-party? I hardly knew her name, and I marvelled at her summons. But the thing was done, and she did not know what she was doing for me. She was an agent of destiny.

Quite calmly and languidly she asked me whether I would like to buy a Sealyham puppy for my daughter. There were six Sealyham puppies, and I could have the pick of the six. I did not know what a Sealyham was. I had never heard of a Sealyham. But I instantly declared that I would buy a Sealyham.

My impetuosity alarmed the lady. She advised me to consult my wife and my daughter. They might not want a Sealyham. They might want a fox terrier, or an Aberdeen terrier, or an Irish terrier, or a Cairn, or an Irish wolf-hound, or an Alsatian, or a collie, or a dachshund, or a Pekinese, or a spaniel. No. I was sure they would have nothing but a Sealyham, and then I asked her to spell it.

The reason I asked her to spell Sealyham may seem frivolous to you. But I happened to have met a many called Seely, and I disliked him more than any man I have ever known. If Sealyham had been spelled Seelyham all would have been finished and done with. As it was, I could put up with Sealyham, and no more. It may be said that Bunch and I might have been separated for ever over a gangrenous punctilio of vowels.

Do not imagine that all was smooth and plain sailing after I had promised to consult my wife and my daughter. Long before I reached their bathing cabin my heart began to sink into my shoes, not because I had done something wrong, but because I knew that I could not do anything right. It is the boon, privilege, and glory of a husband and father to carry in his breast a perpetual sense of guilt and conviction of sin.

Doubts crept down my spine, and I nearly turned tail and begged the Sealyham lady to let me cry off my precipitate decision. But a man fears to look like a fool, or at any rate more like one. It would have been wiser to beard one woman than to beard two. I could have quarrelled for life with the Sealyham lady and no harm would have been done. I might have lied to her. I might have airily informed her that my daughter had changed her mind and had decided to have a cat instead of a dog. I might have done nothing at all, and pretended, if it came to an explanation, that I had forgotten all about the appointment for three o'clock.

I was still vacillating and oscillating between at least a hundred excuses and pretexts when my feet walked me into the lion's mouth, or, to be genderically accurate, the lioness's mouth. It is my misfortune to be an easy blusher. Some men blush after they tell a lie. I blush about ten minutes before I tell one.

I blushed as I met Eva Alexandra's cold blue eye.

'What have you been up to?' said Eva Alexandra.

I read her thoughts in a flash. She had jumped to the conclusion that I had been furtively and stealthily having a cocktail with some male miscreant at the Golf Club.

'No,' I explained. 'This is no cocktail matter.'

'Then what have you been doing?' said Eva Alexandra. 'Do not try to deceive me. I can see that you have been doing something. You are keeping something from me.'

'You are right, my dear,' said I. 'You are always right.'

'Don't "my dear" me,' said she. 'I can't let you out of my sight for a second.'

'I have bought a dog,' said I.

'I knew it,' said she. 'I won't have a dog in my house. I have enough trouble without a dog. It is like a man to go and buy a dog.'

'All right,' I said, 'I will go and unbuy it.'

'Have you paid for it?' said she. 'Can you get the money back?'

'I can,' said I. 'I will go now and get it.'

I went for a walk, and as I came back I met Carmen. She was breathless with excitement.

'Daddy,' she said, 'is it true?'

'Is what true?' said I.

'Have you really bought a dog for me?'

'Who told you I had bought a dog for you?'

'Mums,' said Carmen. 'She sent me to search for you.'

'Was she angry?' I cautiously explored. 'Does she want a dog?'

'She said you could please yourself, and that you would do that anyhow. Where is the dog?'

'We are to see it at three o'clock,' said I. 'but your mother does not want a dog, and I am not going to be dogged by her reproaches for the rest of my life. If you want a dog you must get round her. I can't.'

Carmen got round her and round me. A treaty was drawn up. It was agreed that the dog would not be a burden on Eva Alexandra. She would have nothing to do with the dog. She would not feed it, wash it, comb it, brush it, or teach it manners. She would not walk it.

The entire toil and labour would be borne by us. We promised to devote our life to the dog. It would be our dog, and if it was a nuisance it would be our nuisance.

I vowed and Carmen vowed. We were both one large and enthusiastic vow.

'And what will happen when Carmen goes to school in Paris next month? Will you take charge of the dog till Christmas?'

'Certainly,' said I light-heartedly, lying hard.

'I know you,' said Eva Alexandra. 'I will be left with the dog. But I warn you both that I will have nothing to do with it. If you think I can run the house and look after a dog, you are mistaken.'

There we wisely left it, knowing well that Eva Alexandra's bark was worse than her bite.

*

Carmen and I sedulously dissembled our excited impatience during one of the longest mornings in history, for we knew that one rash word might wreck the fair prospect and promise of three o'clock. We were afraid to take anything as settled and decisive, so we warily avoided any gesture or phrase of assurance and certainty.

But we could not control our thoughts, and we knew that Eva Alexandra could hardly control hers, but we helped her by preserving an appearance of calm indifference. Perhaps we overdid our obsequious subservience to every flicker of her embattled eyelid. Our sycophancy was almost sickening, but she nobly ignored it, although we felt that she was seeing through it as she sees through everything.

Luncheon was the slowest meal we ever ate, and every bite tasted of deferred dog. We doubled and redoubled our hypocrisy, taking second helpings of boiled cod and rice pudding, and talking eagerly and eloquently to conceal our concentrated obsession. Eva Alexandra let us stew in our juice. If we were slow, she was slower. Not a word said she and not a word said we about three.

After luncheon we sat in the garden in the sun and Eva Alexandra fell asleep or pretended to fall asleep. She slept or pretended to sleep for what seemed to our imagination eternity. We waited and watched her till we could wait and watch no longer.

Then I upset the coffee tray with a clatter of china and teaspoons. Eva Alexandra opened her eyes.

'Why did you wake me?' said Eva Alexandra.

'My dear,' said I recklessly, 'it is time to go.'

'Go where?' said Eva Alexandra.

'To see the Sealyham puppy,' I brutally replied.

'What Sealyham puppy?' said Eva Alexandra.

We humbly pretended to believe that she had forgotten, and went through the delicate process of jogging her memory. I think she was sorry for us, for she put us out of our misery.

'I suppose I must go to please you,' said Eva Alexandra, 'but I'm sure I'll hate the puppy.'

'Oh, Mummy,' cried Carmen earnestly and deceitfully, 'if you don't like him we won't have him.'

'No, my dear,' said I fervently and mendaciously, 'we won't.'

Behold us three, then, marching solemnly along the rose-hung avenues and converging at the gate of fate on the very stroke of three. And there in the garden lay Mother Sealyham with her six fat, foolish puppies, yelping, nuzzling, nibbling, and rolling on the grass round her maternal indifference and aloofness.

Her name was Rebecca—Becky for short, and the Sealyham lady's little girl had bestowed on the six puppies Christian names each beginning with a B. If a wise and beneficent Providence had not led and guided us to the choice of the right B this book would never have been written.

The choice fell upon the funniest, silliest, comicalist, drollest, absurdest and grotesquest of the six. He captured and captivated Carmen. She would have him and none other. And his name was Bunch of Blackadder, and even in his babyhood he possessed in miniature all the mature Bunchical qualities, characteristics, and idiosyncrasies.

He was manifestly a fool of a puppy, a born clown, and he at once started his laughter-provoking career. We laughed at his foolish face with its gigantic eyes and its gigantic nose and its lamentably receding chin. We laughed at his waddling walk. We laughed at his fat feet and his fat tail.

Some of the other B's had square chins, but we preferred Bunch's heterodox recessional because it heightened and enhanced his general air and mien of jolly imbecility. We agreed that he had all the charm of the idiot, and we did not care a hang about the show-bench and its punctilios.

We also resolved to overlook his pigeon chest, which even in his infancy protruded and projected like a bow-window. It reminded me of William Makepeace Thackeray's house in Young Street, Kensington. This puppy, I said, is a humorist. He is Thackerayan. He is Dickensian. He is Elian. He is Shandean.

We divined and foreknew a lifetime of laughter in his company. Our divination and foreknowledge were abundantly fulfilled, for Bunch became the Dan Leno of dogdom, the Charlie Chaplin of caninity. He has never failed to excite and extort laughter from every stranger in the street—not derisive laughter, not contemptuous laughter, but the laughter of love.

His father, we learned, was a celebrated and illustrious

Sealyham with the ringing, royal and sonorous name of Senny Ding. And Bunch was endowed and endued with the badger marking of his sire. The badger marking on his head and ears filled us with pride in his pedigree and with hope in his pugnacity. And we liked the sound of Senny Ding. We had never heard of Senny Ding, but we made up our minds that it would be jolly to be able to retort to cynical questions and denigrations, 'Bunch is a son of Senny Ding.'

We have never known the retort to fail. It silences every sceptic who informs us that Bunch's jaw is undershot and that he could not get his teeth into a badger. After all, we did not buy him for badger-baiting. We have never met and we never expect to meet a badger, which the Concise Oxford Dictionary describes as a 'grey-coated, strong-jawed nocturnal, hibernating, plantigrade quadruped between weasels and bears.' A plantigrade is an animal that walks on its soles, placing the whole sole on the ground at once in walking. I am happy to say that Bunch is not interested in plantigrades and their soles. His tastes and interests are more fastidious.

Eva Alexandra behaved well until we got Bunch out of the garden and he was wobbling on his short legs along the road. Then without warning she dumbfounded us with this question:

'How much did you say you paid for him?'

'As a matter of fact I have not paid for him yet,' I stammered.

'How much is he?' said Eva Alexandra. 'I suppose, five shillings.'

'Well,' said I, 'you could not expect to get a son of Senny Ding for five shillings.'

'I wouldn't give more than five shillings for any dog,' said Eva Alexandra. 'Why, his licence will cost seven and sixpence.'

'I don't think we could get him for five shillings,' said I.

'What!' said Eva Alexandra. 'You don't know his price! You have bought a pig in a poke.'

'He is not a pig,' said I; 'he is a puppy.'

'Go straight back,' said Eva Alexandra, 'and take the puppy with you, and find out his price. If he is more than five shillings, you may leave him.'

'But we have bought him,' said I. 'We will wait till we get the bill.'

'Certainly not,' said Eva Alexandra. 'Most certainly not!'

Ruefully I marched off with Bunch. Too well I knew the price. I had kept the dark secret to myself. Bunch's price was six guineas.

Eva Alexandra watched me till I opened the gate. I hid behind a rhododendron bush for ten minutes, and then I went back to Eva Alexandra.

'He's a guinea,' said I.

'You've been done,' said Eva Alexandra. 'I could have got him for half a guinea. Did you bargain?'

Miserably I confessed that I did not bargain.

'Just like a man!' said Eva Alexandra. 'And now let me tell you something. He's not a guinea. He's six guineas!'

'How did you know?' I gasped.

'She told me,' said Eva Alexandra bitterly. 'I could buy a new hat for it.'

'My dear,' said I, 'you shall have a new hat. But Bunch will last longer than a new hat. He will wear for years and years and years.'

And he did!

*

It is the law of life in an hotel that everybody talks about everybody and nobody talks to anybody else. Any infringement of this law is defined and described as breaking the ice. The process of breaking the ice is long, slow and painful, and he who breaks it runs the risk of being regarded as an enemy of society.

Before the advent of Bunch the ice was without a flaw or a crack. He immediately ground it into powder. He set everybody smiling as soon as he tumbled through the swing door, and he made for us more friends in two minutes than we had made in two weeks.

We basked in his reflected popularity. As his proprietors we became persons of importance. He was ready to lick any hand or any face. All puppies are friendly, but Bunch's friendliness was a tornado of affection. It perturbed us a little to perceive that he was eager to give himself with his whole heart to the whole human race. It was clear that he would never be a one-man dog, or a one-woman dog, or a one-girl dog. He was destined to be everybody's dog. I do not know how long our journey from the front door to the bedroom lasted, but I think it was nearly an hour before we had Bunch safely and securely extricated from his worshippers. His tongue was dry after all his lickings, and as it hung out pink and parched we hastened to set a bowl of water before him.

He stepped into it and upset it on the carpet. We filled it again and held him down to drink, and he upset it again. Then we held the bowl and held Bunch while he lapped so violently that we all got more water than he got. We could not persuade him to lap only with his tongue.

He lapped with every leg, with both ears, with his tail, with his backbone, and with every nerve in his body. After he had lapped the three of us till we were soaked and drenched, we vainly tried to quiet and calm him. He seemed to be determined to eat the whole room, and when he was not eating something he was rushing about, banging his head against bed-legs, chair-legs, table-legs, and anything bangable.

'This is not a dog you have bought,' said Eva Alexandra. 'It's an earthquake.'

'Let us give him an aspirin,' said I. 'He is feverish.'

'It is not an aspirin he needs,' said Eva Alexandra. 'It's chloroform.'

'I will hold him,' said Carmen.

Unhappily, Carmen has only two hands and two arms. She is not descended from the Hetatoncheires, the hundred-handed ones. Bunch would have been a handful for Briareus, Cottus and Gyes, who, according to Homer's opposite number, cannot tell you why fifty of their arms were handless, for plainly an arm without a hand is useless.

Perhaps the three giants were pirates and wore hooks, like Captain Hook. But even a giant with a hundred hands and fifty hooks might have found it hard to hold Bunch.

At any rate, Carmen, using two hands, two knees, and two feet, utterly failed to control, master, and subjugate his myriad paroxysms, contortions, wriggles, and spasms. He leaped from her lap, overturned a table, and rushed out of the French window, hurling his panting body against a deck chair on the balcony, which collapsed and closed on him in a chaos of canvas, joints, and cushions.

'This is not a dog,' said Eva Alexandra. 'It is a whirlwind.'

We closed the French window and held a council of war, while Bunch tried to scale the balcony balustrade.

'He will kill himself,' said I.

'He will kill us,' said Eva Alexandra, as four dogs on the lawn below burst into a volley of barks and howls at Bunch, who was now giving an imitation of a hyæna shuttle, darting up and down the balcony at an estimated speed of sixty miles an hour.

'We must buy a dog collar,' said Carmen, 'and a lead.'

'Lead!' said Eva Alexandra. 'That avalanche needs a chain.'

'A chain cable,' said I.

'We can get them at Woolworth's, Daddy,' said Carmen.

'My dear,' said I, 'this is not a job for Mr Woolworth. We must try a marine store. Bunch requires a chain and anchor. I wonder whether we could moor him to a bed.'

'Let us leave him ramping on the balcony,' said Eva Alexandra, 'and we will go down to tea.'

We were drinking the first cup when we heard a terrible din at the top of the landing, and suddenly a fat man rolled down the stairs with Bunch coiled round his legs.

The fat man lay swearing upside down with Bunch buried somewhere in his waistcoat. I helped him to rise, and there on the mat lay Bunch flattened out with his eyes goggling and his tongue lolling sideways out of his slavering little mouth.

'You have killed my poor dog!' cried Carmen, as she carried the inert carcase to a sofa.

'He has nearly killed me,' groaned the fat man, mopping his red face with a purple handkerchief.

'Have a drink,' said I, calling a waiter out of the crowd. 'Quick! Two double whiskies and a large soda.'

'He is only a puppy,' said I, as we drank deep.

'Heaven help you when he grows up!' said the fat man.

'If you will excuse me,' said I, 'I will go for a chain before he recovers.'

'I'll come with you,' said the fat man. 'This hotel will not be safe while he is loose.'

'Don't be long,' said Eva Alexandra. 'He has opened one eye.'

On our way to the ship chandler I asked the fat man whether he played golf. He did.

'Very well,' said I. 'Tomorrow let us play golf all day, and lunch at the Club. I need a rest.'

'So do I,' said the fat man.

We brought back a collar that had been made for a bulldog and a chain that had been made for preventing a motor-car from skidding on a frozen road.

'Brutes!' said Carmen. 'He's as quiet as a lamb now. You must have frightened the darling.'

There lay Bunch like a large powder puff.

'He's swollen,' said I.

'He has eaten all the tea,' said Eva Alexandra. 'Everybody has been feeding him.'

'I think he's going to be sick,' said Carmen, hastily picking him up and hurrying out to the garden.

Presently she returned with Bunch trotting behind her.

'Well?' said I.

'He has been sick,' said Carmen.

'We'll all be sick,' said Eva Alexandra, 'before we are much older. Sick and sorry! There is only one thing to be done.'

'What is that?' said I.

'Poison him!' said the fat man, grinning from ear to ear. 'Any chemist would do it for five bob.'

'Daddy!' said Carmen. 'You won't poison him?'

'No, my dear,' said I. 'I will tie a brick round his neck and row him out to sea and drown him.'

'If you do that,' said Carmen, 'I will drown myself.'

'Very well,' said I. 'That will save a lot of worry. I will get two bricks, and you can come with us. There is just time before dinner.'

'It's a good thing we have a balcony,' said Eva Alexandra.

'Then you mean to keep him?' said I.

'I like him,' said Eva Alexandra, 'and he likes me. He will be company for me when Carmen goes to school in Paris.'

'Company!' said the fat man. 'He will be more than company. He will be a regiment. He will be an army corps.'

And he was!

Dogs In a Big Way

KENNETH AND ANNA ROBERTS

D OGS have always seemed to me an essential part of every well-conducted home. When I say always, I mean practically always.

Like most persons engaged in what income-tax experts jocularly term gainful endeavour, I long had visions of leading an ideal life in a rambling farmhouse of great simplicity but extreme comfort—a farmhouse containing one hundred and thirty thousand dollars' worth of conveniences, but costing about four thousand dollars.

Those visions were rosy and indefinite, except for the dogs. I had clear ideas on the dogs that would surround and inhabit the farm. I would have several utilitarian dogs: a few setters to assist me in gunning for partridges; two springer spaniels to precede me through swamps and alder thickets during the woodcock season; a dachshund to make things uncomfortable for foxes and woodchucks that have retired to their holes; and above all I wished a lot of wire-haired terriers, for no particular reason except that they pleased me, even in their obtuse and imbecilic moments. In all, I figured, I would need about forty dogs.

I clung to this idea even when, in moving about my home, I stepped on the wire-haired terrier who had the freedom of the premises at the moment. On such occasions my nerves were harrowed by a scream more blood-curdling than that of a panther. Such screams, I regret to say, more often caused irritation than sympathy, and occasionally resulted in book throwing.

I have also found my terriers capable of staging disappearing acts more baffling than those evolved by Herman the Great.

One incumbent, Serena Blandish, developed disappearing

almost to a science. At one moment she reclined on the front porch, staring somnolently into space. The next moment she was gone—vanished—evaporated. All work ceased while she was hunted. I liked her, and she also had an economic value, having won blue ribbons, together with those more concrete rewards of blue-ribbon winning: canned kennel ration, bagged dog biscuit, flea powder, condition pills, and worm capsules. The countryside was scoured. The neighbourhood echoed to shrill whistles. Hearts were filled with rage and despondency. Eventually she materialized from space, like an ectoplasm. At one moment the front porch was empty—deserted. The next moment she was there, staring somnolently at nothing and smelling richly of ripe fish or rotted seaweed.

Subconsciously I realized that if one lost dog can cause anguish, the losses among forty would be harrowing; while cold common sense told me that if I were in a position to step on forty dogs, I would soon be removed to a cell for observation and treatment.

Yet I continued to dream my dreams of a healthy outdoor life, surrounded by a seething mass of wire-hairs, springers, cockers, setters—almost all kinds except the little pop-eyed ones that snore.

Because of these dreams, I went into the dog-raising business —or, more properly speaking, the dog-breeding game— determined to have plenty of dogs on hand when my visionary farm should become a fact.

In the beginning it seemed a mere accident. Later it took on the aspects of a catastrophe. What happened was this:

Some years ago, with the kind assistance of American consular officers stationed in Germany, I brought home from Munich a beautiful wire-haired terrier—the dog Dick. His background was as pleasing as his appearance; for his grand-father, a French messenger dog, had been discovered in a dazed state by a German regiment out for an early morning stroll behind a heavy barrage; and the Krauts, as they were then known in American military circles, had adopted him.

Dick answered to my notion of what a good terrier should be. His facial expression was both worried and assured, and set off by fine whiskers modelled on those of Chief Justice Charles Evans Hughes. He was tough and mean where woodchucks and other vermin were concerned, but amiability itself around the house, wholeheartedly joining in dinner parties and table games by placing himself among the guests' feet and silently enduring accidental or intentional kicks.

His reputation was excellent and widespread; and it was not long before an Englishman living in a near-by town approached me with a matrimonial project for him. When the puppies should be born, I was to have the one I liked best. My frugal New England nature was pleasantly excited at the thought of obtaining, at no expenditure, an amiable descendant of a dog whose amiability was beyond question; and consequently the marriage took place.

All this occurred during that golden period when everyone was keeping cool with Coolidge; and when it was known that Dick was a proud father, a number of neighbours requested permission to pay high for the descendants of such an amiable parent. Ordinarily a dog buyer is not interested in buying anything but just plain dog; but these were boom times, when people buy unaccountable things in the line of real estate, antiques, and dogs; and on the strength of the dog Dick's amiability, his puppies brought $75 and $100 apiece. Since the Englishman seemed to be and indeed was financially embarrassed, I waived my right of selecting the pick of the litter and allowed the Englishman to sell it for his own account and risk.

In the course of time a second litter arrived. The Englishman's fortunes had not exactly improved, yet he urged me to take the best puppy for my own. I felt that a bargain was a bargain, so I thought I ought to act on his suggestion. Still, the puppy was an extra-good one—too good to take for nothing, really; so although I scarcely needed another dog at the moment, I took him home with me and arranged matters satisfactorily by making a donation to the kennel. I think I might even have kept this puppy if it had not been for the inhospitable and unnatural attitude of Dick toward his own child. He not only failed to recognize it, but in its presence his amiability vanished. When people were in sight, he affected a cold indifference; but when he thought himself free of observation, he studied it with malevolent hatred. Anybody with half an eye could see that the little newcomer had what is known as a Chinaman's chance of reaching maturity in the neighbourhood of the dog Dick. Consequently I was obliged to return him to the kennels.

He was an excellent specimen of puppyhood—one of those dogs known to English terrier experts as 'reg'lar little lions'; and since I had taken him, I had to do something with him. The only solution seemed to be to give him away; so I decided to send him to a friend, a former general in the American army, who had recently lost a favourite wire-haired terrier.

The puppy was duly registered in the American Kennel Club under an important-sounding title, as is the custom in the dog-breeding game—some such name as Wild Oat of Hoosegow or Royal Asafœtida Persimmon; and then, as is also the custom among dog breeders, he was given a working or everyday name. Since he was to be given to a general, he was, with striking originality, dubbed 'General' in order to distinguish him from his brothers and sisters. In those days I knew little or nothing about dog breeding; and since he was learning to answer when addressed as 'General', I thought it might simplify matters to register him under that name. I was at once made to realize that this is not in accordance with the best practice among the fancy. The fancy, incidentally, is the epithet applied to persons who raise dogs—particularly to those who raise dogs in England. I don't know why a dog breeder is said to belong to the fancy, and I also don't know why it isn't considered good practice by the fancy to register a dog under his everyday name.

Unfortunately for me, when the time arrived for shipping General to the general, the general's wife wrote me an almost tearful letter begging me to keep the dog. It would be her lot, she said, to attend to the upbringing of any dog that entered the home; and since she had a number of things on her mind, she was afraid that if she attempted to add dog rearing to them, she might crack. Those were not her exact words; but the underlying sentiments were even stronger.

So there I was with General on my hands, wondering what to do with him. While I was still wondering, a dog show was announced in a near-by city. Lacking anything better to do, I entered him in eight classes at this show, at two dollars per class, and had my colleague groom him for it.

The grooming of a wire-haired terrier for a show is a protracted proceeding. Six weeks before the show he is smeared with wet chalk, so that the fingers can obtain a secure grip on his wiry hair. A large part of the hair is then wrenched from him by main force—a proceeding not without peril when the hair on the tenderer portions of the stomach is attacked.

A conscientious dog plucker will spend six or eight hours on the initial grooming of a wire-haired terrier, clutching the chalk-covered and fretful dog to his bosom with one arm, and deftly wielding a stripping comb with his free hand, or pulling manfully at clumps of chalky hair. When the job is half done, the plucker has the appearance of having slept for a week in a half-filled flour barrel and of having passed his hands through a meat grinder.

Following the initial plucking, the dog is chalked and trimmed at intervals until he rounds into shape and begins to look like the pictures of wire-haired terriers in magazines. In a state of nature, the coat of a wire-haired terrier is inclined to be long and unkempt. This sometimes proves annoying to persons who buy wire-haired terriers for fifty or seventy-five dollars in the mistaken belief that their dogs will always look like the pictures of two-thousand-dollar dogs newly groomed for a show.

General rounded into shape handsomely. In private life he had developed into an arbitrary and assertive dog, strongly anti-social where cats and woodchucks were concerned. He was also insolent in his bearing, and walked proudly on his toes when taken out in public; so there was reason to think he would win enough prizes at the show to keep his mother in kennel rations, dog biscuit, and tar soap for six months.

Unfortunately he proved to be show shy. When set down in the show hall, carefully chalked and with whiskers neatly brushed, he wrenched loose from his leash, shot through the door and headed homeward with low, quavering howls. When caught, after a two-mile chase, he was chalked and combed for two hours before the road tar could be extracted from his whiskers. On being placed in the show ring, he struggled to conceal himself beneath spectators. When hauled into the open, he cowered, panting, his tail between his legs, and grovelled before the judge. He was awarded two yellow ribbons and a white—two Thirds and a Fourth. When a member of the fancy wins a yellow ribbon at a dog show, he is as proud of it as of a tube of cholera bacilli. It is something to be hidden from human sight; something to be mentioned only in hushed whispers up an alley.

Notwithstanding this catastrophe, my accomplice in the venture insisted that General was a good dog—a grand dog—a reg'lar little lion. Worth keeping, he insisted, in case anything happened to the dog Dick. It was about this time that I had the thought of going into dog breeding in a big way, so to be sure of stocking my visionary farm with blue-ribbon winners, all replicas of the pictures of wire-haired terriers in the magazines. It occurred to me that if I could pick up a few lady dogs to act as wives for General, I could leave him in the kennels and let Nature take its course. My colleague approved heartily of the idea. He was to manage the kennels and let me have—if I wanted it—one dog out of each litter. The rest of the progeny were to be his.

I distinctly remember that the phrase 'pick up' was always used in connection with acquiring the lady dogs. My under-standing was that if you weren't in a hurry, lady dogs of sterling parentage could be 'picked up' for next to nothing. That phrase 'next to nothing' was also in heavy use for a time. I do not yet know its exact meaning; but in recent years I have become wary of any commodity that is picked up for next to nothing. Roughly speaking, 'next to nothing' usually proves to be twice as much as I can afford.

I had several reasons to advance to myself as to why dog raising was advisable. For one thing, I argued, it would provide work for my English confederate, who was a mill worker and had recently lost his position. For another thing, I would pay nothing for dogs in the future. If I wanted a dog, or a dozen dogs, I would merely appropriate the best ones in the kennels.

And it would be a diversion to watch the little rascals at play. Nothing like it, I told myself, for freshening up the old bean when it went stale in the middle of a novel. And who could tell, I asked myself—who could tell what great oak might someday grow from this little acorn of an idea? I knew that usually there were seven or eight puppies in a litter. Sometimes there were as many as ten. I was sure that I had heard of litters containing all of twelve, even. Still, call it seven. Suppose, just to be conservative, we had tough luck and got a mere contemptible seven. If, out of each litter, five were sold and two were kept—one a male and one a female—the kennels would grow and grow until they—well, you could never tell what would come of it!

A short time after that I heard of a lady in Washington, D.C., who had wire-haired terriers for sale. To be brief, I went there and was shown an attenuated female certain, I was assured, to make a fine matron. Just the type, she was. I picked her up for $100 and shipped her to my colleague.

She was a disappointment. It was nobody's fault: not that of the lady who sold her to me, and certainly not mine. Her chief trouble was that she was interested in everything except the charms of motherhood.

We waited an unconscionable time for her first litter. It consisted of two puppies. We waited even longer for the second. It contained three. Since my partner was obliged to subsist during this period, it was obviously impossible for me to claim any of the puppies for myself, even if I had wanted them. None, even, could be retained to build up the kennels. In fact, it became necesary for me to make a few donations to the good of the cause; for anybody could see that my colleague could hardly be expected to board two full-grown dogs for nothing, especially since they were doing next to nothing to justify their existence.

It was around this time that I became aware of a singular peculiarity of men who wished to buy dogs. They spoke freely of their experiences with liquor dealers, and of the poor quality of the stimulants for which they were obliged to pay from sixty to eighty dollars a case. Usually these gentlemen were buying dogs for their children. Good-natured ones, they asked for—'a good-natured dog that'll be a companion for my wife and kiddies.' The peculiarity was that they seemed willing, if not eager, to pay sixty dollars for twelve bottles of whisky, but protested at dispensing fifty dollars for a good dog that was to be a companion to their wives and children for years to come.

My confrere felt, I think, that I had been—to put it crudely—a bit of a sucker in my first pickup. That feeling seemed to be justified, shortly after the arrival of the second small litter, when another Englishman, living in an adjoining state, reported to my partner that he was confronted with a financial stringency. He must, he wrote, part with a wire-haired terrier matron of proven worth for a mere twenty-five dollars. Obviously this was a genuine pickup, and my colleague was at once dispatched to the neighbouring state in a dented automobile to do the picking.

The transaction was marred by two slips. The owner of the pickup was hospitable; and when the sale had been made, he produced a bottle of homemade ale and shared it with my partner. That was the first slip. Having consumed half the bottle, my partner took the new pickup under his arm, climbed back into his dented automobile, and rattled off toward Maine. He had rattled about seven miles when a lady charged out of a side street in a hearselike sedan and struck his dented conveyance with a sickening crash. That was the second slip. A fragment of flying glass laid open his forehead, and the steering wheel almost pushed his nose into his ear. When, therefore, a crowd assembled and hauled him out of his machine, along with a dazed wire-haired terrier, his appearance was not one to inspire confidence.

Under the best of circumstances my partner is uncommonly hard of hearing; so when an impatient policeman appeared and hurled questions at him, the replies were not satisfactory. The policeman, in short, could get nothing from him but a faint, elusive fragrance of the half bottle of ale; and in a few moments my colleague was introduced into a cell in the local jail, charged with driving while under the influence of liquor. When money had been telegraphed to straighten things out, and the dented automobile had been nursed back to health, the cost of our latest pickup had bounded up into the neighbourhood of the market price on elephants.

Around this period I came across a book on wire-haired terriers; and in it were references to the manner in which a number of the most celebrated English wire-haired terriers had been picked up for next to nothing during their adolescence. I spoke to my colleague about it, and he confirmed what the book said. According to him, there were mill towns and colliery towns in England where a wire-haired terrier was as much a part of every man's personal property as his trousers. Because of that, he said, you could pick up wire-haired terriers in England—rare 'uns, too: reg'lar little lions—for a song. I asked him if he meant they could be purchased for next to nothing, and he said, 'Aye! You can pick 'em up for next to nothing!'

He agreed that if we could pick up a good English dog for our kennels, it would be an excellent thing. I felt instinctively that he was right: that if we could pick up a good English dog, a new strain would be introduced into the kennels; that the very presence of an imported dog was bound to be beneficial.

Almost everyone in the dog-breeding game seems to know subconsciously that an imported dog cannot help but have a beneficial effect on American kennels. It is one of the few things a dog breeder doesn't have to be told; it appears in his head from nowhere, without warning, just as dog hairs appear on his coat sleeve.

At all events, when I next returned to my home in Maine from the half-baked palace, I returned by way of England for the express purpose of picking up a new strain for the kennel. It seemed to me that the surest way to get plenty of new strain was to pick up a young wire-haired terrier matron in a delicate condition and carry her to America for her accouchement. To show that my intentions were serious, I advertised for the matron in the London *Times*, specifying that I wished a small-sized one.

Apparently, however, something was wrong. What it was, I have no way of knowing. It hardly seems possible that in such a country of dog lovers as England there should have been no wire-haired terriers in a delicate condition; and I find it hard to believe that only one dog owner reads the London *Times*.

The fact remains that the only persons who answered the advertisement were

(a)   A man in Leeds who had invented a compound for both internal and external use, guaranteed to cure mange, eczema, ringworm, inflamed eyes, colic, and sore gums, and to be an excellent preservative for shoes and harness;

(b)   A young woman graduate of a nursing home for dogs, who wished to give and receive references preliminary to obtaining employment as a kennel assistant; and

(c)   An ex-army officer in Bath who had in his kennels a fine young wire-haired terrier matron, exactly what I wanted, keen as mustard, price three guineas.

Bath is a five-hour train ride from London, and I had no particular desire to make a ten-hour trip unless the outlook was promising. Even though hunting a pickup, I had planned to pay considerably more than three guineas—fifteen dollars—for the new strain I proposed to inject into our tottering American kennels, and I could scarcely believe a three-guinea dog would be much of a bracer. I called the Bath gentleman on the phone, therefore, and had a chat with him—a chat couched in the British manner, so there might be no misunderstanding—and misunderstandings inevitably fall to the lot of American tele-phoners in England unless the recurrent form of address is used. To say, 'Hello, are you the man that answered a *Times* ad yesterday?' may readily baffle all but the most cosmopolitan Englishman. It is far safer to steal up on the subject, somewhat as follows:

'I say, I say! Are you there, what? Are you there? Oh, yes, yes, yes; I say did you, I mean, I say, did you write a note in arnser to an advertisement in the *Times*, eh?'

The gentleman in Bath understood me at once, and assured me he had just the thing—cleverest little tyke in the world—keen as mustard—a pal if ever there was one; so without more ado I caught the next express to Bath.

Dog buying in England is less of a business transaction than a social function. You cannot point at a dog and say, 'I'll take that one,' and leave the premises. First you must have a spot of whisky, and a little friendly chat about the war and repara-tions, and whether these banker johnnies know what they're about. Then you can look over the kennels; and after that your future little pal is brought out for inspection.

English kennel owners have an interesting obsession, which is that any shortcoming in a dog can be effectively concealed by assuring a possible purchaser that the dog is a pal. 'You'll be getting a pal,' they say, with all the tremolo stops pulled out, and with the clear implication in eye and voice that if you buy any other dog, you'll be getting a dog fiend—a sort of hyena—that will gnaw off your ears at the earliest opportunity. If I

161

learned anything in England, it was to take a second and more careful look at any dog as soon as the word 'pal' was mentioned in connection with him.

In the case of the Bath breeder, the mustard-keen little pal was a dwarfish animal whose tangled coat gave her the look of an animated mop, but not very animated. She moved reluctantly when called; and if her owner had not given her age as five years, I would have suspected her of having reached eighteen, which is about the limit for dogs. Still, if she was expecting, as they say—

'When are the puppies due?' I asked.

'I beg your pardon?' he said vacantly.

'I advertised for one that was going to have puppies,' I reminded him.

'Oh, quite! Quite!' he said. 'Ah, but this little thing is such a pal! Such a pal! Just a pal, she is! Keen as mustard!'

The little pal stared at him mournfully and collapsed under a table.

'You mean she's not going to have puppies?' I asked, thinking of the five-hour train ride before me.

'Ah,' he said hastily, 'how'd you like to take that rangy one in the kennels, eh? Make you a good price on her, by Jerve! Forty-two pounds!'

'Is she going to have puppies?' I asked hopefully.

He shook his head and sucked thoughtfully at his pipe. 'Tell you what, old chap!' he said at length. 'Put the thing in my hands, eh? Something's sure to turn up, what I mean! Get you a pickup for forty pounds and ship it along to you in the States.'

'The fact is,' I said, 'this is my first visit to Bath, so I think I'll be running along to have a look at the antique shops. It must be two miles back to town, so if you wouldn't mind calling a taxi—'

'Oh, I say!' he protested. 'This is Saturday! Nothing open Saturday afternoon! Whole town's shut up tight as tight! How about a spot of tea and a muffin, what?'

'Well,' I said, 'maybe I could catch an earlier train back to London. Long ride, you know, ha, ha, ha!'

'No train but the six-o'clock,' he said. 'Do you no good, going into town this hour, I mean to say. Now, see here, old chap, take that rangy one, eh? We'll say forty pounds. Dirt cheap, old fellow!'

I reached the station, minus a pal, at seven minutes before six, after having passed the wide-open doors of seven antique shops.

It began to look, then, as if I was licked. It was obvious that if I travelled to many parts of England, accepting undesired spots of whisky from kennel owners who didn't have what I wanted, my funds would soon be so depleted that I would be obliged to swim home. Even more than that, my health would be undermined. I was, in a word, despondent.

At that juncture a friend told me about a lady who had kennels in a Surrey village—one of those invariably referred to, by British real estate dealers, as Old-World Villages.

I at once made an appointment with the lady; and on arriving in the old-world village I took an old-world taxi to her home and was thoughtfully given a glass of milk and a bun before being subjected to the fatiguing experience of viewing the kennels.

I do not know the reason for the widespread belief that the English are a cold and inhospitable people; but I do know that anybody who furthers that rumour has never tried to buy a dog in England.

Almost immediately I learned from the kennel owner that she didn't have exactly what I wanted; but she had what was known to the fancy as a débutante—a lady dog, that is to say, aged eight months, who was a trifle lame from having been caught under a gate, but was being massaged daily by one of the kennel assistants—a graduate of an accredited school of dog nurses—so that she was soon expected to walk without limping. This débutante, moreover, had won a blue ribbon at a local show at the age of six months, and was regarded as a comer.

I was, as I say, despondent; and when the owner suggested that I purchase the débutante for $100 and leave her in England until she had been successfully wedded, I agreed to everything. It was not expensive, the owner assured me, to send a dog to America; and it was easy, too: as easy as—well, as easy as easy.

Probably, she said, I would have my little pal within a week or two of the day when I myself entered my own home. No trouble at all! Just go home and whitewash the kennel, and before I knew it the little pal would be there, nosing about for rats, eh?

I recall thinking that this was really a simpler and better plan than my original one, since I would not have the débutante on my hands during the ocean voyage; and because—ah well, because it was.

The débutante was bought and paid for on May 6. A few days later I sailed for home. On September 20 a cable reached me saying that the débutante —a débutante no longer, but a prospective mother—had that day been shipped from Southampton aboard the mail packet *Aquitania*.

A week or so later the little pal herself arrived in a state of almost complete collapse; and with her arrived a bulky assortment of bills calling for payment of board and lodging for one dog for several weeks, transportation of one dog and accredited dog nurse from old-world Surrey village to port of Southampton and return of nurse to old-world village, passage for one dog aboard mail packet *Aquitania*, cost of one magnificent dog house with grilled door and grilled rear window to ensure perfect ventilation, export licence from His Imperial Majesty's government, fees for customs brokers, tips to stewards, transportation across the city of New York, and expressage to final destination.

I meditated, when writing the necessary cheques, that while the débutante's final cost seemed enormous, it really wasn't high, since out of the litter of seven or eight puppies soon to arrive, there would be three that would go to building up the kennels; while the other four or five, being practically imported, would sell for such stiff prices that my partner would be spurred to greater endeavours.

As the weeks passed, it seemed possible that our rosiest expectations would be realized. It looked, for a time, as though the little pal might have as many as eight or nine offspring. Unfortunately she failed to produce a single progeny. All that the kennels gained, as a result of my excursion to Merrie England, was a pal; and I might add that the pal was apparently permanently unbalanced by her lonely travels. For nearly a year her timidity was such that any sudden noise sent her into a corner, from which she emerged only when encouraged with a broom. She became a mother a year later, but had cannibalistic tendencies. Her first litter contained three. Two of these she ate. Later her tastes improved a little, but not much.

As I progressed in the dog-breeding game, I slowly realized that one of its outstanding features is the difficulty of retaining in the kennels a sufficient number of dogs to provide for future growth. When large litters are needed, the litters are usually small — so small that all of them must be sold. When large litters arrive, dog buyers are stubborn about paying reasonable prices, so that the puppies are sold cheaply — so cheaply that all of them must be sold. In either case somebody is obliged to make a donation to the kennels if the kennels are to continue to exist. I scarcely need to point out who it is that must make the donation.

The very best puppies — the ones that should be saved for breeding purposes — are fairly certain to find and swallow a splintered chicken bone or a peculiarly succulent cinder and perish unexpectedly of a punctured intestine. And too often puppies must be given away. This is something that few dog breeders can escape. Maybe the out-and-out professionals can escape it, but not a part-time member of the fancy like myself. One of the singularities of the human race is that people who would shudder at the thought of soliciting a half-pound box of candy from a confectioner, or of suggesting to a grocer that he send them without charge a dozen cans of tomato soup, will freely importune a dog breeder for a dog or an author for a book. It is an understandable frailty; for to any layman it is manifestly incredible that an author should have to pay for a book he has written, or that a kennel-bred puppy represents a large part of the sole income of the kennels from which he comes. This is a painful subject; and I will content myself with remarking that whenever a puppy is given away, somebody usually has to donate its equivalent to the kennels in real money. The donor is never the Rockefeller Foundation or the Carnegie Institute.

In spite of everything, the kennels continued to exist and to provide a bare existence for my partner. Therefore, when the dog Dick went racing importantly into the dog heaven, his whiskers abristle and his black nose quivering eagerly on the scent of the ghostly rabbits, woodchucks, and foxes that must inhabit those celestial meadows, I knew exactly where to go for one of his descendants. Here at last was the justification for the time, thought, profanity, and largesse I had lavished on what is known as the dog-breeding game.

I then discovered I had no particular yearning to replace the dog Dick. He had been a good dog, and good dogs are difficult to replace. However, the house was lonely, and the rugs looked bare without a terrier lying on them and cocking his eye at me whenever I moved; so it seemed advisable to take another dog. Unfortunately, the kennels were depleted of puppies at the moment, and harboured only one of Dick's descendants—a dog a year and a half old. I knew vaguely that when a dog has lived in kennels for a year and a half he has become a kennel dog and should usually be left there. However, I wanted one of Dick's children; so I took him.

Since my partner had fed him and boarded him for eighteen months, I could scarcely expect to take him without making some sort of return; and since he was a healthy, mature dog, I knew he was worth a great deal more than a puppy. So I made a substantial donation to the kennels, and was glad to do it.

In the kennels this new acquisition had been a hearty welterweight fighter; but when removed to unfamiliar surroundings, he lost his assurance. I took him to Italy with me; and at his first sight of a donkey he was so terror-stricken that he ran nine kilometres. I thought sadly of how the dog Dick would have acted. If he had considered himself threatened by a donkey, he would have gathered up a mouthful of loose skin on the donkey's cheek and done his best to slam him over the nearest stone wall.

Still, there was nothing to be done about it; and since it is impossible to set foot out of doors in the Italian countryside without meeting from one to fifty donkeys, the new dog lived in a perpetual state of consternation. It was doubtless due to this that he quickly fell ill. Medicines were rushed from London by air mail, and other medicines were hurriedly purchased by the American consul in Florence; but in spite of everything, he died after we had owned him three months.

It was at this juncture that I began to wonder whether I

wouldn't have been happier if I had never been struck by the idea of breeding dogs. Life, it seemed to me, was just one fruitless donation after another.

When I returned to America again, I found three new litters, among them several reg'lar little lions. As a matter of fact, one was a lioness, some six inches in length, with a ferocious bark similar to the noise made by the removal of five champagne corks in rapid succession.

She seemed to have brains; for when her approach to the dinner bowl was blocked by two larger brothers, she impulsively inserted her head beneath one and bit the other on the stomach. In the ensuing fracas the lioness made for the dish and helped herself until her abdomen resembled a pale pink cantaloupe.

It seemed to me this lioness would, when grown, have possibilities; so I took her home to see how she blended with the rugs. Since she blended well, I made the customary donation to the kennels and went to work teaching her to keep her nose out of candy and sandwiches.

She was given the name Serena Blandish, won two blue ribbons on the only occasion when she was placed in a prize ring, and by the time she was one year old was under the impression she had terrorized all the donkeys in Italy.

In casting up my accounts, I did a little figuring on my venture into the dog-breeding game. Unless I am greatly mistaken, Serena Blandish represented an expenditure of a trifle more than two thousand dollars, not counting dogs withdrawn from the kennels as gifts and so paid for at regular market rates. On that basis, the forty dogs I planned to have on my visionary farm would represent an outlay of $80,000; but if they should be as good as Serena Blandish, they'd be worth it.

Montmorency

JEROME K. JEROME

T O look at Montmorency you would imagine that he was an angel sent upon the earth, for some reason withheld from mankind, in the shape of a small fox-terrier. There is a sort of Oh—what—a—wicked—world—this—is—and—how—I—wish—I—could—do—something—to—make—it—better—and—nobler expression about Montmorency that has been known to bring the tears into the eyes of pious old ladies and gentlemen.

When first he came to live at my expense, I never thought I should be able to get him to stop long. I used to sit down and look at him, as he sat on the rug and looked up at me, and think: 'Oh, that dog will never live. He will be snatched up to the bright skies in a chariot, that is what will happen to him.'

But, when I had paid for about a dozen chickens that he had killed; and had dragged him, growling and kicking, by the scruff of his neck, out of a hundred and fourteen street fights; and had had a dead cat brought round for my inspection by an irate female, who called me a murderer; and had been summoned by the man next door but one for having a ferocious dog at large, that had kept him pinned up in his own toolshed, afraid to venture his nose outside the door for over two hours on a cold night; and had learned that the gardener, unknown to myself, had won thirty shillings by backing him to kill rats against time, then I began to think that maybe they'd let him remain on earth for a bit longer, after all.

The only subject on which Montmorency and I have any serious difference of opinion is cats. I like cats; Montmorency does not.

When I meet a cat, I say, 'Poor Pussy!' and stoop down and tickle the side of its head; and the cat sticks up its tail in a rigid, cast-iron manner, arches its back, and wipes its nose up against my trousers; and all is gentleness and peace. When Montmorency meets a cat, the whole street knows about it; and there is enough bad language wasted in ten seconds to last an ordinary respectable man all his life, with care.

I do not blame the dog (contenting myself, as a rule, with merely clouting his head or throwing stones at him), because I take it that it is his nature. Fox-terriers are born with about four times as much original sin in them as other dogs are, and it will take years and years of patient effort on the part of us Christians to bring about any appreciable reformation in the rowdiness of the fox-terrier nature.

I remember being in the lobby of the Haymarket Stores one day, and all round about me were dogs, waiting for the return of their owners, who were shopping inside. There were a mastiff, and one or two collies, and a St Bernard, a few retrievers and Newfoundlands, a boar-hound, a French poodle, with plenty of hair round its head, but mangy about the middle; a bulldog, a few Lowther Arcade sort of animals, about the size of rats, and a couple of Yorkshire tykes.

There they sat, patient, good, and thoughtful. A solemn peacefulness seemed to reign in that lobby. An air of calmness and resignation—of gentle sadness pervaded the room.

Then a sweet young lady entered, leading a meek-looking little fox-terrier, and left him, chained up there, between the bulldog and the poodle. He sat and looked about him for a minute. Then he cast up his eyes to the ceiling, and seemed, judging from his expression, to be thinking of his mother. Then he yawned. Then he looked round at the other dogs, all silent, grave, and dignified.

He looked at the bulldog, sleeping dreamlessly on his right. He looked at the poodle, erect and haughty, on his left. Then, without a word of warning, without the shadow of a provocation, he bit that poodle's near foreleg, and a yelp of agony rang through the quiet shades of that lobby.

The result of his first experiment seemed highly satisfactory to him, and he determined to go on and make things lively all round. He sprang over the poodle and vigorously attacked a collie, and the collie woke up, and immediately commenced a fierce and noisy contest with the poodle. Then Foxey came back to his own place, and caught the bulldog by the ear, and tried to throw him away; and the bulldog, a curiously impartial animal, went for everything he could reach, including the hall-porter, which gave that dear little terrier the opportunity to enjoy an uninterrupted fight of his own with an equally willing Yorkshire tyke.

Anyone who knows canine nature need hardly be told that, by this time, all the other dogs in the place were fighting as if their hearths and homes depended on the fray. The big dogs fought each other indiscriminately; and the little dogs fought among themselves, and filled up their spare time by biting the legs of the big dogs.

The whole lobby was a perfect pandemonium, and the din was terrific. A crowd assembled outside in the Haymarket, and asked if it was a vestry meeting; or, if not, who was being murdered, and why? Men came with poles and ropes, and tried to separate the dogs, and the police were sent for.

And in the midst of the riot that sweet young lady returned, and snatched up that sweet little dog of hers (he had laid the tyke up for a month, and had on the expression, now, of a new-born lamb) into her arms, and kissed him, and asked him if he was killed, and what those great nasty brutes of dogs had been doing to him; and he nestled up against her, and gazed up into her face with a look that seemed to say: 'Oh, I'm so glad you've come to take me away from this disgraceful scene!'

She said that the people at the stores had no right to allow great savage things like those other dogs to be put with respectable people's dogs, and that she had a great mind to summon somebody.

Such is the nature of fox-terriers; and, therefore, I do not blame Montmorency for his tendency to row with cats, but he wished he had not given way to it that morning.

We were, as I have said, returning from a dip, and half-way up the High Street a cat darted out from one of the houses in front of us, and began to trot across the road. Montmorency gave a cry of joy—the cry of a stern warrior who sees his enemy given over to his hands—the sort of cry Cromwell might have uttered when the Scots came down the hill—and flew after his prey.

His victim was a large black tom. I never saw a larger cat, nor a more disreputable-looking cat. It had lost half its tail, one of its ears, and a fairly appreciable proportion of its nose. It was a long, sinewy-looking animal. It had a calm, contented air about it.

Montmorency went for that poor cat at the rate of twenty miles an hour; but the cat did not hurry up—did not seem to have grasped the idea that its life was in danger. It trotted quietly on until its would-be assassin was within a yard of it, and then it turned round and sat down in the middle of the road, and looked at Montmorency with a gentle, inquiring expression, that said:

'Yes? You want me?'

Montmorency does not lack pluck; but there was something about the look of that cat that might have chilled the heart of the boldest dog. He stopped abruptly, and looked back at Tom.

Neither spoke; but the conversation that one could imagine was clearly as follows:

THE CAT: 'Can I do anything for you?'

MONTMORENCY: 'No—no, thanks.'

THE CAT: 'Don't you mind speaking, if you really want anything, you know.'

MONTMORENCY (*backing down the High Street*): 'Oh no—not at all—certainly—don't you trouble. I—I am afraid I've made a mistake. I thought I knew you. Sorry I disturbed you.'

THE CAT: 'Not at all—quite a pleasure. Sure you don't want anything, now?'

MONTMORENCY (*still backing*): 'Not at all, thanks—not at all— very kind of you. Good morning.'

THE CAT: 'Good morning.'

Then the cat rose, and continued his trot; and Montmorency, fitting what he calls his tail carefully into its groove, came back to us, and took up an unimportant position in the rear.

To this day, if you say the word 'Cats!' to Montmorency, he will visibly shrink and look up piteously at you, as if to say: 'Please don't.'

Some Sunnybank Dogs

ALBERT PAYSON TERHUNE

A SCHOOLTEACHER, looking back over his experiences with more than a thousand pupils, would find himself dwelling with special interest in recollections of at least nine or ten of them; nine or ten personalities so outstanding, for one reason or another, that they will not let themselves be forgotten or grouped with the vast majority.

It is so with my memories of the long line of Sunnybank dogs.

Soon or late, every dog master's memory becomes a graveyard; peopled by wistful little furry ghosts that creep back unbidden, at times, to a semblance of their olden lives. To outsiders, the past deeds and misdeeds of these loved canine wraiths may hold no great interest.

With this somewhat windy apology, which really is no apology at all, let's go:

Lad stands out as foremost of the dogs of Sunnybank. I have written his life saga; stretching its exploits through no fewer than three 'Lad' books. So I need not go in for a wearisome retelling of his biography. A few episodes and characteristics, and then we'll pass on to the next cage.

He was a big and incredibly powerful collie, with a massive coat of burnished mahogany-and-snow and with absurdly small fore-paws (which he spent at least an hour a day in washing) and with deep-set dark eyes that seemed to have a soul behind them. So much for the outer dog. For the inner: he had a heart that did not know the meaning of fear or of disloyalty or of meanness.

But it was his personality, apart from all these things, which made—and still makes—him so impossible to forget. As I have tried clumsily to bring out in my three books about him.

He was immeasurably more than a professionally loyal and heroic collie. He had the most elfin sense of fun and the most human-like reasoning powers I have found in any dog.

Suppose we talk about those traits for a minute or two.

The Mistress and I went to pay a call of sympathy on a lachrymose old woman whose arm had been broken. The fracture had knit. The victim was almost as well as ever. But she revelled in giving dramatic recitals of her mishap to anyone and everyone who would listen.

We took Lad along with us when we dropped in on the invalid-emeritus. Before we had been there five minutes, we had every reason to wish we had left him at home.

Not that he failed to behave with entire outward decorum. But he took much uncalled-for part in the conversation. The woman launched forth on a detailed report of her accident. She sprinkled the lamentable recital thickly with moans and groans and belching sighs.

Lad was enormously pleased with the performance. So much so that he elected to turn the dolorous solo into a still more doleful duet. Every time our hostess gave forth one of the many successive sounds of grief, Lad copied it with startling realism and in precisely the same key. In perfect imitation, he moaned and whimpered and sighed and emitted ghastly groanings.

Throughout, he was lying demurely at the Mistress's feet. But his eyes were a-dance. The plumed tip of his tail twitched uncontrollably. Lad was having a beautiful time. The Mistress and I were not.

We sought to keep our faces straight, as the woman's narrative waxed in noisy intensity and as Lad's accompaniment swelled to a crescendo.

Groan for groan he gave her and moan for moan. Carried away by his own brilliant enactment, his ululations increased in volume until they all but drowned out the sufferer's performance. It was a horrible duel of emotional expression. And Lad won it. For the woman paused in her jeremiad, and stared down at the statuesquely couchant collie in tearful admiration.

'Oh, he's wonderful!' she exclaimed. 'Just *wonderful*! He understands all the agonies I've been through! And it almost breaks his heart. I wish some people were half as sympathetic as this poor dumb beast.'

Lad, who for five minutes had been anything but dumb, eyed her in happy expectation; waiting for her to strike the next imitable note of grief, and yearning for a chance to resume his own performance. But there was no opening. The lament had shifted to clamorous praise of the dog's unbelievable comprehension and sympathy. And in the hymn of praise there were no alluring groans to copy.

We got away as soon as we could. If ever a dog merited rebuke for disgraceful impudence, Lad was that dog. But neither the Mistress nor myself had the heart to scold him for it.

With uncanny wisdom the collie had realized from the outset that the old lady was in no pain, in no real distress, that she was just airing her past trouble in maudlin quest for sympathy and in an orgy of self-pity. And he had joined blithely in the scene; in a spirit of straight ridicule.

In cases of genuine human distress or pain or misfortune, Lad's sympathy was ever eager and heart-sick. But he had a whole-souled disgust for any form of faking; a disgust he took pleasure in showing most unmistakably.

Sometimes his guying took a subtler form. As when a man came here to see me on business—a man Lad disliked and distrusted as much as I did. The day was hot. The visitor took off his new pongee coat and laid it on the edge of the veranda. Then he began to talk.

He had an unpleasant manner and he was saying unpleasant things. I was hard put to it to remember I was his host, and to behave civilly to him. I found the effort more and more difficult as the talk went on.

Lad was lying beside my chair. As always, he sensed my mood.

With a collie's odd psychic powers he knew I was increasingly angry and that I yearned to kick the visitor off my land. The dog looked worriedly up into my face. Then he eyed my caller, and the tip of one of his long white eye-teeth peeped from under the lip that had begun to curl ever so slightly.

I could see the tiger muscles go taut beneath Lad's coat. I laid my hand on his head and whispered sharply:

'Quiet, Lad. Let him *alone!'*

All his adult life the dog had known the meaning of both those commands and the stark necessity of obeying them. Yet the Master was pestered by this obnoxious stranger. And, with Lad, that was not on the free list. Glumly he lay down, his eyes fixed alertly on the guest.

Then, stealthily, he got to his feet. With catlike softness of foot he crossed to the veranda edge where was draped the visitor's imported white coat—a garment of much value, even if not of many colours. To my shame I admit I saw the collie's progress without checking it. I had used up my whole day's stock of hospitality.

Lad lifted the snowy and costly coat from its place. He carried it out on to the muddy gravel of the driveway as tenderly as though it were a sick puppy. The owner was too busy orating to notice the rape of the garment. And I had not the good breeding to call Lad back.

On the driveway, Lad sought out a spot where was a smear of surface mud and silt as wide as a dining-room table—the effluvia of that morning's heavy rain.

With the same exaggerated tenderness he laid the coat on top of the area of mud. Then, in very evident relish, he proceeded to roll on it, back and forth, several times. After which he proceeded to rub one of his heavy shoulders into the muddily crumpled British imported pongee, and then the other shoulder. He ended the desecration by rolling once more upon it.

Now to an outsider this shoulder rubbing and rolling might have had no significance, apart from crass mischief. A dogman would have understood the unspeakable black insult implied. For only into carrion—liquescent and putrescent carrion—does a dog roll and rub his body in that fashion. It is the foulest affront he can offer.

It was when Lad had completed his task of defilement as I have told it and was pacing back in majestic dignity to his place beside my chair, that the visitor's eye chanced to rest—first inquisitively and then in swift horror—upon his treasured white coat; or at the befouled bunch of muddy cloth which had been that coat.

Again I should have reprimanded Lad right ferociously. Again I did not.

In October of 1912 the Mistress was stricken with a long and
perilous attack of pneumonia. It was a time of horror which
even yet I don't like to recall. Through the endless days and the
interminable nights Lad crouched against the door of her
sickroom. He would not eat. If he were put out of the house,
he would smash a cellar window, and, two minutes later, he
would be back at his post outside the shut door.

Day and night he lay there, shivering, moaning softly under
his breath. Doctor and nurse, coming or going, would tread
accidentally on his sensitive body a dozen times a day.

Outside, the October woods were full of chaseable rabbits
and squirrels: Lad's lifelong pacemakers in wild-forest chases.
But the dog paid no heed. Miserable and sick with dread, he
lay there.

Then, of a glorious Sunday morning, the death danger was
past. I called Lad into the sickroom. Trembling, ecstatic, he
made his way to the side of the bed, moving as softly as any
nurse or mother. The Mistress was told of his long vigil.
And she patted his classic head and told him what a grand dog
he was.

Then I told him to go outdoors. He obeyed.

Once outside, he proceeded to comport himself in a manner
unworthy of a three-months puppy.

For the next ten hours complaints came pouring in on me:
complaints ranging from tearful to blasphemous; complaints I
was too happy to heed.

Lad had broken into the dairy, by hammering open its door
with his head. There he had pulled, one by one, every milk or
cream pan from the shelves, and had left the stone floor deep
in a white covering.

Lad had chased the Mistress's cat up a tree. And the poor
little feline was stranded out on the end of a wabbly bough
whence only a long ladder could rescue her.

Lad had gushed forth among the cows and had driven them
into stampede flight. One of them, tethered to a long chain,
he had chased in a circle till the chasee was too exhausted
to stand.

Lad had cantered up to the gate lodge. There he had slipped
into the kitchen and had yanked from the open cover a ten-
pound leg of mutton designed for the Sunday dinner of my

superintendent and his family. This hotly savoury trophy he had been burying deep in a flower-bed when the superintendent's wife rescued it in sorry plight.

Lad had nipped the heels of an elderly horse which drew a carry-all wherein his owner and the latter's children were driving to church. The horse had run away, more in conscientiousness than in terror, for several yards, before the driver could rein him in.

Meantime, Lad had sprung upward and had caught between his teeth the corner of an elaborate laprobe. He had dragged this for a quarter-mile, and at last had deposited it in the dead centre of a half-impenetrable berry patch.

Lad had hunted up three neighbours' dogs and had routed them out of their kennels and had bestowed on them a series of terrific thrashings.

Lad had ripped the nurse's best newly starched uniform from the clothes-line (he hated the antiseptic-smelling and abhorredly efficient nurse from the first) and had deposited it in the black lakeside mud.

In brief, Lad had misbehaved as never before in all his stately life had he dreamed of misbehaving. He had been, for ten hours, a Scourge, a neighbourhood Pest.

Fast and furious poured in the complaints from everywhere. To my lasting discredit, I must say I made the same reply to every weeping or cursing complainant:

'Let him alone. Send me the bill and I'll settle it. Lad and I have been through the red flames of hell, this past fortnight. To-day he's doing the things *I'd* do if I had the nerve. We're celebrating, he and I.'

(I don't need to point out to any of you that this was an inanely drunken speech for any grown man to keep on repeating as I repeated it on that golden Day of Deliverance.)

A year later, Lad took upon himself, of his own accord, a man's size job. Namely, the task of shaping his harum-scarum young son, Wolf, into a decent canine citizen. Patiently, the big dog wrought at this chore. At first the results were slow and uncertain.

For one thing, Wolf's inborn sense of mischief made his sedate sire's life a burden. The worst form of plaguing was the stealing by Wolf of Lad's most cherished meat bones.

At first the older collie suffered these thefts without resentment or punishment. Lad could thrash (and *did* thrash) every dog of his size, or much larger, which attacked him. But against a silly half-grown pup he would not employ his fearsome punitive powers. He hit on a better trick for keeping his beloved bones from Wolf's thieving teeth. I was lucky enough to be on hand, at a distance, to see this ruse carried out more than once. And, to me, it savours, not of blind atavistic canine instinct, but of true human sense of reasoning.

Lad received, as part of his dinner, a gorgeously meatful beef bone. He had eaten to repletion. Thus he planned to bury this delicious two-pound morsel for future exhuming and gnawing. First, he took preliminary steps.

Then with no show of caution at all he carried the red-streaked bone to a sheltered spot in a flower border. There he laid it down and proceeded to dig a hole in the soft loam—a hole deeper than he usually dug.

In the bottom of this pit he placed the bone. With his nose, he shoved an inch or so of earth on top of the buried treasure. (A dog digs holes with his forepaws, you know. But he uses his nose, never his paws, for filling such holes. I don't know why.)

After the bone was comfortably if lightly covered, Lad dived into a clump of shrubbery hard by, and reappeared carrying a bare and sterile bone he had hidden there—a bone which long ago had lost its last iota of dog appeal and which had been bleached white by many rains.

This forlorn relic he dropped into the cavity. Then he proceeded to push back all the displaced dirt, up to the level of the rest of the ground; and walked unconcernedly away, not once turning to glance back at the cache.

Wolf had been watching from a safe distance, and with avid interest. As soon as Lad left the scene of interment, the puppy danced over to it and began to dig. Thus, often, he had rifled his sire's underground bone-repositories. Presently, Wolf had dug down to the first bone.

In disgust he sniffed at its meatless aridity. Then he turned away. Apparently he had had all his toil for nothing, for less than nothing, for a bone a starving coyote would have turned up its nose at. Off trotted the baffled puppy without the faintest suspicion that a right toothsome meat-fringed bone was lying less than two inches beneath the decoy bone he had disinterred.

Now, unless I am more in error than usual, that ruse of old Lad's called for something like human reasoning and powers of logic. Assuredly it was not based on mere instinct. Every move was thought out and executed in crafty sequence.

I have heard of two other dogs, since then, whose owners saw them do the same thing.

Let's go back to an aftermath of Lad's crazy spree of relief when he knew the Mistress was out of danger. A week or so later, the convalescent was carried downstairs, one Indian summer morning, and ensconced in a porch hammock. Lad, as always, lay on the veranda floor beside her.

During the forenoon, two or three neighbours came to see the Mistress, to congratulate her on her recovery and to bring her gifts of flowers and candy and fruit and the like. These presents they placed in her lap for inspection. Lad watched interestedly. Soon he got up and loped away towards the woods.

Somewhere far back in the forests he found—much more likely *re*found—the carcass of an excessively dead horse. From it he wrenched part of a rib. Then, dragging his heavy burden, he made his way home.

None of us noticed the collie's approach; the wind blowing from the wrong direction. Our first knowledge of his return to the porch was when he came alongside the hammock and dropped his awful gift across the Mistress's lap.

And why not? To a dog, such far-gone carrion is a rare delicacy. Not for food, but to roll in. To him the odour must seem delicious, if one may judge by his joy in transferring it to his own coat.

Lad had followed the example of the morning's visitors by bringing his dear deity a present—the choicest he could find.

After all, the reek of carrion cannot be much more offensive to us than is the smell of tobacco and of booze and of costly imported perfumes to dogs. Yet for the incomprehensible pleasure of being near us, our dogs endure those rank smells; while we banish from the house any dog whose fur has even the faintest reek of carrion.

*

179

Of all my countless ignorances of dog nature, the densest is his yearning to be near his master or mistress.

I don't know why my collies will leave their dozing in front of the living-room hearth for the privilege of following me out into a torrent of winter rain. They hate rain.

I don't know why all folk's dogs risk gladly a scolding or a whipping by breaking out of a room or a kennel into which they have been shut, and galloping down the street or over the fields to catch up with the master who purposely has left them behind.

To-day (for another and non-thrilling instance) I am writing at my hammock desk, a hundred yards or more from the house. Seven dogs are with me. It is a cool, brilliant afternoon; just the weather for a romp. The lawns and the woods and the lake all offer allurement to my collies.

What are the seven doing? Each and every one of them is lounging on the ground, close to the hammock.

Even crippled and ancient Sandy (Sunnybank Sandstorm) has left the veranda mat where he was so comfortable. To him all movement nowadays is a source of more or less keen discomfort. Yet he limped painfully down the six steps from the veranda to the driveway, and came slowly over to me, as soon as he found I was here; stretching himself at my feet, on bumpy ground much less comfortable than his porch bed. And here for the past two hours he has been drowsing with the others.

Why? I don't know. There must be some mysterious lure in the presence of their human gods which gives dogs that silly yearning to stay at their sides; rather than do more amusing and interesting things.

When I chance to go from the house towards the stables, a cloud of the white doves of Sunnybank fly to meet me and to escort me in winnowing flight to my destination. There is no mystery about this semblance of devotion. They know their food-box is in a shed there.

The same cause was assignable to the welcoming whinnies of my horses (when I still kept horses) that greeted me as I passed in through the stable doors in the early mornings.

It is the same with the goldfish, when a hundred of them converge in fiery streams to where I halt at the kerb of the wide lily-pool; and when they wriggle fearlessly in and out among my dabbling fingers. They know—or hope—I am there to feed them.

No, none of those phenomena holds a single half-grain of mystery, any more than does human fawning on a rich relative. But the dogs—mine and everyone's—stick around where we are and go where we go, through no graft motive at all.

They are absurd enough to want to be with us, and with no hope of reward. That is an impulse I have sought hard and vainly to explain to myself.

In the bunch of Sunnybank collies, as they lie around me here on the grass, there is no trace of the flattering attention they show towards the maids, who love to feed them surreptitiously from the kitchen windows; none of the still more rapt interest they bestow on my superintendent as he prepares their one ample daily meal.

There is no such patently self-seeking tinge in their attitude towards me as they lie here on the lawn. There was none of it in the canine procession which followed me to the house, three minutes ago, when I went to my study for a new supply of typewriter paper, and which waited at the door for me and then convoyed me back here to the hammock.

No, it is a trait I can't figure out. As I think I have said several times in the past page or two.

Which is a long digression from our story. I like to hope it hasn't bored you overmuch. And now let's get back to Lad.

I have dealt here only with a few of the queerly human and mischievous and logic-guided happenings in Laddie's life. Not with his actual history.

His death battle with two younger and stronger dogs in the snow-choked forests back of Sunnybank, his deeds of dashingly worshipful service to the Mistress and to myself during his full sixteen years of life, the series of stark adventures that starred his long career—are not these chronicled to perhaps tiresome length in my three books about him?

Foremost among the Sunnybank dogs of my childhood and young boyhood was my father's over-sized pointer, Shot. He is worth your notice. Naturally, in any modern dog show Shot would be 'gated' most unmercifully.

He was of royally pure blood. But his head lacked the so-styled refinement of to-day's show pointer. His mighty chest and shoulders and hindquarters that carried him tirelessly for ten hours a day through the stiffest kinds of shooting country, and the harsh coat and thick skin which served as armour against briar and bramble and kept him unscathed through the thorniest copses—these were at laughable variance with the silken skin and dainty narrow-chested body lines of the show-type pointer of nowadays.

At 'laughable' variance. But to me the laugh would not be on Shot. For, to me, he still is, in memory, the grandest pointer of my rather long experience.

My mother's health broke. My father took her and all of us to Europe, in the hope of curing her. (The cure was made. She lived more than forty healthy years longer.)

Sunnybank was rented during our two-year absence from America. Shot was sent to one of my uncles to be cared for until we should come back for him.

This uncle, Colonel G.P. Hawes, Sr., was an ideal sportsman. He understood dogs as it is given to few men to understand them. He and Shot had been good friends, since the pointer came to us as a just-weaned puppy. The dog could not have had a better home and a more congenial guardian.

Yet Colonel Hawes wrote my father that the usually gay dog had grown sullen and mopey and spiritless. Shot went through his duties in the hunting field as honestly as ever, but with no interest. He was grieving sorely for his absent master and for Sunnybank.

After our two-year exile we came back to America. One of my father's first moves was to go to my uncle's home and bring Shot to Sunnybank. He took me along on this errand. Its details are as clear in my memory as if they had occurred last month.

As soon as we were seated, Colonel Hawes sent a man to bring Shot into the house. The dog was kennelled some distance away and had not seen or scented our arrival. Into the living-room plodded the pointer, at my uncle's summons.

He was thinner, much thinner, than I remembered him. His gait and his every line and motion were listless. He seemed wholly without spirit and devoid of any interest in life. My father had arranged the scene beforehand. He had told me what to do. I did it.

He and I sat motionless and without speaking. We were at the end of the room farthest from the door, and we were seated perhaps ten feet from each other.

Lifelessly, Shot came through the doorway. Just inside the threshold he halted. Up went his splendid head. His eyes sought out my father's mute and moveless figure. For a second or more the dog stood so.

Then he began to creep towards my father, hesitantly, one slow step at a time, crouching low and shuddering as with ague. Never did his dazed eyes leave my father's face. Inch by inch he continued that strangely crawling advance.

He did not so much as glance towards where I was sitting. His whole mind was focused on the unmoving and unspeaking man in the chair ahead of him. So might a human move towards the ghost of a loved one; incredulous, hypnotized, awed. Then my father spoke the one word:

'Shot!'

The dog screamed; as though he had been run over. He hurled himself on his long-lost master, sobbing and shrieking, insane with joy. Then the sedate pointer whirled round him in galloping circles, and ended the performance by dropping to my father's feet; laying his head athwart his shoe and chattering and sobbing.

I drew a shaky breath. At the sound Shot raised his head from its place of adoration.

He dashed over to me and accorded me a welcome which ordinarily would have seemed tumultuous, but which was almost indifferent, compared to the greeting he had accorded my father. Then, all at once, he was back to his master again, laying his head on the man's knee and still sobbing in that queerly human fashion.

(Yet not long ago I read a solemn scientific preachment to the effect that no dog could remember a lost master's face and scent for the space of eighteen months! Shot beat that record by half a year. And I believe he could have beaten it by a decade.)

To Sunnybank we came; Shot with us. The dog's sullen apathy was gone—gone for all time. He was jubilantly happy at his return to the home of his earliest memories. But for weeks he would not willingly let my father out of his sight. He seemed to fear he would lose his master again.

My father taught me to shoot. A few years after our return to America he and I went out quail-hunting with Shot. At the base of a steep hill there was a brambly meadow. The meadow was cut midway by a railroad track. As he neared the track, the dog came to a dead point. He was facing a clump of low bushes on the far side of the rails.

Statue-still, Shot stood, at point, waiting my father's signal to move forward towards the clump. Before that signal could be spoken an express train came whizzing round the curve at the foot of the hill, and bore down towards us. Under its wheels and in its wake was a fog of dust and of flying hot cinders.

Shot stood, rocklike, on his point. The train roared past, not ten inches from his nose. The dog did not stir or falter, though he was peppered with burning cinders and choked by the whirlwind of dust and soot.

After the train had rattled its ill-smelling length out of the way, my father signalled Shot to move forward. The pointer took two stealthy steps ahead: steps that carried him to the centre of the railroad track. From the clump just in front of him three quail whirred upward like a trio of fluffy little bombs. I suppose they had been too scared by the passage of the train to break cover until then.

Shot dropped to the ground, tense and waiting. My father brought down two of the birds in one of his customary brilliant left-and-right volleys.

I missed the third.

I was too shaky over the dog's peril and his plucky ignoring of it to do any creditable shooting just then. Shot lived to a ripe—an over-ripe—old age. We buried him in a strip of lakeside land a furlong or more from the house: a strip where sleep the Sunnybank dogs of almost eight decades. He was interred next to a grave whose little marble headstone's blurred lettering still may be deciphered as

FRANK Our Dog. For Thirteen Years
Our Faithful Friend. Died 1876.

Frank was Shot's immediate predecessor as my father's hunting companion.

Frank bit me when I was at the age of two. I had tried to bite off one of his floppy ears. It was a punitive nip Frank gave me rather than a real incision. I am told I wept loudly at the scare and hurt of it.

(If 'when a man bites a dog, that's *news*,' I wonder if it is tabloid news when a two-year-old boy chews a dog's ear.)

It was long before my birth that my father bought Frank. The dog was just past puppyhood. The time was winter. So my parents were at Newark, where my father was pastor of the old First Reformed Church. Not at Sunnybank. (Even as, to my sorrow, I was not born at Sunnybank like three of my nephews, but at Newark; because my birth date fell on December 21st — my mother's forty-second birthday.)

Young Frank was restless in his new home. On the day after his arrival he ran away. My father and my mother and my two elder sisters and the servants went to look for him. All in different directions.

My mother wandered about for an hour, calling the pointer's name from time to time. At last, just in front of her, in the twilight, she saw him emerge from an alleyway. She called to him. He paid no heed, but walked away. She gave chase and overhauled him. The dog showed his teeth as she grabbed him by the collar. This though he had seemed to take a genuine liking to her after his arrival at our home.

She ripped a flounce or something from an underskirt — women wore a labyrinth of underskirts and petticoats in those prehistoric days — and fastened it to his collar. Then she proceeded to drag him homeward.

'Drag' is the right word. For the pointer fought and held back every step of the way. A small but enthusiastic crowd formed, and followed the pair with shouts of gay encouragement. After a mile of hard going they reached our house, at 476, High Street.

In triumph, if in much weariness, my mother hauled the snappingly protesting dog indoors and into the firelit living-room.

There, in front of the hearth, lounged my father. Frank was asleep on the rug at his feet.

The runaway dog had tired of his roamings and, half an hour earlier, had come back home of his own accord; just as my father was returning from a fruitless search for him.

The dog my mother had kidnapped was enough like him to have been Frank's twin brother. They never knew who the other pointer belonged to. But when they let him escape into the night he bounded off as with some evident destination in view. For weeks thereafter my mother dreaded arrest on a charge of dog stealing.

Never again did Frank run away, throughout the thirteen happy years of his life. Every winter he stayed on at Sunnybank when the family returned to Newark. There, in the absence of his gods, he made himself a member of the superintendent's family at the gate lodge; waiting in weary impatience for the family's return home.

When in early spring our carriage and the baggage wagon turned in at the gate, Frank would follow them down the winding furlong driveway to Sunnybank House. Here, till our departure in late autumn, he remained. And he would bark harrowingly at the superintendent or at anyone of the gate-lodge household who might venture to come near our door.

He was a peerless field dog and a peerless watchdog. To the inch, he knew the boundaries of our land. No unauthorized outsider might pass those boundaries without instant challenge and assault from Frank. He treed several innocent (if any of their foul breed can merit the term, 'innocent') sightseers. He was a Neighbourhood Terror.

Nightly, at stated intervals, he would leave his porch mat and would patrol the outside of the house and every part of Sunnybank's home tract. He was perhaps the best of all the great Sunnybank watchdogs we have had over a period of nearly eighty years.

I never liked him. And he didn't like me. Thus, my praise of his worth comes from my brain and from my conscience, not from my heart. He was bitterly and justly resentful, too, when in his old age young Shot came here to take his place in the field work he no longer had the strength or endurance to perform. I can't blame the ancient dog for that.

*

186

It was soon after Frank's death that someone gave my mother a miniature black-and-tan terrier. She named her 'Jip,' after Dora Copperfield's tiny dog. Though Jip nominally was my mother's, yet the little terrier chose my father as her only god. Her devotion to him was all-engrossing. She insisted on going everywhere with him. Sometimes this was not wholly pleasant.

As when, one Sunday, she was locked safely at home in his study while the rest of us went to church. My father was in the midst of his sermon when Jip came strutting proudly up the aisle.

A servant had gone into the study to replenish its fire. Jip had sneaked out, unseen. Somehow she had made her way to the street. There she had had no trouble at all in picking up my father's trail and following it.

Happy at the reunion with her adored master, Jip eluded easily the grabbing hands of the sexton and of one or two of the worshippers whose pews she went past. Up the pulpit steps she bounded, and leaped to the pulpit itself, landing squarely if scramblingly on the open Bible.

My father did not so much as pause in the delivery of his sermon, nor did he heed the snickers of the congregation. Which showed fairly good self-control, I think, as he had not noticed the terrier's progress up the aisle, and as his first intimation of her presence was when she appeared, wagging her tail and wriggling with joy, on the top of the pulpit's Bible.

Without checking his discourse, my father picked up the little morsel of caninity very gently and thrust her into one of the flowing sleeves of his black clerical gown.

From that exalted position, her beady eyes surveyed the congregation in triumph. Throughout the rest of the long church service she did not stir. She just cuddled deep in the fold of her master's silken sleeve, her alert head alone visible to the grinning onlookers.

If she shamed us on that day, she more than atoned for her sin a few nights later.

Always she slept on the foot of my father's bed. He woke to hear her growling with falsetto intensity far down in her throat. Then she sprang to the floor and scampered out of the room and downstairs.

A moment later, the house re-echoed to her furious barking. My father went down to investigate. For never before had the good little dog done such a thing as to disturb the slumbers of the family. Others of the household also went downstairs to find what it was all about. As a result, a burglar was nabbed and jailed. In his cell, later, the man gave this testimony:

'The thing we're most scared of in a house is a small dog that barks and keeps backing away, like that black cur at Dominie Terhune's last night. You can't make them shut up and you can't get close enough to them to land a kick. They wake up everybody.'

So much for gallant and adoring Jip. I don't remember what became of her. And now, a good deal more than a half-century later, there is nobody I can ask. Peace to her, anyhow! She stood patiently for a godless lot of mauling from my grubby childish hands. I recall that much, very distinctly.

Jock and Jean were son and mother. Both were children of my great collie, Bruce, 'The Dog without a Fault'; the hero of my book that bears his name.

Usually a mother dog loses all special interest in her pups soon after she has weaned them. That was what Jean did, in regard to most of her many offspring. But never with Jock.

To the day of Jock's death he was still her cherished baby. Daily—though he grew to be almost twice her size—she would make him lie down, first on one side and then on the other, while with her untiring pink tongue she washed him from nose to tail tip.

She superintended his eating. Daintily she would transfer from her own food dish to his the choicest tidbits of her dinner.

It was pretty: this love and care of the little brown collie mother for her big brown collie son. And Jock reciprocated it all to the utmost. He and Jean were wretchedly unhappy when either was forced to be away from the comradeship of the other for more than an hour at a time.

Jock was one of the best collies, from a show point, I have bred. Close he was to complete perfection. In his only dog show he cleaned up everything in his classes against strong competition; and he was beaten for 'Best of Breed' only by his own peerless sire, Bruce.

This meant immeasurably less to me than did my success in breeding into him a clever and gay and courageous spirit and a flavour of wise 'folksiness' which made him an ideal companion. Mentally, spiritually, in disposition, he was a replica of Bruce. I asked (and ask) better of no dog on earth. As to his jolly pluck:

From the time he could leave the brood nest, Jock feared nothing. He would tackle any peril, any adversary, with a queerly happy and defiant high-pitched bark whose duplicate I have yet to hear.

That queer bark of glad defiance was ever his war cry.

On a day, while I sat writing in my outdoor hammock, young Jock lounged at my feet. He leapt up, suddenly, with that jocund challenge bark of his.

I looked behind me. There I saw on the lawn a big and thick-girthed copperhead snake. The serpent had been gliding through the grass towards the hammock and towards my unheeding ankles, when Jock either had sighted him or else had become aware of the nauseous viperine odour—a stench as of stale cucumbers—which clings to such venomous snakes.

In some occult way, Jock had seemd to divine my possible peril. He had sprung up from his doze and had rushed at the copperhead, sounding his glad battle cry. The snake checked its own slithery advance. It coiled, and prepared itself to face this plangent new adversary.

Many a fool dog would have plunged forward to death. Many a more prudent dog would have avoided the issue. Jock was neither a fool nor prudent.

It was a new experience to me to watch his duel with the copperhead. Never before, I think, had he encountered a snake. Yet he fought with consummate skill. In and out he flashed, tempting the copperhead to strike, and then dodging back, barely an inch out of reach of the death-dealing fangs; and immediately flashing in with an effort to slay the serpent before it could coil afresh.

Each combatant was a shade too swift for the other. Back and forth for some seconds waged the death duel. Neither adversary scored the fatal bite, though more than once each was within a hair's breadth of it. And ever rang forth that odd battle bark of my young collie.

Then I had sense enough to realize that I was allowing an untried paragon to pit his skill, for life or for death, against the most deadly type of viper in this region. And I went to his help.

I smashed the copperhead's ugly triangular skull under my heel.

This with no zest at all. For I was wearing low shoes of canvas at the time. And if I had missed, the snake might well have scored on my unprotected ankle. I had a twinge of mental nausea as I gauged the distance and the required speed and accuracy for my head blow.

(There is little of the hero and a goodly modicum of the coward in my make-up. I detest danger and all its by-products. But Jock was my chum. And he was risking his life for me.)

The heel came down fatally on the fat copperhead. The fight

was ended. So was the snake's life. And for two days thereafter Jock would have nothing whatever to do with me. I had spoiled his jolly life battle by butting in on it and by slaying his very entertaining opponent. He viewed me with cold aversion, until his youth and his inborn love for me overcame his disapproval.

But we were chums, he and I, for a pitifully short time after that.

For, a week later, like the fool I was, I took him to the dog show I have mentioned. He had been inoculated twice against distemper, and I used every other preventive and safeguard I knew of. (Doses of Delcreo in advance, a sponging of mouth and of pads with grain alcohol directly after the show, followed by the rubbing of flaked naphthaline into his luxuriant coat and a liberal dosage of castor oil.)

But a distemper-sickening chow had touched noses with him briefly at the big show. And that was enough. Jock was the more delicate because he was so closely inbred. He was infected. Ten days afterwards he developed a dry cough and a wet nose.

The disease had set in. The malady which kills more purebred dogs than do all other diseases put together; the malady which took horrible toll from that same show and which has killed more than a thousand dogs a month, in its flood tide, after other shows.

Distemper practically never kills a mongrel (cross-breed is a better term) which it assails. The afflicted dog crawls under the barn or into some other cool and dark hiding-place. Thence he emerges a few days later, bone thin and weak, but cured. But it slays at least fifty per cent of the thoroughbreds it attacks. Sometimes more.

It is a disease which, like typhoid, its human counterpart, calls for twenty-four hours a day of nursing. And, as in typhoid, nursing is ninety per cent of the cure.

Not often does actual distemper kill its victims. Oftener they die of its sequel illnesses: pneumonia or pleurisy or chorea. Chorea is a form of St Vitus dance. With dogs, almost always it is fatal.

Jock weathered the distemper itself. I nursed him, twenty-four hours a day, through the pneumonia which followed upon it. Then through the long siege of chorea which came after pneumonia. I cured him of each successive one of these scourges, though I waxed dead on my feet from sleeplessness and from eternal vigilance during every one of them.

I gave up all attempt to work. And I spent my days and my eternally long nights in the wide box stall that was Jock's sickroom. Then, just as success seemed ahead, the youngster somehow acquired 're-infection.' At least that is what the two vets named it.

At grey dawn of one November morning I sat on the floor in a dim corner of the box stall, with Jock's head and shoulders pillowed on my aching knees. I had had seven weeks of the conflict, with not one night's rest. Yet I was thrilled at the idea I was gradually winning the battle for the good collie comrade I loved.

Jock had been sleeping peacefully for hours. Suddenly he lurched to his feet. His fevered eyes were fixed on something in the black shadows at the far opposite corner of the wide stall; something my own gross human gaze could not see.

Forward he sprang, voicing that same strange high challenge bark of his. Then he fell dead, across my outstretched feet.

What did he see—if anything—lurking there in the stall's far corner? Probably nothing. Perhaps 'the Arch Fear in visible shape.' Whatever It was, brave young Jock had no dread of It. With his olden glad bark of defiance he had staggered forward to meet It.

Perhaps some of us soul-possessing humans may die a less valiant death.

At sunrise I had my men dig a grave for Jock, far from the house, and in the centre of the line of Sunnybank dogs' graves I have spoken of, at the lake edge and on the border of the more distant woods. There we buried the fearless young collie; buried him almost six feet deep, before we fumigated his box-stall sickroom.

For the past weeks Jean had been shut up in her own spacious kennel yard. That day I let her out for the first time since her loved son had fallen ill. Eagerly, unwearyingly, the little she-collie searched every inch of the forty-acre Place. Back and forth and in narrowing circles she coursed and cast, in quest of Jock.

After several hours she came to the grave of her puppy.

There she halted; first sniffing about, then waving happily her plumed tail and nestling down beside the mound of new earth.

There was nothing sad or hopeless in her attitude and aspect. It was as if, after long search, she had arrived by chance at a spot nearer her precious son than she had been for weeks.

Presently she got up and ran to find me. Then she led me joyously to the grave; and once more she snuggled down to it, with waving tail and happy, smiling eyes. There she stayed all day. Not mournfully, but in pleasant expectation.

There was no taint of exhibitionism or of the role of professional mourner, or even of grief, in her bearing. She had missed her dear son all these weeks. Now at last she was nearer to him than she had been throughout that long time of waiting. Her sense of smell told her that.

Several times before settling down there she circled the ground, nose to earth, for a radius of perhaps thirty feet, as if in search of some newer trail to follow. There was none. She realized she was closer to him, at his grave, than anywhere else. Presumably she believed Jock would come back to her, there, in course of time. So she waited, in happy eagerness.

She did not establish a senseless twenty-four-hour-a-day vigil. But every morning, as soon as she was let out of her kennel yard, she would canter to Jock's grave in that same blithe expectation of finding he had returned. There she would stand or lie for a few minutes before going back to the day's usual routine.

She was a strangely lovable little collie, was Sunnybank Jean; with a hundred pretty ways that were all her own. The Mistress, whose property she was, used to say:

'Any burglar could steal Jean if only he'd pat her while he was doing it.'

Unlike most of our collies, she loved petting, even from strangers. And she delighted in the arrival of guests.

At sight or sound of a car coming down the furlong of winding wooded driveway from the high road above, Jean would run to the foot of the drive at the veranda's edge and stand wriggling with jolly anticipation, thrusting forward one of her white forepaws in an effort to shake hands with the approaching visitors—even while their car still was many yards away.

193

Two minor mishaps were for ever befalling Jean. One was the wedging of some fragment of bone into the hinges of her jaw at the very back of her mouth. This propped her jaws wide apart and she could not close them or get rid of the obstacle. The other was throwing her shoulder out of joint during a gallop or a romp.

Both these things happened again and again. But they did not bother her. Invariably she would come straight to me with a flatteringly trustful expression on her visage; an aspect which said as plainly as could any shouted words:

'Boss, I'm in a jam again. But it's all right, now that you're here. *You'll* fix it for me. You always do.'

With plumed tail awag, she would stand patiently and even gaily while I pried loose the lump of knuckle-bone from between her jaw hinges, or pulled the dislocated shoulder joint back into place.

One morning, when she was let out for a run, she went as always to Jock's grave. On her way back to the house she heard a car starting down the drive from the high road. In her role of Reception Committee, she raced to her usual place of welcome and stood with forepaw out-thrust in a hand-shaking gesture.

The car, laden with sightseeing strangers from far away, had crashed the gates at the lodge and had sped down the drive at perhaps forty miles an hour. This with the customary sweet disregard for the several 'Please Drive Slowly' signs which disfigure our trees along the way.

Perhaps the driver did not notice the beautiful little collie near the veranda; the canine Reception Committee with waving tail and politely extended forepaw, waiting so happily to welcome the newcomers.

The car went over Jean, disembowelling her and breaking most of her bones.

She must have been in hideous agony during the few minutes before she died. But not so much as a whimper escaped her. She was as plucky as they make them.

When I ran out of the house, towards her, Jean lifted her head and turned it towards me with the same flatteringly trustful expression that always had been hers when her jaw hinge was blocked by a bone or when her shoulder was out of joint; the expression that said:

'It's all right, now that *you're* here. *You'll* fix it for me.'

A large woman in bright blue was among the tourists who debarked tumultuously from the killer car. Breezing over to where I knelt beside my dead little collie friend she made graceful amends for everything by assuring me with a gay smile:

'I am really VERY sorry this has happened.'

(What a heaven-sent gift it must be, to know how to say just the right thing at just the right time! Hers was a talent to be envied. Yet for the only time in my life I replied to a woman's words with a torrent of indescribably foul blasphemy.)

A local magistrate fined the head of the party one hundred dollars for trespass and for malicious mischief or for some such fault. He wanted to make the sum much larger. I persuaded him not to. I told him the mischief had not been malicious, but idiotic. Which was far worse, but not so heinous in the eyes of the law. Also that if he should fine every unwarranted sight-seer motorist who trespasses on Sunnybank's posted grounds the national debt could be wiped out in no time at all.

I told him to divide the hundred dollars between two village charities. Which he did. I wanted no part of the blood money that he imposed for my collie chum's killing.

As far as I was concerned I thought the rotten incident was closed. It was not.

A syndicated newspaper column's space, two days later, was devoted to the affair and to denouncing me venomously for my boorishness in penalizing a party of 'kindly meaning hero worshippers who had travelled so far to see me.' Several papers throughout the country—one of them a religious weekly—printed editorials along the same general line of invective.

Thus I lost not only good little Jean, but much popular approval and, doubtless, many readers.

Let Us Have
a Mongrel Dog Show

CECIL ALDIN

IN England we have a season for everything, a flat-racing season, a football season, a shooting and hunting season, even a greyhound racing season—in fact a season for all our sports and pastimes. Now at the moment of writing I find that the mongrel, or comic, dog show season has commenced. This is vividly brought to my notice by my morning mail increasing to an alarming extent. Lady promoters of comic dog shows all over the country so deluge my desk with anxious enquiries as to the rules, regulations and classes, that my time, about the spring of the year, looks like being fully occupied in answering my numerous correspondents on the subject.

But this correspondence *must* cease—I have to work for my living—and the simplest way for me to get this done will be for me to tell you here and now what little is known of mongrel dog shows.

First of all, mongrel dog shows should only be held in aid of charities, but besides mongrel dogs there are two or three things necessary for a successful show. The first of these is a promoter or ringmaster with a strongly developed sense of humour.

A show of this kind is not a serious thing at all, and it must always have a feeling of flippancy and irresponsibility. At the same time in running it there must not be any 'waits,' or, as they say in the theatre world, 'hold-ups.' The ring should not be too large, as the show, if successful, has to be a very intimate affair, and the ringmaster should be in close touch with his audience all the afternoon. It must not last more than two or

LET US HAVE A MONGREL DOG SHOW

three hours, and only ten minutes should ever be allowed to judge each class.

To see that this time limit is not exceeded is one of the ringmaster's duties, nothing being more tiring for spectators than long-drawn-out judging.

The judges also, as well as the ringmaster, should be humorists, and the less they know about dogs the better. When I first started these shows an official from the English Kennel Club, obviously *not* a humorist, wrote me a series of letters, threatening dire and terrible consequences and extradition from all Kennel Club shows for myself and all entrants for my mongrel dog shows. I replied that, as far as I had been able to discover, mongrel dogs were not very likely to be entered for any Kennel Club show, and that the threatened consequences would therefore be null and void.

I also explained that my best judges and stewards were chosen from those who knew nothing whatever about dogs, the only qualification necessary being that they must know something of arithmetic (see Class V, the dog with the most spots), be expert judges of sympathetic eyes, fancy dress, long tails and short noses, and have infinite patience in order to judge the dogs with the longest 'begs.'

My correspondent, however, still continued to write most serious letters on the subject, and I believe I am now living in a state of excommunication by the Club. All promoters of comic dog shows are therefore warned, as they will probably receive voluminous correspondence on the subject from this austere authority.

Before advertising a mongrel dog show make up your schedule of events and advertise the classes on your posters, or in whatever way you propose to announce your show.

Entries are always made on the ground. The simplest way is to charge 6d each event and guarantee 5s to the winner, 2s 6d to the second, and 6d or 1s to the third.

Exhibitors pay their entrance money as they enter the ring for each class, and receive their prize money as they go out of it. There is a sinister motive in the paying of prize money by the management at once, for those who receive it—like the winners at the tables at continental casinos—invariably return a shilling to the show funds before the day is over in further entries.

The mongrel programme should begin with some very simple class such as:

(I) *The dog with the longest tail.*

This is a good start, because exhibitors are generally shy at first, and everyone can understand a class of this description. To get over 'exhibitor fright' is a very simple matter. A friend of the management first pays his 6d to enter the ring with a schipperke or some similar breed with a very small caudal appendage. Other exhibitors, seeing the length of his dog's tail, soon grasp the fact that these shows are 'money for nothing.' That five shillings can easily be won on a capital expenditure of 6d, and they immediately pay their sixpences and enter their longer-tailed dogs, every fresh entry having a tail a little longer than those already in the ring. We as a nation—at least everyone except myself—are financiers; we have the financial spirit strongly developed, and you can rely on making your first class go with a swing if this little ruse is carried out.

Once this class has started and got a laugh, the anxieties of the ringmaster are at an end.

Class II can be for

The smallest dog (over one year).

Here, again, if an Irish wolfhound comes into the ring first he soon brings a full house. But do not overdo this. Even financiers are sometimes suspicious.

Class III we have for

The worst mongrel.

Here everyone on the ground has a chance with their dog. In fact, I have known exhibitors rush out into the street and annex a dog for the occasion in the hope of winning 5s for 6d.

The ringmaster, or collecting ring stewards, should not make the mistake of advising the owner of a pet Peke to enter for this class on the assurance that her dog is sure to win. She will probably leave the show in high dudgeon and never speak to him again. Judges should be warned that untrimmed Sealyhams, Welsh corgi dogs, and long-haired dachshunds are *not* mongrels. I once saw quite a good Border terrier awarded the worst mongrel prize, much to his owner's disgust.

Next comes Class IV,

The dog with the most sympathetic eyes.

Here you always have a 'winner' among the ladies. They simply crowd into the ring, and the ringmaster must warn both judges (male) and exhibitors (female) that the owner's eyes cannot in any way influence the judges' verdict. It is also advisable, before giving the awards in this class, for the judges to take out a life insurance policy.

Class V can be for

The dog with the most spots,

and a couple of qualified medical practitioners often make the best judges of this class.

Some people bar Dalmatians, or plum-pudding dogs, as it takes too long to count *their* spots. I think this is wrong, as the judges can always get the help of a bank clerk to assist them quickly in their addition, a bank employee being able to run his finger up the side of a Dalmatian and tell you at once the total figure.

In Class VI we can have

The dogs' fancy dress competition,

and an astonishing amount of time and trouble is always taken
by exhibitors on this event.

I have had between thirty and forty entries in this class, some
of the costumes worn by the exhibited being well worthy of the
Lord Mayor's children's fancy dress ball at the Mansion House.
Pierrots, policemen, hospital nurses, columbines, babies, and
bathing costumes make a variegated kaleidoscope all over the
ring. The fancy dress parade is always a success.

Class VII,

The dog with the bandiest legs.

The funny part about this class is that exhibitors invariably
try to make their own legs as bandy as possible when showing
their dogs before the judges. After a few minutes' parade
in the ring even the judges themselves begin to get that
'bandy feeling'.

Quite knock-kneed judges get bandy-legged before their ten
minutes of judging this class has expired, and even members of
the audience have been known to develop sympathetic bow-
legs while watching the dogs in the ring.

Although not strictly among the classes authorized by the
International Mongrel Dog Show Association Incorporated, a
good class to once more straighten the legs of the exhibitors
and audience is to insert here as Class VIII an interval of

Mongrel dog racing

after the mechanical rabbit or cat.

This can be done under special licence from the Greyhound
Racing Association, Jockey Club, or some other august body,
but it was originally invented by my own bull-terrier Cracker.

The mechanical part of this invention consists of a machine
containing the stomach and hindquarters of a high-geared
bicycle. Its mechanism is simple but effective, for when two
hundred yards of strong fishing line are attached to one end
and a nursery or woolly rabbit or cat attached to the other,
and then rapidly wound up, no mongrel dog can possibly resist
chasing it.

You can, if you are rash, allow dogs to run after it *not attached* to their owners, but my advice is DON'T!!! You will have quite enough to do to settle jealous canine disputes when the quarry arrives at the winning-post *with* the owners attached, without asking for trouble by allowing the competitors to run loose and start their quarrels during the race. *Safety First. All dogs must be on leads* is the best watchword for these shows.

If you have large numbers of entries divide your classes into two sections, dogs over sixteen inches at the shoulder and dogs under that height.

The method of running these races is also simple, and it is better not to have more than four dogs (*with* owners attached) in each heat.

The quarry is unostentatiously taken almost to the starting-point and placed gently in a sitting position in a tuft of long grass.

The four competitors are then brought by their respective owners to the start, and stand at least eight yards behind the squatting hare. When all are ready the man at the wheel, from the winning-post end of the course, moves the hare very slowly for a few feet, and as the starter gives the word 'Go!' to the competitors, keeps it going just in front of the leading dog. If the gear of the bicycle is high enough this is quite easy to do with the fastest mongrel.

As they race up the course every dog in the field gives tongue, but this only excites the competitors to further effort, and the race ends with a rough house at the winning-post, runners and dogs being mixed up in friendly fracas. It beats greyhound racing to a frazzle.

When the wounded dogs and owners have been cleared off the field by the red or blue cross vans in waiting, the show can continue; but by some authorities it is considered best to have this mongrel dog racing last of all, as the fights can then be continued to a finish.

Other classes, if required, can be

The fattest dog.
The dog with the shortest nose.
The dog with the curliest tail.

But any promoter of these shows can invent for himself as many varieties as he or she likes.

If the semi-electric hare racing does not come last, finish with

The dog with the longest beg,

because it may mean an all-night sitting for the judges.

Competitors, with owners in front of them holding sugar or chocolate, line up in a straight row down the centre of the ring. The ringmaster counts twenty in loud ringing tones, and when he shouts the number twenty each competitor must be seated on his hindquarters with his forefeet in the air—the last one to stop begging being, of course, the winner.

On one occasion I remember a Sealyham, specially built for begging, and a greedy Peke were the only two left in. Nothing would move either of them until the Pekinese sneezed, and that brought him to earth, otherwise I fancy they might still be begging.

It is the unexpected that usually ends these competitions—a dog fight at the other end of the ground, a fly on the nose, or a cold in the head.

In any case, the longest beg class is an excellent way to close the day and finish the show.

Dandy, the Story of a Dog

W. H. HUDSON

H
E WAS of mixed breed, and was supposed to have a strain of Dandy Dinmont blood which gave him his name. A big ungainly animal with a rough shaggy coat of blue-grey hair and white on his neck, and clumsy paws. He looked like a Sussex sheep-dog with legs reduced to half their proper length. He was, when I first knew him, getting old and increasingly deaf and dim of sight, otherwise in the best of health and spirits, or at all events very good-tempered.

Until I knew Dandy I had always supposed that the story of Ludlam's dog was pure invention, and I dare say that is the general opinion about it; but Dandy made me reconsider the subject, and eventually I came to believe that Ludlam's dog did exist once upon a time, centuries ago perhaps, and that if he had been the laziest dog in the world Dandy was not far behind him in that respect. It is true he did not lean his head against a wall to bark; he exhibited his laziness in other ways. He barked often, though never at strangers; he welcomed every visitor, even the tax-collector, with tail-waggings and a smile. He spent a good deal of his time in the large kitchen, where he had a sofa to sleep on, and when the two cats of the house wanted an hour's rest they would coil themselves up on Dandy's broad shaggy side, preferring that bed to cushion or rug. They were like a warm blanket over him, and it was a sort of mutual benefit society. After an hour's sleep Dandy would go out for a short constitutional as far as the neighbouring thoroughfare, where he would blunder against people, wag his tail to everybody, and then come back. He had six or eight or more outings each day, and, owing to doors and gates being closed and to his lazy disposition, he had much trouble in getting out and in. First he would sit down in the hall and bark, bark,

bark, until someone would come to open the door for him, whereupon he would slowly waddle down the garden path, and if he found the gate closed he would again sit down and start barking. And the bark, bark would go on until someone came to let him out. But if after he had barked about twenty or thirty times no one came, he would deliberately open the gate himself, which he could do perfectly well, and let himself out. In twenty minutes or so he would be back at the gate and barking for admission once more, and finally, if no one paid any attention, letting himself in.

Dandy always had something to eat at meal-times, but he too liked a snack between meals once or twice a day. The dog biscuits were kept in an open box on the lower dresser shelf, so that he could get one 'whenever he felt so disposed,' but he didn't like the trouble this arrangement gave him, so he would sit down and start barking, and as he had a bark which was both deep and loud, after it had been repeated a dozen times at intervals of five seconds, any person who happened to be in or near the kitchen was glad to give him his biscuit for the sake of peace and quietness. If no one gave it him, he would then take it out himself and eat it.

Now it came to pass that during the last year of the war dog biscuits, like many other articles of food for man and beast, grew scarce, and were finally not to be had at all. At all events, that was what happened in Dandy's town of Penzance. He missed his biscuits greatly and often reminded us of it by barking; then, lest we should thnk he was barking about something else, he would go and sniff and paw at the empty box. He perhaps thought it was pure forgetfulness on the part of those of the house who went every morning to do the marketing and had fallen into the habit of returning without dog biscuits in the basket. Once day during that last winter of scarcity and anxiety I went to the kitchen and found the floor strewn all over with fragments of Dandy's biscuit-box. Dandy himself had done it; he had dragged the box from its place out into the middle of the floor, and then deliberately set himself to bite and tear it into small pieces and scatter them about. He was caught at it just as he was finishing the job, and the kindly person who surprised him in the act suggested that the reason of his breaking up the box in that way was that he got

something of the biscuit flavour by biting the pieces. My own theory was that as the box was there to hold biscuits and now held none, he had come to regard it as useless—as having lost its function, so to speak—also that its presence there was an insult to his intelligence, a constant temptation to make a fool of himself by visiting it half a dozen times a day only to find it empty as usual. Better, then, to get rid of it altogether, and no doubt when he did it he put a little temper into the business!

Dandy, from the time I first knew him, was strictly teetotal, but in former and distant days he had been rather fond of his glass. If a person held up a glass of beer before him, I was told, he wagged his tail in joyful anticipation, and a little beer was always given him at meal-time. Then he had an experience,

207

which, after a little hesitation, I have thought it best to relate, as it is perhaps the most curious incident in Dandy's somewhat uneventful life.

One day Dandy, who after the manner of his kind, had attached himself to the person who was always willing to take him out for a stroll, followed his friend to a neighbouring public-house, where the said friend had to discuss some business matter with the landlord. They went into the tap-room, and Dandy, finding that the business was going to be a rather long affair, settled himself down to have a nap. Now it chanced that a barrel of beer which had just been broached had a leaky tap, and the landlord had set a basin on the floor to catch the waste. Dandy, waking from his nap and hearing the trickling sound, got up, and going to the basin quenched his thirst, after which he resumed his nap. By and by he woke again and had a second drink, and altogether he woke and had a drink five or six times; then, the business being concluded, they went out together, but no sooner were they out in the fresh air than Dandy began to exhibit signs of inebriation. He swerved from side to side, colliding with the passers-by, and finally fell off the pavement into the swift stream of water which at that point runs in the gutter at one side of the street. Getting out of the water, he started again, trying to keep close to the wall to save himself from another ducking. People looked curiously at him, and by and by they began to ask what the matter was. 'Is your dog going to have a fit—or what is it?' they asked. Dandy's friend said he didn't know; something was the matter, no doubt, and he would take him home as quickly as possible and see to it.

When they finally got to the house Dandy staggered to the sofa, and succeeded in climbing on to it and, throwing himself on his cushion, went fast to sleep, and slept on without a break until the following morning. Then he rose quite refreshed and appeared to have forgotten all about it; but that day when at dinner-time some one said 'Dandy' and held up a glass of beer, instead of wagging his tail as usual he dropped it between his legs and turned away in evident disgust. And from that time onwards he would never touch it with his tongue, and it was plain that when they tried to tempt him, setting beer before him and smilingly inviting him to drink, he knew they were mocking him, and before turning away he would emit a low growl and show his teeth. It was the one thing that put him out and would make him angry with his friends and life companions.

I should not have related this incident if Dandy had been alive. But he is no longer with us. He was old—half-way between fifteen and sixteen: it seemed as though he had waited to see the end of the war, since no sooner was the armistice proclaimed than he began to decline rapidly. Gone deaf and blind, he still insisted on taking several constitutionals every day, and would bark as usual at the gate, and if no one came to let him out or admit him, he would open it for himself as before. This went on till January 1919, when some of the boys he knew were coming back to Penzance and to the house. Then he established himself on the sofa, and we knew that his end was near, for there he would sleep all day and all night, declining food. It is customary in this country to chloroform a dog and give him a dose of strychnine to 'put him out of his misery.' But it was not necessary in this case, as he was not in misery; not a groan did he ever emit, waking or sleeping; and if you put a hand on him he would look up and wag his tail just to let you know that it was well with him. And in his sleep he passed away—a perfect case of euthanasia—and was buried in the large garden near the second apple-tree.

Verdun Belle

ALEXANDER WOOLLCOTT

I FIRST heard the saga of Verdun Belle's adventure as it was being told one June afternoon under a drowsy apple-tree in the troubled valley of the Marne.

The story began in a chill, grimy Lorraine village, where, in hovels and haymows, a disconsolate detachment of United States marines lay waiting the order to go up into that maze of trenches of which the crumbling traces still weave a haunted web around the citadel bearing the immortal name of Verdun.

Into this village at dusk one day in the early spring of 1918 there came out of space a shabby, lonesome dog—a squat setter of indiscreet, complex and unguessable ancestry.

One watching her as she trotted intently along the aromatic village street would have sworn that she had an important engagement with the mayor and was, regretfully, a little late.

At the end of the street she came to where a young buck private lounged glumly on a doorstep. Halting in her tracks, she sat down to contemplate him. Then, satisfied seemingly by what she sensed and saw, she came over and flopped down beside him in a most companionable manner, settling herself comfortably as if she had come at last to her long journey's end. His pleased hand reached over and played with one silken chocolate-coloured ear.

Somehow that gesture sealed a compact between those two. There was thereafter no doubt in either's mind that they belonged to each other for better or for worse, in sickness and in health, through weal and woe, world without end.

She ate when and what he ate. She slept beside him in the day, her muzzle resting on his leg so that he could not get up in the night and go forgetfully back to America without her noticing it.

210

VERDUN BELLE

To the uninitiated onlookers her enthusiasm may not have been immediately explicable. In the eyes of his top sergeant and his company clerk he may well have seemed an undistinguished warrior, freckle-faced and immensely indifferent to the business of making the world safe for democracy.

Verdun Belle thought him the most charming person in all the world. There was a loose popular notion that she had joined up with the company as mascot and belonged to them all. She affably let them think so, but she had her own ideas on the subject.

When they moved up into the line she went along and was so obviously trench-broken that they guessed she had already served a hitch with some French regiment in that once desperate region.

They even built up the not implausible theory that she had come to them lonely from the grave of some little soldier in faded horizon blue.

Certainly she knew trench ways, knew in the narrowest of passages how to keep out from underfoot and was so well aware of the dangers of the parapet that a plate of chicken bones up there would not have interested her. She even knew what gas was, and after a reminding whiff of it became more than reconciled to the regulation gas mask, which they patiently wrecked for all subsequent human use because an unimaginative War Department had not foreseen the peculiar anatomical specifications of Verdun Belle.

In May, when the outfit was engagd in the exhausting activities which the High Command was pleased to describe as 'resting,' Belle thought it a convenient time to present an interested but amply forewarned regiment with seven wriggling casuals, some black and white and mottled as a mackerel sky, some splotched with the same brown as her own.

These newcomers complicated the domestic economy of the leathernecks' haymow, but they did not become an acute problem until that memorable night late in the month when breathless word bade these troops be up and away.

The Second Division of the A.E.F. was always being thus picked up by the scruff of the neck and flung across France. This time the enemy had snapped up Soissons and Rheims and were pushing with dreadful ease and speed towards the remembering Marne.

Foch had called upon the Americans to help stem the tide. Ahead of the marines, as they scrambled across the monotonous plain of the Champagne, there lay amid the ripening wheat fields a mean and hilly patch of timber called Belleau Wood. Verdun Belle went along.

The leatherneck had solved the problem of the puppies by drowning four and placing the other three in a basket he had begged from a village woman.

His notion that he could carry the basket would have come as a shock to whatever functionary back in Washington designed the marine pack, which, with its neat assortment of food supplies, extra clothing, emergency restoratives, and gruesome implements for destruction, had been so painstakingly calculated to exhaust the capacity of the human back. But in his need the young marine somehow contrived to add an item not in the regulations—namely, one basket containing three unweaned and faintly resentful puppies.

By night and by day the troop movement was made, now in little wheezing trains, now in swarming lorries, now afoot.

Sometimes Belle's crony rode. Sometimes (under pressure of popular clamour against the room he was taking up) he would yield up his place to the basket and jog along with his hand on the tail-board, with Belle trotting behind him.

All the soldiers in Christendom seemed to be moving across France to some nameless crossroads over the hill. Obviously this was no mere shift from one quiet sector to another. They were going to war.

Everyone had assured the stubborn youngster that he would not be able to manage, and now misgivings settled on him like crows.

He guessed that Verdun Belle must be wondering too. He turned to assure her that everything would be all right. She was not there. Ahead of him, behind him, there was no sign of her. No one within call had seen her quit the line. He kept telling himself she would show up. But the day went and the night came without her.

He jettisoned the basket and pouched the pups in his forest-green shirt in the manner of kangaroos. In the morning one of the three was dead. And the problem of transporting the other two was now tangled by the circumstance that he had to feed them.

213

An immensely interested old woman in the village where they halted at dawn, vastly amused by this spectacle of a soldier trying to carry two nursing puppies to war, volunteered some milk for the cup of his mess kit, and with much jeering advice from all sides, and, by dint of the eye-dropper from his pack, he tried sheepishly to be a mother to the two waifs. The attempt was not shiningly successful.

He itched to pitch them over the fence. But if Verdun Belle had not been run over by some thundering camion, if she lived she would find him, and then what would he say when her eyes asked what he had done with the pups?

So, as the order was shouted to fall in, he hitched his pack to his back and stuffed his charges back into his shirt.

Now, in the morning light, the highway was choked. Down from the lines in agonized, grotesque rout came the stream of French life from the threatened countryside, jumbled fragments of fleeing French regiments. But America was coming up the road.

It was a week in which the world held its breath.

The battle was close at hand now. Field hospitals, jostling in the river of traffic, sought space to pitch their tents. The top sergeant of one such outfit was riding on the driver's seat of an ambulance. Marines in endless number were moving up fast.

It was one of these who, in a moment's halt, fell out of line, leaped to the step of the blockaded ambulance, and looked eagerly into the medico top sergeant's eyes.

'Say, buddy,' whispered the youngster, 'take care of these for me. I lost their mother in the jam.'

The Top found his hands closing on two drowsy pups.

All that day the field-hospital personnel was harried by the task of providing nourishment for the two casuals who had been thus unexpectedly attached to them for rations. Once established in a farmhouse (from which they were promptly shelled out), the Top went over the possible provender and found that the pups were not yet equal to a diet of bread, corn syrup and corned willy. A stray cow, loosed from her moorings in the great flight, was browsing tentatively in the next field, and two orderlies who had carelessly reminisced of life on their farms back home were detailed to induce her co-operation.

But the bombardment had brought out a certain moody

214

goatishness in this cow, and she would not let them come near her. After a hot and maddening chase that lasted two hours, the two milkmen reported a complete failure to their disgusted chief.

The problem was still unsolved at sundown, and the pups lay faint in their bed of absorbent cotton out in the garden, when, bringing up the rear of a detachment of marines that straggled past, there trotted a brown-and-white setter.

'It would be swell if she had milk in her,' the top sergeant said reflectively, wondering how he could salvage the mascot of an outfit on the march.

But his larcenous thoughts were waste. At the gate she halted dead in her tracks, flung her head high to sniff the air, wheeled sharp to the left and became just a streak of brown and white against the ground. The entire staff came out and formed a jostling circle to watch the family reunion.

After that it was tacitly assumed that these casuals belonged. When the hospital was ordered to shift farther back beyond the reach of the whining shells, Verdun Belle and the pups were entrusted to an ambulance driver and went along in style. They all moved—bag, baggage and livestock—into the deserted little Château of the Guardian Angel, of which the front windows were curtained against the eyes and dust of the road, but of which the rear windows looked out across drooping fruit trees upon a sleepy, murmurous, multi-coloured valley, fair as the Garden of the Lord.

The operating tables, with acetylene torches to light them, were set up in what had been a tool shed. Cots were strewn in the orchard alongside. Thereafter for a month there was never rest in that hospital.

The surgeons and orderlies took spells, snatching morsels of sleep and returning a few hours later to relieve the others. But Verdun Belle took no time off. Between cat naps in the corner, due attentions to her restive brood and an occasional snack for herself, she managed somehow to be on hand for every ambulance, cursorily examining each casualty as he was lifted to the ground.

Then, in the four o'clock dark of one morning, the orderly bending over a stretcher that had just been rested on the ground was hit by something that half-bowled him over.

The projectile was Verdun Belle. Every quivering inch of her proclaimed to all concerned that here was a case she was personally in charge of. From nose to tail tip she was taut with excitement, and a kind of eager whimpering bubbled up out of her as if she ached to sit back on her haunches and roar to the star-spangled sky but was really too busy at the moment to indulge herself in any release so satisfying to her soul. For here was this mess of a leatherneck of hers to be washed up first. So like him to get all dirty the moment her back was turned! The first thing he knew as he came to was the feel of a rough pink tongue cleaning his ears.

I saw them all next day. An ambling passer-by, I came upon two cots shoved together under an apple-tree. Belle and her ravenous pups occupied one of these. On the other the young marine—a gas case, I think, but maybe his stupor was shell-shock and perhaps he had merely had a crack on the head—was deep in a dreamless sleep. Before drifting off he had taken the comforting precaution to reach out one hand and close it tight on a silken ear.

Later that day he told me all about his dog. I doubt if I ever knew his name, but some quirk of memory makes me think his home was in West Philadelphia and that he had joined up with the marines when he came out of school.

I went my way before dark and never saw them again, nor ever heard tell what became of the boy and his dog. I never knew when, if ever, he was shipped back into the fight, nor where, if ever, those two met again. It is, you see, a story without an end, though there must be those here and there in this country who witnessed and could set down for us the chapter that has never been written.

I hope there was something prophetic in the closing paragraph of the anonymous account of Verdun Belle which appeared the next week in the A.E.F. newspaper, *The Stars and Stripes*. That paragaph was a benison which ran in this wise:

Before long they would have to ship him on to the evacuation hospital, on from there to the base hospital, on and on and on. It was not very clear to anyone how another separation could be prevented. It was a perplexing question, but they knew in their hearts they could safely leave the answer to someone else. They could leave it to Verdun Belle.

The Oracle of the Dog

G.K. CHESTERTON

'YES,' said Father Brown, 'I always like a dog, so long as he isn't spelt backwards.'

Those who are quick in talking are not always quick in listening. Sometimes even their brilliancy produces a sort of stupidity. Father Brown's friend and companion was a young man with a stream of ideas and stories, an enthusiastic young man named Fiennes, with eager blue eyes and blond hair that seemed to be brushed back, not merely with a hair-brush but with the wind of the world as he rushed through it. But he stopped in the torrent of his talk in a momentary bewilderment before he saw the priest's very simple meaning.

'You mean that people make too much of them?' he said. 'Well, I don't know. They're marvellous creatures. Sometimes I think they know a lot more than we do.'

Father Brown said nothing, but continued to stroke the head of the big retriever in a half-abstracted but apparently soothing fashion.

'Why,' said Fiennes, warming again to his monologue, 'there was a dog in the case I've come to see you about: what they call the "Invisible Murder Case," you know. It's a strange story, but from my point of view the dog is about the strangest thing in it. Of course, there's the mystery of the crime itself, and how old Druce can have been killed by somebody else when he was all alone in the summer-house—'

The hand stroking the dog stopped for a moment in its rhythmic movement, and Father Brown said calmly: 'Oh, it was a summer-house, was it?'

'I thought you'd read all about it in the papers,' answered Fiennes. 'Stop a minute; I believe I've got a cutting that will give you all the particulars.' He produced a strip of newspaper

217

from his pocket and handed it to the priest, who began to read it, holding it close to his blinking eyes with one hand while the other continued its half-conscious caresses of the dog. It looked like the parable of a man not letting his right hand know what his left hand did.

Many mystery stories, about men murdered behind locked doors and windows, and murderers escaping without means of entrance and exit, have come true in the course of the extraordinary events at Cranston on the coast of Yorkshire, where Colonel Druce was found stabbed from behind by a dagger that has entirely disappeared from the scene, and apparently even from the neighbourhood.

The summer-house in which he died was indeed accessible at one entrance, the ordinary doorway which looked down the central walk of the garden towards the house. But, by a combination of events almost to be called a coincidence, it appears that both the path and the entrance were watched during the crucial time, and there is a chain of witnesses who confirm each other. The summer-house stands at the extreme end of the garden, where there is no exit or entrance of any kind. The central garden path is a lane between two ranks of tall delphiniums, planted so close that any stray step off the path would leave its traces; and both path and plants run right up to the very mouth of the summer-house, so that no straying from that straight path could fail to be observed, and no other mode of entrance can be imagined.

Patrick Floyd, secretary of the murdered man, testified that he had been in a position to overlook the whole garden from the time when Colonel Druce last appeared alive in the doorway to the time when he was found dead; as he, Floyd, had been on the top of a step-ladder clipping the garden hedge. Janet Druce, the dead man's daughter, confirmed this, saying that she had sat on the terrace of the house throughout that time and had seen Floyd at his work. Touching some part of the time this is again supported by Donald Druce, her brother—who overlooked the garden— standing at his bedroom window in his dressing-gown, for he had risen late. Lastly, the account is consistent with that given by Dr Valentine, a neighbour, who called for a time to talk with Miss Druce on the terrace, and by the Colonel's solicitor, Mr Aubrey Traill, who was apparently the last to see the murdered man alive—presumably with the exception of the murderer.

All are agreed that the course of events was as follows: About half-past three in the afternoon, Miss Druce went down the path to ask her father when he would like tea; but he said he did not want any and was waiting to see Traill, his lawyer, who was to be sent to him in the summer-house. The girl then came away and met Traill coming down the path; she directed him to her father and he went in as directed. About half an hour afterwards he came out again, the Colonel coming with him to the door and showing himself to all appearance in health and even high spirits. He had been somewhat annoyed earlier in the day by his son's irregular hours, but seemed to recover his temper in a perfectly normal fashion, and had been rather markedly genial in receiving other visitors, including two of his nephews, who came over for the day. But as these were out walking during the whole period of the tragedy, they had no evidence to give. It is said, indeed, that the Colonel was not on very good terms with Dr Valentine, but that gentleman only had a brief interview with the daughter of the house, to whom he is supposed to be paying serious attentions.

Traill, the solicitor, says he left the Colonel entirely alone in the summer-house, and this is confirmed by Floyd's bird's-eye view of the garden, which showed nobody else passing the only entrance. Ten minutes later, Miss Druce again went down the garden and had not reached the end of the path when she saw her father, who was conspicuous by his white linen coat, lying in a heap on the floor. She uttered a scream which brought others to the spot, and on entering the place they found the Colonel lying dead beside his basket-chair, which was also upset. Dr Valentine, who was still in the immediate neighbourhood, testified that the wound was made by some sort of stiletto, entering under the shoulder-blade and piercing the heart. The police have searched the neighbourhood for such a weapon, but no trace of it can be found.

219

'So Colonel Druce wore a white coat, did he?' said Father Brown as he put down the paper.

'Trick he learnt in the tropics,' replied Fiennes, with some wonder. 'He'd had some queer adventures there, by his own account; and I fancy his dislike of Valentine was connected with the doctor coming from the tropics, too. But it's all an infernal puzzle. The account there is pretty accurate; I didn't see the tragedy, in the sense of the discovery; I was out walking with the young nephews and the dog—the dog I wanted to tell you about. But I saw the stage set for it as described; the straight lane between the blue flowers right up to the dark entrance, and the lawyer going down it in his blacks and his silk hat, and the red head of the secretary showing high above the green hedge as he worked on it with his shears. Nobody could have mistaken that red head at any distance; and if people say they saw it there all the time, you may be sure they did. This red-haired secretary, Floyd, is quite a character; a breathless bounding sort of fellow, always doing everybody's work as he was doing the gardener's. I think he is an American; he's certainly got the American view of life—what they call the view-point, bless 'em.'

'What about the lawyer?' asked Father Brown.

There was a silence and then Fiennes spoke quite slowly for him. 'Traill struck me as a singular man. In his fine black clothes he was almost foppish, yet you can hardly call him fashionable. For he wore a pair of long, luxuriant black whiskers such as haven't been seen since Victorian times. He had rather a fine grave face and a fine grave manner, but every now and then he seemed to remember to smile. And when he showed his white teeth he seemed to lose a little of his dignity, and there was something faintly fawning about him. It may have been only embarrassment, for he would also fidget with his cravat and his tie-pin, which were at once handsome and unusual, like himself. If I could think of anybody—but what's the good, when the whole thing's impossible? Nobody knows who did it. Nobody knows how it could be done. At least there's only one exception I'd make, and that's why I really mentioned the whole thing. The dog knows.'

Father Brown sighed and then said absently: 'You were there

220

as a friend of young Donald, weren't you? He didn't go on your walk with you?'

'No,' replied Fiennes smiling. 'The young scoundrel had gone to bed that morning and got up that afternoon. I went with his cousins, two young officers from India, and our conversation was trivial enough. I remember the elder, whose name I think is Herbert Druce and who is an authority on horse-breeding, talked about nothing but a mare he had bought and the moral character of the man who sold her; while his brother Harry seemed to be brooding on his bad luck at Monte Carlo. I only mention it to show you, in the light of what happened on our walk, that there was nothing psychic about us. The dog was the only mystic in our company.'

'What sort of a dog was he?' asked the priest.

'Same breed as that one,' answered Fiennes. 'That's what started me off on the story, your saying you didn't believe in believing in a dog. He's a big black retriever, named Nox, and a suggestive name, too; for I think what he did a darker mystery than the murder. You know Druce's house and garden are by the sea; we walked about a mile from it along the sands and then turned back, going the other way. We passed a rather curious rock called the Rock of Fortune, famous in the neighbourhood because it's one of those examples of one stone barely balanced on another, so that a touch would knock it over. It is not really very high but the hanging outline of it makes it look a little wild and sinister; at least it made it look so to me, for I don't imagine my jolly young companions were afflicted with the picturesque. But it may be that I was beginning to feel an atmosphere; for just then the question arose of whether it was time to go back to tea, and even then I think I had a premonition that time counted for a good deal in the business. Neither Herbert Druce nor I had a watch, so we called out to his brother, who was some paces behind, having stopped to light his pipe under the hedge. Hence it happened that he shouted out the hour, which was twenty past four, in his big voice through the growing twilight; and somehow the loudness of it made it sound like the proclamation of something tremendous. His unconsciousness seemed to make it all the more so; but that was always the way with omens; and particular ticks of the clock were really very ominous things

221

that afternoon. According to Dr Valentine's testimony, poor Druce had actually died just about half-past four.

'Well, they said we needn't go home for ten minutes and we walked a little farther along the sands, doing nothing in particular—throwing stones for the dog and throwing sticks into the sea for him to swim after. But to me the twilight seemed to grow oddly oppressive, and the very shadow of the top-heavy Rock of Fortune lay on me like a load. And then the curious thing happened. Nox had just brought back Herbert's walking-stick out of the sea and his brother had thrown his in also. The dog swam out again, but just about what must have been the stroke of the half-hour, he stopped swimming. He came back again on to the shore and stood in front of us. Then he suddenly threw up his head and sent up a howl or wail of woe—if ever I heard one in the world.

' "What the devil's the matter with the dog?" asked Herbert; but none of us could answer. There was a long silence after the brute's wailing and whining died away on the desolate shore; and then the silence was broken. As I live, it was broken by a faint and far-off shriek, like the shriek of a woman from beyond the hedges inland. We didn't know what it was then; but we knew afterwards. It was the cry the girl gave when she first saw the body of her father.'

'You went back, I suppose,' said Father Brown patiently. 'What happened then?'

'I'll tell you what happened then,' said Fiennes with a grim emphasis. 'When we got back into that garden the first thing we saw was Traill, the lawyer; I can see him now with his black hat and black whiskers relieved against the perspective of the blue flowers stretching down to the summer-house, with the sunset and the strange outline of the Rock of Fortune in the distance. His face and figure were in shadow against the sunset; but I swear the white teeth were showing in his head and he was smiling.

'The moment Nox saw that man the dog dashed forward and stood in the middle of the path barking at him madly, murderously, volleying out curses that were almost verbal in their dreadful distinctness of hatred. And the man doubled up and fled along the path between the flowers.'

Father Brown sprang to his feet with a startling impatience.

'So the dog denounced him, did he?' he cried. 'The oracle of the dog condemned him. Did you see what birds were flying and are you sure whether they were on the right hand or the left? Did you consult the augurs about the sacrifices? Surely you didn't omit to cut open the dog and examine his entrails. That is the sort of scientific test you heathen humanitarians seem to trust when you are thinking of taking away the life and honour of a man.'

Fiennes sat gaping for an instant before he found breath to say: 'Why, what's the matter with you? What have I done now?'

A sort of anxiety came back into the priest's eyes—the anxiety of a man who has run against a post in the dark and wonders for a moment whether he has hurt it.

'I'm most awfully sorry,' he said with sincere distress. 'I beg your pardon for being so rude; pray forgive me.'

Fiennes looked at him curiously. 'I sometimes think you are more of a mystery than any of the mysteries,' he said. 'But anyhow, if you don't believe in the mystery of the dog, at least you can't get over the mystery of the man. You can't deny that at the very moment when the beast came back from the sea and bellowed, his master's soul was driven out of his body by the blow of some unseen power that no mortal man can trace or even imagine. And as for the lawyer—I don't go only by the dog—there are other curious details, too. He struck me as a smooth, smiling, equivocal sort of person; and one of his tricks seemed like a sort of hint. You know the doctor and the police were on the spot very quickly; Valentine was brought back when walking away from the house, and he telephoned instantly. That, with the secluded house, small numbers, and enclosed space, made it pretty possible to search everybody who could have been near; and everybody was thoroughly searched—for a weapon. The whole house, garden, and shore were combed for a weapon. The disappearance of the dagger is almost as crazy as the disappearance of the man.'

'The disappearance of the dagger,' said Father Brown, nodding. He seemed to have become suddenly attentive.

'Well,' continued Fiennes, 'I told you that man Traill had a trick of fidgeting with his tie and tie-pin—especially his tie-pin. His pin, like himself, was at once showy and old-fashioned. It had one of those stones with concentric coloured rings that look like an eye; and his own concentration on it got on my nerves, as if he had been a Cyclops with one eye in the middle of his body. But the pin was not only large but long; and it occurred to me that his anxiety about its adjustment was because it was even longer than it looked; as long as a stiletto in fact.'

Father Brown nodded thoughtfully. 'Was any other instrument ever suggested?' he asked.

'There was another suggestion,' answered Fiennes, 'from one of the young Druces—the cousins, I mean. Neither Herbert nor Harry Druce would have struck one at first as likely to be of assistance in scientific detection; but while Herbert was really the traditional type of heavy Dragoon, caring for nothing but horses and being an ornament to the Horse Guards, his younger brother Harry had been in the Indian Police and knew something about such things. Indeed, in his own way he was quite clever; and I rather fancy he had been too clever; I mean he had left the police through breaking some red-tape regulations and taking some sort of risk and responsibility of his own. Anyhow, he was in some sense a detective out of work, and threw himself into this business with more than the ardour of an amateur. And it was with him that I had an argument about the weapon—an argument that led to something new. It began by his countering my description of the dog barking at Traill; and he said that a dog at his worst didn't bark, but growled.'

'He was quite right there,' observed the priest.

'This young fellow went on to say that, if it came to that, he'd heard Nox growling at other people before then; and among others at Floyd, the secretary. I retorted that his own argument answered itself; for the crime couldn't be brought home to two or three people, and least of all to Floyd, who was as innocent as a harum-scarum schoolboy, and had been seen by everybody all the time perched above the garden hedge with his fan of red hair as conspicuous as a scarlet cockatoo. 'I know there's difficulties anyhow,' said my colleague; 'but I wish you'd come with me down the garden a minute. I want to show you something I don't think any one else has seen.' This was on the very day of the discovery, and the garden was just as it had been. The step-ladder was still standing by the hedge, and just under the hedge my guide stopped and disentangled something from the deep grass. It was the shears used for clipping the hedge, and on the point of one of them was a smear of blood.'

There was a short silence and then Father Brown said suddenly, 'What was the lawyer there for?'

'He told us the Colonel sent for him to alter his will,' answered Fiennes. 'And, by the way, there was another thing about the business of the will that I ought to mention. You see, the will wasn't actually signed in the summer-house that afternoon.'

'I suppose not,' said Father Brown; 'there would have to be two witnesses.'

'The lawyer actually came down the day before and it was signed then; but he was sent for again next day because the old man had a doubt about one of the witnesses and had to be reassured.'

'Who were the witnesses?' asked Father Brown.

'That's just the point,' replied his informant eagerly, 'the witnesses were Floyd, the secretary, and this Dr Valentine, the foreign sort of surgeon or whatever he is; and the two have a quarrel. Now I'm bound to say that the secretary is something of a busybody. He's one of those hot and headlong people whose warmth of temperament has unfortunately turned mostly to pugnacity and bristling suspicion; to distrusting people instead of to trusting them. That sort of red-haired red-hot fellow is always either universally credulous or universally incredulous; and sometimes both. He was not only a Jack-of-all-trades, but he knew better than all tradesmen. He not only knew everything, but he warned everybody against everybody. All that must be taken into account in his suspicions about Valentine; but in that particular case there seems to have been something behind it. He said the name of Valentine was not really Valentine. He said he had seen him elsewhere known by the name of De Villon. He said it would invalidate the will; of course he was kind enough to explain to the lawyer what the law was on that point. They were both in a frightful wax.'

Father Brown laughed. 'People often are when they are to witness a will,' he said; 'for one thing, it means that they can't

225

have any legacy under it. But what did Dr Valentine say? No doubt the universal secretary knew more about the doctor's name than the doctor did. But even the doctor might have some information about his own name.'

Fiennes paused a moment before he replied.

'Dr Valentine took it in a curious way. Dr Valentine is a curious man. His appearance is rather striking but very foreign. He is young but wears a beard cut square; and his face is very pale, dreadfully pale and dreadfully serious. His eyes have a sort of ache in them, as if he ought to wear glasses, or had given himself a headache with thinking; but he is quite handsome and always very formally dressed, with a top hat and a dark coat and a little red rosette. His manner is rather cold and haughty, and he has a way of staring at you which is very disconcerting. When thus charged with having changed his name, he merely stared like a sphinx and then said with a little laugh that he supposed Americans had no names to change. At that I think the Colonel also got into a fuss and said all sorts of angry things to the doctor; all the more angry because of the doctor's pretensions to a future place in his family. But I shouldn't have thought much of that but for a few words that I happened to hear later, early in the afternoon of the tragedy. I don't want to make a lot of them, for they weren't the sort of words on which one would like, in the ordinary way, to play the eavesdropper. As I was passing out towards the front gate with my two companions and the dog, I heard voices which told me that Dr Valentine and Miss Druce had withdrawn for a moment into the shadow of the house, in an angle behind a row of flowering plants, and were talking to each other in passionate whisperings — sometimes almost like hissings; for it was something of a lovers' quarrel as well as a lovers' tryst. Nobody repeats the sort of things they said for the most part; but in an unfortunate business like this I'm bound to say that there was repeated more than once a phrase about killing somebody. In fact, the girl seemed to be begging him not to kill somebody, or saying that no provocation could justify killing anybody; which seems an unusual sort of talk to address to a gentleman who has dropped in to tea.'

'Do you know,' asked the priest, 'whether Dr Valentine seemed to be very angry after the scene with the secretary and the Colonel—I mean about witnessing the will?'

'By all accounts,' replied the other, 'he wasn't half so angry as the secretary was. It was the secretary who went away raging after witnessing the will.'

'And now,' said Father Brown 'what about the will itself?'

'The Colonel was a very wealthy man, and his will was important. Traill wouldn't tell us the alteration at that stage, but I have since heard only this morning in fact—that most of the money was transferred from the son to the daughter. I told you that Druce was wild with my friend Donald over his dissipated hours.'

'The question of motive has been rather over-shadowed by the question of method,' observed Father Brown thoughtfully. 'At that moment, apparently, Miss Druce was the immediate gainer by the death.'

'Good God! What a cold-blooded way of talking,' cried Fiennes, staring at him. 'You don't really mean to hint that she—'

'Is she going to marry that Dr Valentine?' asked the other.

'Some people are against it,' answered his friend. 'But he is liked and respected in the place and is a skilled and devoted surgeon.'

'So devoted a surgeon,' said Father Brown, 'that he had surgical instruments with him when he went to call on the young lady at teatime. For he must have used a lancet or something, and he never seems to have gone home.'

Fiennes sprang to his feet and looked at him in a heat of inquiry. 'You suggest he might have used the very same lancet—'

Father Brown shook his head. 'All these suggestions are fancies just now,' he said. 'The problem is not who did it or what did it, but how it was done. We might find many men and even many tools—pins and shears and lancets. But how did a man get into the room? How did even a pin get into it?'

He was staring reflectively at the ceiling as he spoke, but as he said the last words his eye cocked in an alert fashion as if he had suddenly seen a curious fly on the ceiling.

'Well, what would you do about it?' asked the young man. 'You have a lot of experience; what would you advise now?'

'I'm afraid I'm not much use,' said Father Brown with a sigh. 'I can't suggest very much without having ever been near the place or the people. For the moment you can only go on with local inquiries. I gather that your friend from the Indian Police is more or less in charge of your inquiry down there. I should run down and see how he is getting on. See what he's been doing in the way of amateur detection. There may be news already.'

As his guests, the biped and the quadruped, disappeared, Father Brown took up his pen and went back to his interrupted occupation of planning a course of lectures on the Encyclical *Rerum Novarum*. The subject was a large one and he had to recast it more than once, so that he was somewhat similarly employed some two days later when the big black dog again came bounding into the room and sprawled all over him with enthusiasm and excitement. The master who followed the dog shared the excitement if not the enthusiasm. He had been excited in a less pleasant fashion, for his blue eyes seemed to start from his head and his eager face was even a little pale.

'You told me,' he said abruptly and without preface, 'to find out what Harry Druce was doing. Do you know what he's done?'

The priest did not reply, and the young man went on in jerky tones:

'I'll tell you what he's done. He's killed himself.'

Father Brown's lips moved only faintly, and there was nothing practical about what he was saying—nothing that has anything to do with this story or this world.

'You give me the creeps sometimes,' said Fiennes. 'Did you—did you expect this?'

'I thought it possible,' said Father Brown; 'that was why I asked you to go and see what he was doing. I hoped you might not be too late.'

'It was I who found him,' said Fiennes rather huskily. 'It was the ugliest and most uncanny thing I ever knew. I went down that old garden again, and I knew there was something new and unnatural about it besides the murder. The flowers still tossed about in blue masses on each side of the black entrance into the old grey summer-house; but to me the blue flowers looked like blue devils dancing before some dark cavern of the underworld. I looked all round, everything seemed to be in its ordinary place. But the queer notion grew on me that there was something wrong with the very shape of the sky. And then I saw what it was. The Rock of Fortune always rose in the background beyond the garden hedge and against the sea. And the Rock of Fortune was gone.'

Father Brown had lifted his head and was listening intently.

'It was as if a mountain had walked away out of a landscape or a moon fallen from the sky; though I knew, of course, that a touch at any time would have tipped the thing over. Something possessed me and I rushed down that garden path like the wind and went crashing through that hedge as if it were a spider's web. It was a thin hedge really, though its undisturbed trimness had made it serve all the purposes of a wall. On the shore I found the loose rock fallen from its pedestal; and poor Harry Druce lay like a wreck underneath it. One arm was thrown round it in a sort of embrace as if he had pulled it down on himself; and on the broad brown sands beside it, in large crazy lettering, he had scrawled the words: "The Rock of Fortune falls on the Fool." '

'It was the Colonel's will that did that,' observed Father Brown. 'The young man had staked everything on profiting himself by Donald's disgrace, especially when his uncle sent for him on the same day as the lawyer, and welcomed him with so much warmth. Otherwise he was done; he'd lost his police job; he was beggared at Monte Carlo. And he killed himself when he found he'd killed his kinsman for nothing.'

'Here, stop a minute!' cried the staring Fiennes. 'You're going too fast for me.'

'Talking about the will, by the way,' continued Father Brown calmly, 'before I forget it, or we go on to bigger things, there was a simple explanation, I think, of all that business about the doctor's name. I rather fancy I have heard both names before somewhere. The doctor is really a French nobleman with the title of the Marquis de Villon. But he is also an ardent Republican and has abandoned his title and fallen back on the forgotten family surname. "With your Citizen Riquetti you have puzzled Europe for ten days." '

'What is that?' asked the young man blankly.

'Never mind,' said the priest. 'Nine times out of ten it is a rascally thing to change one's name; but this was a piece of fine fanaticism. That's the point of his sarcasm about Americans having no names—that is, no titles. Now in England the Marquis of Hartington is never called Mr Hartington; but in France the Marquis de Villon is called M. de Villon. So it might well look like a change of name. As for the talk about killing, I fancy that also was a point of French etiquette. The doctor was talking about challenging Floyd to a duel, and the girl was trying to dissuade him.'

'Oh, I *see*,' cried Fiennes slowly. 'Now I understand what she meant.'

'And what is that about?' asked his companion, smiling.

'Well,' said the young man, 'it was something that happened to me just before I found that poor fellow's body; only the catastrophe drove it out of my head. I suppose it's hard to remember a little romantic idyll when you've just come on top of a tragedy. But as I went down the lanes leading to the Colonel's old place I met his daughter walking with Dr Valentine. She was in mourning, of course, and he always wore black as if he were going to a funeral; but I can't say that their faces were very funereal. Never have I seen two people looking in their own way more respectably radiant and cheerful. They stopped and saluted me, and then she told me they were married and living in a little house on the outskirts of the town, where the doctor was continuing his practice. This rather surprised me, because I knew that her old father's will had left her his property; and I hinted at it delicately by saying I was going along to her father's old place and had half expected to meet her there. But she only laughed and said: 'Oh, we've given up all that. My husband doesn't like heiresses.' And I discovered with some astonishment they really had insisted on restoring the property to poor Donald; so I hope he's had a healthy shock and will treat it sensibly. There was never much really the matter with him; he was very young and his father was not very wise. But it was in connexion with that that she said something I didn't understand at the time; but now I'm sure it must be as you say. She said with a sort of sudden and splendid arrogance that was entirely altruistic:

' "I hope it'll stop that red-haired fool from fussing any more about the will. Does he think my husband, who has given up a crest and a coronet as old as the Crusades for his principles, would kill an old man in a summer-house for a legacy like that?" Then she laughed again and said, "My husband isn't killing anybody except in the way of business. Why, he didn't even ask his friends to call on the secretary." Now, of course, I see what she meant.'

'I see part of what she meant, of course,' said Father Brown. 'What did she mean exactly by the secretary fussing about the will?'

Fiennes smiled as he answered. 'I wish you knew the secretary, Father Brown. It would be a joy to you to watch him make things hum, as he calls it. He made the house of mourning hum. He filled the funeral with all the snap and zip of the brightest sporting event. There was no holding him, after something had really happened. I've told you how he used to oversee the gardener as he did the garden, and how he instructed the lawyer in the law. Needless to say, he also instructed the surgeon in the practice of surgery; and as the surgeon was Dr Valentine, you may be sure it ended in accusing him of something worse than bad surgery. The secretary got it fixed in his red head that the doctor had committed the crime, and when the police arrived he was perfectly sublime. Need I say that he became, on the spot, the greatest of all amateur detectives? Sherlock Holmes never towered over Scotland Yard with more Titanic intellectual pride and scorn than Colonel Druce's private secretary over the police investigating Colonel Druce's death. I tell you it was a joy to see him. He strode about with an abstracted air, tossing his scarlet crest of hair and giving curt impatient replies. Of course it was his demeanour during these days that made Druce's daughter so wild with him. Of course he had a theory. It's just the sort of theory a man would have in a book; and Floyd is the sort of man who ought to be in a book. He'd be better fun and less bother in a book.'

'What was his theory?' asked the other.

'Oh, it was full of pep,' replied Fiennes gloomily. 'It would have been glorious copy if it could have held together for ten minutes longer. He said the Colonel was still alive when they found him in the summer-house, and the doctor killed him with the surgical instrument on pretence of cutting the clothes.'

'I see,' said the priest. 'I suppose he was lying flat on his face on the mud floor as a form of siesta.'

'It's wonderful what hustle will do,' continued his informant. 'I believe Floyd would have got his great theory into the papers at any rate, and perhaps had the doctor arrested, when all these things were blown sky high as if by dynamite by the discovery of that dead body lying under the Rock of Fortune. And that's what we come back to after all. I suppose the suicide is almost a confession. But nobody will ever know the whole story.'

There was a silence, and then the priest said modestly: 'I rather think I know the whole story.'

Fiennes stared. 'But look here,' he cried; 'how do you come to know the whole story, or to be sure it's the true story? You've been sitting here a hundred miles away writing a sermon; do you mean to tell me you really know what happened already? If you've really come to the end, where in the world do you begin? What started you off with your own story?'

Father Brown jumped up with a very unusual excitement and his first exclamation was like an explosion.

'The dog!' he cried. 'The dog, of course! You had the whole story in your hands in the business of the dog on the beach, if you'd only noticed the dog properly.'

Fiennes stared still more. 'But you told me before that my feelings about the dog were all nonsense, and the dog had nothing to do with it.'

'The dog had everything to do with it,' said Father Brown, 'as you'd have found out if you'd only treated the dog as a dog, and not as God Almighty judging the souls of men.'

He paused in an embarrassed way for a moment, and then said, with a rather pathetic air of apology: 'The truth is, I happen to be awfully fond of dogs. And it seemed to me that in all this lurid halo of dog superstitions nobody was really thinking about the poor dog at all. To begin with a small point, about his barking at the lawyer or growling at the secretary. You asked how I could guess things a hundred miles away; but honestly it's mostly to your credit, for you described people so well that I know the types. A man like Traill, who frowns usually and smiles suddenly, a man who fiddles with things, especially at his throat, is a nervous, easily embarrassed man. I

232

shouldn't wonder if Floyd, the efficient secretary, is nervy and jumpy, too; those Yankee hustlers often are. Otherwise he wouldn't have cut his fingers on the shears and dropped them when he heard Janet Druce scream.

'Now dogs hate nervous people. I don't know whether they make the dog nervous, too; or whether, being after all a brute, he is a bit of a bully; or whether his canine vanity (which is colossal) is simply offended at not being liked. But anyhow there was nothing in poor Nox protesting against those people, except that he disliked them for being afraid of him. Now I know you're awfully clever, and nobody of sense sneers at cleverness. But I sometimes fancy, for instance, that you are too clever to understand animals. Sometimes you are too clever to understand men, especially when they act almost as simply as animals. Animals are very literal; they live in a world of truisms. Take this case: a dog barks at a man and a man runs away from a dog. Now you do not seem to be quite simple enough to see the fact: that the dog barked because he disliked the man and the man fled because he was frightened of the dog. They had no other motives and they needed none; but you must read psychological mysteries into it and suppose the dog had super-normal vision, and was a mysterious mouth-piece of doom. You must suppose the man was running away, not from the dog but from the hangman. And yet, if you come to think of it, all this deeper psychology is exceedingly improbable. If the dog really could completely and consciously realize the murderer of his master he wouldn't stand yapping as he might at a curate at a tea-party; he's much more likely to fly at his throat. And on the other hand, do you really think a man who had hardened his heart to murder an old friend and then walk about smiling at the old friend's family, under the eyes of his old friend's daughter and post-mortem doctor—do you think a man like that would be doubled up by mere remorse because a dog barked? He might feel the tragic irony of it; it might shake his soul, like any other tragic trifle. But he wouldn't rush madly the length of a garden to escape from the only witness whom he knew to be unable to talk. People have a panic like that when they are frightened, not of tragic ironies, but of teeth. The whole thing is simpler than you can understand.

'But when we come to that business by the seashore, things are much more interesting. As you stated them, they were much more puzzling. I didn't understand that tale of the dog going in and out of the water; it didn't seem to me a doggy thing to do. If Nox had been very much upset about something else, he might possibly have refused to go after the stick at all. He'd probably go off nosing in whatever direction he suspected the mischief. But when once a dog is actually chasing a thing, a stone or a stick or a rabbit, my experience is that he won't stop for anything but the most peremptory command, and not always for that. That he should turn round because his mood changed seems to me unthinkable.'

'But he did turn round,' insisted Fiennes; 'and came back without the stick.'

'He came back without-the stick for the best reason in the world,' replied the priest. 'He came back because he couldn't find it. He whined because he couldn't find it. That's the sort of thing a dog really does whine about. A dog is a devil of a ritualist. He is as particular about the precise routine of a game as a child about the precise repetition of a fairy-tale. In this case something had gone wrong with the game. He came back to complain seriously of the conduct of the stick. Never had such a thing happened before. Never had an eminent and distinguished dog been so treated by a rotten old walking-stick.'

'Why, what had the walking-stick done?' inquired the young man.

'It had sunk,' said Father Brown.

Fiennes said nothing, but continued to stare; and it was the priest who continued:

'It had sunk because it was not really a stick, but a rod of steel with a very thin shell of cane and a sharp point. In other words, it was a sword-stick. I suppose a murderer never gets rid of a bloody weapon so oddly and yet so naturally as by throwing it into the sea for a retriever.'

'I begin to see what you mean,' admitted Fiennes; 'but even if a sword-stick was used, I have no guess of how it was used.'

'I had a sort of guess,' said Father Brown, 'right at the beginning when you said the word summer-house. And another when you said that Druce wore a white coat. As long

234

as everybody was looking for a short dagger, nobody thought of it; but if we admit a rather long blade like a rapier, it's not so impossible.'

He was leaning back, looking at the ceiling, and began like one going back to his own first thoughts and fundamentals.

'All that discussion about detective stories like the Yellow Room, about a man found dead in sealed chambers which no one could enter, does not apply to the present case, because it is a summer-house. When we talk of a Yellow Room, or any room, we imply walls that are really homogeneous and impenetrable. But a summer-house is not make like that; it is often made, as it was in this case, of closely interlaced but separate boughs and strips of wood, in which there are chinks here and there. There was one of them just behind Druce's back as he sat in his chair up against the wall. But just as the room was a summer-house, so the chair was a basket-chair. That also was a lattice of loopholes. Lastly, the summer-house was close up under the hedge; and you have just told me that it was really a thin hedge. A man standing outside it could easily see, amid a network of twigs and branches and canes, one white spot of the Colonel's coat as plain as the white of a target.

'Now, you left the geography a little vague; but it was possible to put two and two together. You said the Rock of Fortune was not really high; but you also said it could be seen dominating the garden like a mountain-peak. In other words, it was very near the end of the garden, though your walk had taken you a long way round to it. Also, it isn't likely the young lady really howled so as to be heard half a mile. She gave an ordinary involuntary cry, and yet you heard it on the shore. And among other interesting things that you told me, may I remind you that you said Harry Druce had fallen behind to light his pipe under a hedge.'

Fiennes shuddered slightly. 'You mean he drew his blade there and sent it through the hedge at the white spot. But surely it was a very odd chance and a very sudden choice. Besides, he couldn't be certain the old man's money had passed to him, and as a fact it hadn't.'

Father Brown's face became animated.

'You misunderstand the man's character,' he said, as if he himself had known the man all his life. 'A curious but not unknown type of character. If he had really *known* the money would come to him, I seriously believe he wouldn't have done it. He would have seen it as the dirty thing it was.'

'Isn't that rather paradoxical?' asked the other.

'This man was a gambler,' said the priest, 'and a man in disgrace for having taken risks and anticipated orders. It was probably for something pretty unscrupulous, for every imperial police is more like a Russian secret police than we like to think. But he had gone beyond the line and failed. Now, the temptation of that type of man is to do a mad thing precisely because the risk will be wonderful in retrospect. He wants to say, 'Nobody but I could have seized that chance or seen that it was then or never. What a wild and wonderful guess it was, when I put all those things together; Donald in disgrace; and the lawyer being sent for; and Herbert and I sent for at the same time—and then nothing more but the way the old man grinned at me and shook hands. Anybody would say I was mad to risk it; but that is how fortunes are made, by the man mad enough to have a little foresight.' In short, it is the vanity of guessing. It is the megalomania of the gambler. The more incongruous the coincidence, the more instantaneous the decision, the more likely he is to snatch the chance. The accident, the very triviality of the white speck and the hole in the hedge intoxicated him like a vision of the world's desire. Nobody clever enough to see such a combination of accidents could be cowardly enough not to use them! That is how the devil talks to the gambler. But the devil himself would hardly have induced that unhappy man to go down in a dull, deliberate way and kill an old uncle from whom he'd always had expectations. It would be too respectable.'

He paused a moment, and then went on with a certain quiet emphasis.

'And now try to call up the scene, even as you saw it yourself. As he stood there, dizzy with his diabolical opportunity, he looked up and saw that strange outline that might have been the image of his own tottering soul; the one great crag poised perilously on the other like a pyramid on its point, and remembered that it was called the Rock of Fortune. Can you guess how such a man at such a moment would read such a signal? I think it strung him up to action and even to vigilance. He who would be a tower must not fear to be a toppling tower. Anyhow, he acted; his next difficulty was to cover his tracks. To be found with a sword-stick, let alone a blood-stained sword-stick, would be fatal in the search that was certain to follow. If he left it anywhere, it would be found and probably traced. Even if he threw it into the sea the action might be noticed, and thought noticeable—unless indeed he could think of some more natural way of covering the action. As you know, he did think of one, and a very good one. Being the only one of you with a watch, he told you it was not yet time to return, strolled a little farther and started the game of throwing in sticks for the retriever. But how his eyes must have rolled darkly over all that desolate sea-shore before they alighted on the dog!'

Fiennes nodded, gazing thoughtfully into space. His mind seemed to have drifted back to a less practical part of the narrative.

'It's queer,' he said, 'that the dog really was in the story after all.'

'The dog could almost have told you the story, if he could talk,' said the priest. 'All I complain of is that because he couldn't talk, you made up his story for him, and made him talk with the tongues of men and angels. It's part of something I've noticed more and more in the modern world, appearing in all sorts of newspaper rumours and conversational catchwords; something that's arbitrary without being authoritative. People readily swallow the untested claims of this, that, or the other. It's drowning all your old rationalism and scepticism, it's coming in like a sea; and the name of it is superstition.' He stood up abruptly, his face heavy with a sort of frown, and went on talking almost as if he were alone. 'It's the first effect of not believing in God that you lose your common sense and can't see things as they are. Anything that anybody talks about, and says there's a good deal in it, extends itself indefinitely like a vista in a nightmare. And a dog is an omen, and a cat is a mystery, and a pig is a mascot and a beetle is a scarab, calling up all the menagerie of polytheism from Egypt and old India; Dog Anubis and great green-eyed Pasht and all the holy howling Bulls of Bashan; reeling back to the bestial gods of the beginning, escaping into elephants and snakes and crocodiles; and all because you are frightened of four words: "He was made Man".'

The young man got up with a little embarrassment, almost as if he had overheard a soliloquy. He called to the dog and left the room with vague but breezy farewells. But he had to call the dog twice, for the dog had remained behind quite motionless for a moment, looking up steadily at Father Brown as the wolf looked at St Francis.

The Bitch

COLETTE

WHEN the sergeant arrived in Paris on leave, he found his mistress out. He was all the same greeted with tremulous cries of surprise and joy, embraced and covered with wet kisses. His bitch, Vorace, the sheep dog whom he had left with his young lover, enveloped him like a flame and licked him with a tongue pale with emotion.

Meanwhile, the maid was making as much noise as the dog and kept exclaiming: 'What bad luck! Madame's just gone to Marlotte for a couple of days to close the house there. Madame's tenants have just left and she's going through the inventory of the furniture. Fortunately, it isn't all that far away! Will Monsieur write out a telegram for Madame? If I send it now, Madame will be here tomorrow morning before lunch. Monsieur must sleep here. Shall I turn on the water heater?'

'My good Lucie, I had a bath at home. Soldiers on leave are pretty good at washing!'

He eyed his reflection in the glass; he was both bluish and ruddy, like the granite rocks of Brittany. The Briard sheep dog, standing close to him in a reverent silence, was trembling in every hair. He laughed because she looked so like him, grey and blue and shaggy.

'Vorace!'

She raised her head and looked lovingly at her master, and the sergeant's heart turned over as he suddenly thought of his mistress, Jeannine, so young and so bubbly—a little too young and often too bubbly.

During dinner his dog faithfully observed all the ritual of their old life, catching the pieces of bread he tossed for her and barking at the right words. She was so completely over-

239

whelmed with adoration that she had already forgotten these months of absence.

'I've missed you a lot, too' he whispered to her.

He was smoking now, reclining on the sofa. Crouching like a greyhound on a tombstone, the dog was pretending to be asleep, her ears quite still. Only her eyebrows, twitching at the slightest noise, revealed that she was on the alert.

Worn out as he was, the silence gradually lulled the man, until his hand which held the cigarette slid down the cushion, scorching the silk. He stirred himself, opened a book, fingered a few new ornaments and a photograph, which he had not seen before, of Jeannine in a short skirt, with bare arms, in the country.

'A friend must have taken it . . . How sweet she looks!'

On the back of the unmounted print he read: *'June 5, 1916. Where was I on June the fifth? . . . Oh, I know, over in the direction of Arras. June the fifth. I don't know the writing.'*

He sat down again and was overcome by a sleep which drove all thought away. Ten o'clock struck; he was still just sufficiently awake to smile at the rich and solemn sound of the little clock whose voice, Jeannine used to say, was bigger than its stomach. But as it struck ten the dog got up.

'Quiet!' said the sleepy sergeant. 'Lie down!'

But Vorace did not lie down. She snorted and stretched her paws, which, for a dog, is the same as putting on a hat to go out. She went up to her master and her yellow eyes asked plainly: 'Well?'

'Well,' he answered, 'what's the matter with you?'

Out of respect she dropped her ears while he was speaking, raising them again immediately.

'Oh, what a bore you are!' sighed the sergeant. 'You're thirsty! D'you want to go out?'

At the words 'go out', Vorace grinned and began to pant gently, showing her beautiful teeth and the fleshy part of her tongue.

'All right, then, we'll go out. But not for long, because I'm absolutely dropping with sleep.'

In the road Vorace was so excited that she howled like a wolf, jumped right up to her master's neck, charged a cat, and spun around playing 'inner circle' with her tail. Her master scolded her tenderly as she did all her tricks for him. Finally, she calmed down again and walked along sedately. The sergeant matched his pace to hers, enjoying the warm night and making a little song out of two or three idle thoughts.

'I'll see Jeannine tomorrow morning . . . I'm going to sleep in a comfy bed . . . I've got seven more days to spend here . . .'

He realized that his dog, who had rushed ahead, was waiting for him under a gas lamp with the same look of impatience. Her eyes, her wagging tail, and her whole body asked: 'Well? Come on then.'

As soon as he caught up with her, she turned the corner at a determined trot. Suddenly he realized she was heading somewhere.

'Perhaps,' he thought to himself, 'the maid usually . . . Or Jeannine . . .'

He stopped for a moment, then went on again, following the dog, without even noticing that he had instantly stopped feeling tired, and sleepy, and happy. He quickened his pace and the delighted dog went ahead, like a good guide.

'Go on, go on!' ordered the sergeant from time to time.

He looked at the name of a road, then went on again. They passed gardens with lodges at the gates; the road was dimly lit and they met no one. In her excitement, the dog pretended to bite the hand that hung at his side, and he had to restrain a brutal impulse, which he could not explain, in order not to beat her.

At last she stopped, as though saying: 'Well, here we are!' before an old, broken-down railing, protecting the garden of a little low house smothered in vines and bignonia, a timid, shrouded little house.

'Well, why don't you open it?' said the dog, which had taken up a position before the wooden wicket gate.

The sergeant lifted his hand to the latch and let it fall again. He bent down to the dog, pointed with his finger to a thread of light along the closed shutters, and asked her in a low voice: 'Who's there? . . . Jeannine?'

The dog gave a shrill 'Hi!' and barked.

'Shhh!' breathed the sergeant, clapping his hands over her cool, wet mouth.

Once more he stretched out a hesitant arm toward the gate

241

and the dog bounded forward. But he held her back by her collar and led her to the opposite pavement, whence he stared at the unknown house and the thread of rosy light. He sat down on the pavement beside the dog. He had not yet gathered together all those images and thoughts which spring up around a possible betrayal, but he felt singularly alone, and weak.

'Do you love me?' he murmured in the dog's ear.

She licked his cheek.

'Come on; let's go away.'

They set off, he in front this time. And when they were once more in the little sitting room, she saw that he was putting his linen and slippers in a sack that she knew well. Desperate but respectful, she followed all his movements, while tears, the colour of gold, trembled in her yellow eyes. He laid his hand on her neck to reassure her.

'You're coming too. I'm not going to leave you any more. Next time you won't be able to tell me what happened 'after'. Perhaps I'm mistaken. Perhaps I haven't understood you properly. But you mustn't stay here. Your soul wasn't meant to guard any secrets but mine.'

And while the dog shivered, still uncertain, he held her head in his hands, saying to her in a low voice: 'Your soul . . . Your doggy soul . . . Your beautiful soul . . .'

Intelligent and Loyal

JILLY COOPER

M ANY mongrels have a remarkable ability to distinguish different days of the week and others are excellent timekeepers. A dog is a creature of routine with a built-in time clock. Perhaps the same kind of instinct tells birds it is time to migrate when the days start getting shorter.

What is less easy to explain is how so many dogs anticipate the arrival of their master or mistress even when they don't turn up at a regular time. One mongrel owner, who jets around the world a great deal, said that at first her dog missed her dreadfully when she left home but after a day or two settled into a routine with the housekeeper, of whom he was very fond. Whenever his mistress returned home, however, the moment her plane landed the dog sensed it, and started screaming with excitement. He wouldn't settle until her car finally drew up at the front door.

Kim Spink, a sleek Standard Magpie with a badger stripe down his forehead, always knew when any of the family would be coming home. They all turned up at different times of the day, and there was no routine about this, but Kim always stationed himself at the stairs window, ten minutes before each arrival.

Kim had the badger stripe which seems to be a characteristic of dogs with second sight. He also had a Borderline Collie mother, and mongrels with Collie blood also seem to be particularly psychic. Susie Bill, a red Fetcher, and Ben her stable mate, a smooth black Satin Crammer, always took up their positions on a chair by the window a quarter of an hour before their master returned home—whatever time he arrived. As he worked eight miles away, it was as though they sensed the exact time he left work. When Mr Bill's mother died, he went over to her house to sort out her things, telling his wife he'd be home by seven. During the afternoon he rang to say, there was so much to do he wouldn't be back until long after nine. At six forty-five, the dogs took up their lookout positions on their chair.

'You'll have a long wait,' warned Mrs Bill, but sure enough at seven o'clock Mr Bill arrived, having decided to abandon sorting for the day and come home after all.

The sceptic would insist that the dogs recognize the sound of their owner's car, and also have far superior hearing to humans, but surely this hearing would not be acute enough to pick up a car leaving a quarter of an hour's drive away. Nor does this explain the behaviour of a Rough Diamond called Judy Brown, who lives in a shop where cars are pulling up all day, but who only barks at her master's car, although she can't see him arriving from inside the shop. Nor is it the sound of the engine she recognizes, as she barked the first time he turned up in a new car. She also barks before the telephone rings.

Another inexplicable phenomenon is the mongrel's ability to select the right bus. Bully Latchford, a stalwart rugby player, like many a man before him got bored when he was taken shopping by his mistress and used to sneak off and take the 93 bus home. He always went upstairs and was a great favourite with the conductors. He knew it was time to get off when the bus levelled out at the top of the hill, but, and this is the remarkable part, although there were two bus routes from the town shops, Bully always caught the right bus.

Miss Ellen Coath also remembers a Bertrand Russell called Bobby who was a great wanderer. He used to take free rides from the village, to the end of the road, where Miss Coath lived. One day when she was already on the bus, she saw him board it, run upstairs, crawl under a front seat, then jump out at the right stop. There were two buses which took different routes from Beckenham, but Bobby, like Bully, always took the right one.

Even more impressive at the turn of the century were the navigational skills of a mongrel called Kruger Rogerson.

'He was owned by my dad's Uncle Jim,' writes Mr Rogerson, 'who was a road paver and always took Kruger to work. Each morning Uncle Jim caught a Stockport tram from Cheadle Heath to Mersey Square in the centre of Stockport, changed

trams to take another six mile ride to Hyde Town Hall, then caught a train to Mottram. On several occasions Kruger overslept after a night on the tiles, but nothing daunted would set off, catch all the necessary connections, and get to work only half an hour after his master. All the conductors knew him. On his collar was stamped, "I am Kruger Rogerson, who the hell are you?" '

When Mrs Margaret Turner was a child before the war, she had a little Terrier called Raggy who always picked her up on time from school, and whose bump of locality was as good as his time clock. Every Saturday night he took a train to the other side of Huddersfield to visit an old lady who gave him chocolate biscuits, then caught the right train home again. It must have been easier for dogs in those days when there was less traffic, and no one kicked up a queenie fuss if a stray dog joined them in a bus or train carriage. Raggy's bump of locality also stood him in good stead during a family outing, when he got lost on the moors seven miles from home. Margaret sobbed and sobbed, thinking she'd never see her dog again, but when the family got back home there was Raggy wagging on the doorstep. He was probably guided home by scent, but there are extraordinary tales of dogs finding their way home after travelling to a strange place by car.

Bobby, a two-and-a-half-year-old mongrel belonging to a French florist in the town of La Ferté Alais, got lost in the flower market in the heart of Paris. After a fruitless search his master returned sadly home. Yet five days later an exhausted Bobby arrived on the doorstep. He had covered thirty-five miles and, even more impressive, this rural dog had found his way out of Paris, one of the busiest and most geographically complicated cities in the world.

Dogs who travel to a place by car must notice landmarks on the way. During the war Mr Sharpe, who lived in Finchley, used to drive the family and their dog Chum along a labyrinth of back roads to visit his in-laws in Wood Green. One day Chum, a sleek Standard Magpie with the inevitable badger streak down his forehead, vanished after a bitch. The family searched everywhere, but like the French florist had to return home to Finchley empty-handed. At two-thirty in the morning they were overjoyed to hear a faint scratch on the back door. Bedraggled, exhausted and desperately thirsty, Chum had come the fifteen miles home.

Sometimes by returning to base by a circuitous route a stray mongrel wins its spurs and is allowed to stay. Mr Hutchings tells a touching story of the Standard Magpie bitch he and his sister found wandering in the market when they were children.

'We were convinced it was Floss, our neighbour's bitch. She wagged her tail so hard when we called her that we found an old piece of rope and took her home by tram. When we reached our neighbour's house she was amazed, because her own Floss was already in residence. We realized the two pups were identical. Mother insisted we took our Floss back, so tearfully we boarded the tram and took her back to market. We kept looking back hoping she might follow us, but she didn't. To our delight, when we got home we found her waiting. Mother relented, and she became a member of our family for ten years.'

Whatever good fairy guided Floss and the other dogs back home was aided by the fact that the dogs had been to the place at least once before. Some dogs may have a homing instinct, like carrier pigeons, and are able to navigate by the angle of the sun or the stars. If a dog is separated from home (or the place he considers he ought to be) his internal clock tells him there is an incongruity between the time of day he feels inside him, and the time of day the sun is registering by virtue of its position. He then sets out in the direction that will reduce this internal and external difference. Once he gets near home, he will pick up familiar smells and sights and find his way home easily.

What is far more difficult to explain is how dogs trace owners to places where the dog has never been. There was for example a mongrel in the First World War who, never having been out of England before, crossed the channel and found his master in the trenches. Then there was the mongrel called Tony, who was left in the care of friends because his owners had moved from Illinois to a town in Michigan some 225 miles away. Somehow, six weeks later, Tony, wearing his identifying collar and disc, turned up at the Michigan home. Such feats must defy the rational mind and it is here we enter the tricky world of ESP or 'Psi-trailing', as it is called, which means the psychic location of where someone is. Perhaps in the same way that the mongrel in Australia 'knew' his mistress had landed, Tony and the dog in the First World War were drawn by some sixth sense to their owners. T.S. Eliot wrote of lovers 'who think the same thoughts without need of speech.' Perhaps dogs, whose devotion exceeds that of most lovers, are able to pick up telepathic vibrations from beloved owners who are constantly thinking and worrying about them.

The End

VIRGINIA WOOLF

FLUSH was growing an old dog now. The journey to England and all the memories it revived had undoubtedly tired him. It was noticed that he sought the shade rather than the sun on his return, though the shade of Florence was hotter than the sun of Wimpole Street. Stretched beneath a statue, couched under the lip of a fountain for the sake of the few drops that spurted now and again on to his coat, he would lie dozing by the hour. The young dogs would come about him. To them he would tell his stories of Whitechapel and Wimpole Street; he would describe the smell of clover and the smell of Oxford Street; he would rehearse his memories of one revolution and another—how Grand Dukes had come and Grand Dukes had gone; but the spotted spaniel down the alley on the left—she goes on for ever, he would say. Then violent Mr Landor would hurry by and shake his fist at him in mock fury; kind Miss Isa Blagden would pause and take a sugared biscuit from her reticule. The peasant women in the market-place made him a bed of leaves in the shadow of their baskets and tossed him a bunch of grapes now and then. He was known, he was liked by all Florence—gentle and simple, dogs and men.

But he was growing an old dog now, and he tended more and more to lie not even under the fountain—for the cobbles were too hard for his old bones—but in Mrs Browning's bedroom where the arms of the Guidi family made a smooth patch of scagliola on the floor, or in the drawing-room under the shadow of the drawing-room table. One day shortly after his return from London he was stretched there fast asleep. The deep and dreamless sleep of old age was heavy on him. Indeed to-day his sleep was deeper even than usual, for as he slept the

248

darkness seemed to thicken round him. If he dreamt at all, he
dreamt that he was sleeping in the heart of a primeval forest,
shut from the light of the sun, shut from the voices of mankind,
though now and again as he slept he dreamt that he heard
the sleepy chirp of a dreaming bird, or, as the wind tossed the
branches, the mellow chuckle of a brooding monkey.

Then suddenly the branches parted; the light broke in—here,
there, in dazzling shafts. Monkeys chattered; birds rose crying
and calling in alarm. He started to his feet wide awake. An
astonishing commotion was all round him. He had fallen
asleep between the bare legs of an ordinary drawing-room
table. Now he was hemmed in by the billowing of skirts and
the heaving of trousers. The table itself, moreover, was swaying
violently from side to side. He did not know which way to run.
What on earth was happening? What in Heaven's name
possessed the drawing-room table? He lifted up his voice in a
prolonged howl of interrogation.

To Flush's question no satisfactory answer can here be given.
A few facts, and those of the baldest, are all that can be
supplied. Briefly, then, it would appear that early in the
nineteenth century the Countess of Blessington had bought a
crystal ball from a magician. Her Ladyship 'never could understand the use of it'; indeed she had never been able to see
anything in the ball except crystal. After her death, however,
there was a sale of her effects and the ball came into the
possession of others who 'looked deeper, or with purer eyes',
and saw other things in the ball besides crystal. Whether Lord
Stanhope was the purchaser, whether it was he who looked
'with purer eyes', is not stated. But certainly by the year 1852
Lord Stanhope was in possession of a crystal ball and Lord
Stanhope had only to look into it to see among other things 'the
spirits of the sun'. Obviously this was not a sight that a
hospitable nobleman could keep to himself, and Lord Stanhope
was in the habit of displaying his ball at luncheon parties and of
inviting his friends to see the spirits of the sun also. There was
something strangely delightful—except indeed to Mr Chorley—
in the spectacle; balls became the rage; and luckily a London
optician soon discovered that he could make them, without
being either an Egyptian or a magician, though naturally the
price of English crystal was high. Thus many people in the

early 'fifties became possessed of balls, though 'many persons', Lord Stanhope said, 'use the balls, without the moral courage to confess it'. The prevalence of spirits in London indeed became so marked that some alarm was felt; and Lord Stanley suggested to Sir Edward Lytton 'that the Government should appoint a committee of investigation so as to get as far as possible at the facts'. Whether the rumour of an approaching Government committee alarmed the spirits, or whether spirits, like bodies, tend to multiply in close confinement, there can be no doubt that the spirits began to show signs of restlessness, and, escaping in vast numbers, took up their residence in the legs of tables. Whatever the motive, the policy was successful. Crystal balls were expensive; almost everybody owns a table. Thus when Mrs Browning returned to Italy in the winter of 1852 she found that the spirits had preceded her; the tables of Florence were almost universally infected. 'From the Legation to the English chemists', she wrote, 'people are "serving tables" . . . everywhere. When people gather round a table it isn't to play whist.' No, it was to decipher messages conveyed by the legs of tables. Thus if asked the age of a child, the table 'expresses itself intelligently by knocking with its legs, responses according to the alphabet'. And if a table could tell you that your own child was four years old, what limit was there to its capacity? Spinning tables were advertised in shops. The walls were placarded with advertisements of wonders 'scoperte a Livorno'. By the year 1854, so rapidly did the movement spread, 'four hundred thousand families in America had given their names . . . as actually in enjoyment of spiritual intercourse'. And from England the news came that Sir Edward Bulwer Lytton had imported 'several of the American rapping spirits' to Knebworth, with the happy result—so little Arthur Russell was informed when he beheld a 'strange-looking old gentleman in a shabby dressing-gown' staring at him at breakfast—that Sir Edward Bulwer Lytton believed himself invisible.

When Mrs Browning first looked into Lord Stanhope's crystal ball at a luncheon party she saw nothing—except indeed that it was a remarkable sign of the times. The spirit of the sun indeed told her that she was about to go to Rome; but as she was not about to go to Rome, she contradicted the spirits of the sun.

'But', she added, with truth, 'I love the marvellous.' She was nothing if not adventurous. She had gone to Manning Street at the risk of her life. She had discovered a world that she had never dreamt of within half an hour's drive from Wimpole Street. Why should there not be another world only half a moment's flight from Florence—a better world, a more beautiful world, where the dead live, trying in vain to reach us? At any rate she would take the risk. And so she sat herself down at the table too. And Mr Lytton, the brilliant son of an invisible father, came; and Mr Frederick Tennyson, and Mr Powers and M. Villari—they all sat at the table, and then when the table had done kicking, they sat on drinking tea and eating straw-berries and cream, with 'Florence dissolving in the purple of the hills and the stars looking on', talking and talking: '. . . what stories we told, and what miracles we swore to! Oh, we are believers here, Isa, except Robert. . . .' Then in burst deaf Mr Kirkup with his bleak white beard. He had come round simply to exclaim, 'There is a spiritual world—there is a future state. I confess it. I am convinced at last.' And when Mr Kirkup, whose creed had always been 'the next thing to atheism', was converted merely because, in spite of his deaf-ness, he had heard 'three taps so loud that they made him leap', how could Mrs Browning keep her hands off the table? 'You know I am rather a visionary and inclined to knock round at all the doors of the present world to try to get out', she wrote. So she summoned the faithful to Casa Guidi; and there they sat with their hands on the drawing-room table, trying to get out.

Flush started up in the wildest apprehension. The skirts and the trousers were billowing round him; the table was standing on one leg. But whatever the ladies and gentlemen round the table could hear and see, Flush could hear and see nothing. True, the table was standing on one leg, but so tables will if you lean hard on one side. He had upset tables himself and been well scolded for it. But now there was Mrs Browning with her great eyes wide open staring as if she saw something marvellous outside. Flush rushed to the balcony and looked over. Was there another Grand Duke riding by with banners and torches? Flush could see nothing but an old beggar woman crouched at the corner of the street over her basket of melons. Yet clearly

Mrs Browning saw something; clearly she saw something that was very wonderful. So in the old Wimpole Street days she had wept once without any reason that he could see; and again she had laughed, holding up a blotted scrawl. But this was different. There was something in her look now that frightened him. There was something in the room, or in the table, or in the petticoats and trousers, that he disliked exceedingly.

As the weeks passed, this preoccupation of Mrs Browning's with the invisible grew upon her. It might be a fine hot day, but instead of watching the lizards slide in and out of the stones, she would sit at the table; it might be a dark starry night, but instead of reading in her book, or passing her hand over paper, she would call, if Mr Browning were out, for Wilson, and Wilson would come yawning. Then they would sit at the table together until that article of furniture, whose chief function it was to provide shade, kicked on the floor, and Mrs Browning exclaimed that it was telling Wilson that she would soon be ill. Wilson replied that she was only sleepy. But soon Wilson herself, the implacable, the upright, the British, screamed and went into a faint, and Mrs Browning was rushing hither and thither to find 'the hygienic vinegar'. That, to Flush, was a highly unpleasant way of spending a quiet evening. Better far to sit and read one's book.

Undoubtedly the suspense, the intangible but disagreeable odour, the kicks and the screams and the vinegar, told upon Flush's nerves. It was all very well for the baby, Penini, to pray 'that Flush's hair may grow'; that was an aspiration that Flush could understand. But this form of prayer which required the presence of evil-smelling, seedy-looking men and the antics of a piece of apparently solid mahogany, angered him much as they angered that robust, sensible, well-dressed man, his master. But far worse than any smell to Flush, far worse than any antics, was the look on Mrs Browning's face when she gazed out of the window as if she were seeing something that was wonderful when there was nothing. Flush stood himself in front of her. She looked through him as if he were not there. That was the cruellest look she had ever given him. It was worse than her cold anger when he bit Mr Browning in the leg; worse than her sardonic laughter when the door shut upon his paw in Regent's Park. There were moments indeed when he regretted Wimpole Street and its tables. The tables at No. 50 had never tilted upon one leg. The little table with the ring round it that held her precious ornaments had always stood perfectly still. In those far-off days he had only to leap on her sofa and Miss Barrett started wide-awake and looked at him. Now, once more, he leapt on to her sofa. But she did not notice him. She was writing. She paid no attention to him. She went on writing—'also, at the request of the medium, the spiritual hands took from the table a garland which lay there, and placed it upon my head. The particular hand which did this was of the largest human size, as white as snow, and very beautiful. It was as near to me as this hand I write with, and I saw it as distinctly.' Flush pawed her sharply. She looked through him as if he were invisible. He leapt off the sofa and ran downstairs into the street.

It was a blazing hot afternoon. The old beggar woman at the corner had fallen asleep over her melons. The sun seemed droning in the sky. Keeping to the shady side of the street, Flush trotted along the well-known ways to the market-place. The whole square was brilliant with awnings and stalls and bright umbrellas. The market women were sitting beside baskets of fruit; pigeons were fluttering, bells were pealing, whips were cracking. The many-coloured mongrels of Florence were running in and out sniffing and pawing. All was as brisk as a bee-hive and as hot as an oven. Flush sought the shade. He flung himself down beside his friend Catterina, under the shadow of her great basket. A brown jar of red and yellow flowers cast a shadow beside it. Above them a statue, holding his right arm outstretched, deepened the shade to violet. Flush lay there in the cool, watching the young dogs busy with their own affairs. They were snarling and biting, stretching and tumbling, in all the abandonment of youthful joy. They were chasing each other in and out, round and round, as he had once chased the spotted spaniel in the alley. His thoughts turned to Reading for a moment—to Mr Partridge's spaniel, to his first love, to the ecstasies, the innocences of youth. Well, he had had his day. He did not grudge them theirs. He had found the world a pleasant place to live in. He had no quarrel with it now. The market woman scratched him behind the ear. She had often cuffed him for stealing a grape, or for some other misdemeanour; but he was old now; and she was old. He guarded her melons and she scratched his ear. So she knitted and he dozed. The flies buzzed on the great pink melon that had been sliced open to show its flesh.

The sun burnt deliciously through the lily leaves, and through the green and white umbrella. The marble statue tempered its heat to a champagne freshness. Flush lay and let it burn through his fur to the naked skin. And when he was roasted on one side he turned over and let the sun roast the other. All the time the market people were chattering and bargaining; market women were passing; they were stopping and fingering the vegetables and the fruit. There was a perpetual buzz and hum of human voices such as Flush loved to listen to. After a time he drowsed off under the shadow of the lilies. He slept as dogs sleep when they are dreaming. Now his legs twitched—was he dreaming that he hunted rabbits in Spain? Was he coursing up a hot hill-side with dark men shouting 'Span! Span!' as the rabbits darted from the brushwood? Then he lay still again. And now he yelped, quickly, softly, many times in succession. Perhaps he heard Dr Mitford egging his greyhounds on to the hunt at Reading. Then his tail wagged sheepishly. Did he hear old Miss Mitford cry 'Bad dog! Bad dog!' as he slunk back to her, where she stood among the turnips waving her umbrella? And then he lay for a time snoring, wrapt in the deep sleep of happy old age. Suddenly every muscle in his body twitched. He woke with a violent start. Where did he think he was? In Whitechapel among the ruffians? Was the knife at his throat again?

Whatever it was, he woke from his dream in a state of terror.

THE END

He made off as if he were flying to safety, as if he were seeking refuge. The market women laughed and pelted him with rotten grapes and called him back. He took no notice. Cartwheels almost crushed him as he darted through the streets—the men standing up to drive cursed him and flicked him with their whips. Half-naked children threw pebbles at him and shouted 'Matta! Matta!' as he fled past. Their mothers ran to the door and caught them back in alarm. Had he then gone mad? Had the sun turned his brain? Or had he once more heard the hunting horn of Venus? Or had one of the American rapping spirits, one of the spirits that live in table legs, got possession of him at last? Whatever it was, he went in a bee-line up one street and down another until he reached the door of Casa Guidi. He made his way straight upstairs and went straight into the drawing-room.

Mrs Browning was lying, reading, on the sofa. She looked up, startled, as he came in. No, it was not a spirit—it was only Flush. She laughed. Then, as he leapt on to the sofa and thrust his face into hers, the words of her own poem came into her mind:

> You see this dog. It was but yesterday.
> I mused forgetful of his presence here
> Till thought on thought drew downward tear on tear,
> When from the pillow, where wet-cheeked I lay,
> A head as hairy as Faunus, thrust its way
> Right sudden against my face,—two golden-clear
> Great eyes astonished mine,—a drooping ear
> Did flap me on either cheek to dry the spray!
> I started first, as some Arcadian,
> Amazed by goatly god in twilight grove;
> But, as the bearded vision closlier ran
> My tears off, I knew Flush, and rose above
> Surprise and sadness,—thanking the true Pan,
> Who, by low creatures, leads to heights of love.

She had written that poem one day years ago in Wimpole Street when she was very unhappy. Now she was happy. She was growing old now and so was Flush. She bent down over him for a moment. Her face with its wide mouth and its great eyes and its heavy curls was still oddly like his. Broken asunder, yet made in the same mould, each, perhaps, completed what was dormant in the other. But she was woman; he was dog. Mrs Browning went on reading. Then she looked at Flush again. But he did not look at her. An extraordinary change had come over him. 'Flush!' she cried. But he was silent. He had been alive; he was now dead. That was all. The drawing-room table, strangely enough, stood perfectly still.